OGT Social Studies

THE New! LITTLE BOOK

AMERICAN ASSOCIATION OF UNIVERSITY WOMEN
HEIGHTS – HILLCREST – LYNDHURST, OHIO

The New Little Book: OGT Social Studies is a contribution to the Cleveland Municipal School District by the Heights-Hillcrest-Lyndhurst Branch of the American Association of University Women.

It was prepared with the professional oversight and contributions of Allan Keller, social studies teacher; Linda Wilson, Co-coordinator, The Saturday Tutoring Program at The Church of the Covenant; James Templeman, social studies teacher; Bruce Ransom, social studies teacher/ administrator; and Sean Patton, social studies teacher/ administrator.

The committee who worked on the *The New Little Book: OGT Social Studies:*

Nancy Stellhorn, Coordinator Sarah Maasz, Financial Secretary
Janet Bowden Mary K. Evans
Ranelle Gamble Kathe Mayer
Clara McCann

The Heights-Hillcrest-Lyndhurst Branch of the American Association of University Women also published AAUW's *Eldercare Resources: A Manual for the Elderly and Their Caregivers.*

The study/ review guide follows the *Academic Content Standards: K-12 Social Studies* and the Ohio Graduation Tests published by the Ohio Department of Education. It is supported by grants from The Cleveland Foundation and The Gund Foundation.

The American Association of University Women Heights-Hillcrest-Lyndhurst Branch, Cleveland, Ohio 44124

Copyright © 2007 American Association of University Women Heights-Hillcrest-Lyndhurst, Ohio Branch

Printed by Color Bar Perlmuter, 26310 Emery Road, Warrensville Heights, Ohio 44128

Book and Cover Design by Kim Robinson

ISBN 978-0-9798218-0-6

The New Little Book: OGT Social Studies is protected by United States copyright law. Photocopying of *The New Little Book: OGT Social Studies* that results in profit upon sale is strictly prohibited.

 Printed in the U.S.A. on recycled paper.

Acknowledgments

A special thank you to Neil Murphy, former Cleveland Municipal School District, Social Studies Coordinator, who was a tremendous help in the early stages of the project, and to many other staff members at the Cleveland Municipal School District.

We gratefully acknowledge The Cleveland Foundation and The Gund Foundation for their financial support and the Women Business Owners Educational Foundation, fiscal agent.

Allan Keller's writing, thorough research, and professional experience have been essential to making this a high-quality study/ review book that covers each Ohio indicator. Linda Wilson's unstinting advice about grammar, reading level, and glossary items was invaluable.

The committee offers thanks to other American Association of University Women (AAUW) members and friends of the project who made significant contributions to its success: Cecile Kraus, William Stellhorn, and Debora Fisher, and to many members of the Heights-Hillcrest-Lyndhurst Branch of AAUW and our partners, Delta Sigma Theta and Alpha Kappa Alpha sororities, who helped with glossary definitions and proofreading.

The Church of the Covenant, Cleveland, Ohio granted permission to use copyrighted material from their Ohio Proficiency Test study guide, *The Little Book*. Rev. Laury W. Larson and Robert Ault, clerk of session, encouraged and helped with this process. We especially thank Betty Rose, Louise Steele, and Linda Wilson for their help and advice throughout. They started us on our way and gave us detailed materials from their project.

This study/ review guide and its many contributors and advisors truly demonstrate a large base of support for the children of Ohio – their futures and ours.

Contents

Introduction – Why am I Studying This? 1
How to Use *The New Little Book: OGT Social Studies* .. 3
Test Taking Tips and Strategies 5

1. History
   A – The Enlightenment 12
      Glossary 15

   B – Industrialization 17
      Glossary 21

   C – Imperialism 24
      Glossary 28

   D – Twentieth Century Conflict:
      World War I to World War II 30
      Glossary 43

   E – Twentieth Century Conflict:
      The Cold War and Contemporary Conflicts 51
      Glossary 67

   F – Domestic Affairs in the United States during
      the Twentieth Century 76
      Glossary 98

2. People in Societies
   A – Cultural Perspectives 110
      Glossary 124

   B – Cultural Interaction: Oppression,
      Discrimination, Conflict 129
      Glossary 143

   C – Cultural Diffusion 148
      Glossary 161

3. Geography
- A – Places and Regions 165
  - Glossary 171
- B – Human Environmental Interaction 174
  - Glossary 183
- C – Movement of People, Products, and Ideas 185
  - Glossary 190

4. Economics
- A – Markets 192
  - Glossary 199
- B – Government and the Economy 201
  - Glossary 208

5. Government
- A – Constitutional Amendments and Supreme Court Decisions 211
  - Glossary 216
- B – Systems of Government 218
  - Glossary 220

6. Citizenship Rights and Responsibilities
- A – Citizen Action and Participation 221
  - Glossary 252
- B – Individual Rights and Responsibilities 260
  - Glossary 265

7. Social Studies Skills and Methods
- A – Evaluating Sources of Information 268
  - Glossary 271
- B – How to Support or Refute a Thesis 273
  - Glossary 275

Illustrations Credits 276

Introduction – Why am I Studying This?

The Ohio Graduation Test (OGT) was adopted by the Ohio General Assembly to make sure that when Ohio students graduate from high school, they are ready to be successful members of the work force and in higher education. The test has five areas: Reading, Writing, Mathematics, Science, and Social Studies. The test questions in each area are based on the Ohio Department of Education's *Academic Content Standards* for that area (what they have decided a student needs to know in order to graduate). Every student must pass the OGT in order to graduate from high school. The first time you will take the test is as a high school sophomore.

The New Little Book: OGT Social Studies will help you pass the social studies portion of the OGT. It covers world studies from 1750 to the present and United States studies from 1877 to the present. It is divided into seven areas: History, People in Societies, Geography, Economics, Government, Citizenship Rights and Responsibilities, and Social Studies Skills and Methods.

You are probably saying that social studies is boring, you don't like social studies, and you don't know why you have to learn about social studies. Why does my future depend on how much I know about social studies and how well I do on a social studies test? You are not the first person to say that.

Too often, social studies becomes one fact after another. After all, government is about what happens in Washington DC and geography is about maps and other countries. All anyone needs to know about economics is how to get a job. It also seems like all that happened in history was that there were wars. But there is so much more –

It is true that social studies focuses on facts, but not everyone agrees on what the facts are or what they mean. Historians, for example, don't agree on many things. You can read about Christopher Columbus by different historians and get different points of view. Some historians see Columbus as a brave explorer while others see him as a brutal conqueror. Other historians focus on how Columbus' accidental discovery changed the world. If you learn how to "read" history and to "read" historians, you will find that history is really interesting.

Social studies should expand your understanding of our community, society, and world. It is really about people and events in the past and the present. Social studies is about what we think happens, why it happened, and what we think it means. It uses disciplines such as economics, geography, history, and sociology to understand our world. According to the National Council for the Social Studies, "The primary purpose of social studies is to help young people develop the ability to make informed and reasoned decisions for the public good as citizens of a culturally diverse, democratic society in an interdependent world."

We hope that we have made social studies interesting for you in our "little book." We also hope that it will help you develop your decision-making skills and pass the social studies portion of the Ohio Graduation Test.

How to Use The New Little Book: OGT Social Studies

To get the most out of this study guide, you have to know how to use it. If this is your first time using **The New Little Book,** follow all the steps. If you have used it before, skip to the third step.

FIRST – Read the Table of Contents to see what the book is all about.

Notice that it is divided into sections based on Ohio's seven academic standards. The standards are History, People in Societies, Geography, Economics, Government, Citizenship Rights and Responsibilities, and Social Studies Skills and Methods. Each section is set up as a mini study guide, with its own glossary (an alphabetical list of words with their definitions). The words that are explained for you in the glossary are underlined in the text. Remember that there may be variations of a word (past tense for instance) and that the word is only defined once, but variations of the word appear after it in parentheses.

SECOND – Study one section at a time.

You do not need to study them in order. We suggest everyone starts with social studies skills and methods. It discusses the skills and methods for reading social studies materials, especially history. Eight of the thirty-eight questions on the test come from this standard. Social studies skills and methods will prepare you to study the other six standards. If you have taken the test before, study those standards on which you have the lowest scores. If you have not taken the test before or don't know your scores, we suggest starting with the history standard. Ten of the thirty-eight questions on the test come from this standard.

THIRD – Study the benchmark first. Always look up the definition of the verb under the section titled "Important Performance Verbs."

The multiple choice and short answer test questions are based on the benchmarks. So, you must understand them before you start reading. The benchmark is at the top of each reading selection. It is a specific statement that tells you what you should know and be able to do with the information you are studying. For example, look at the benchmark for History D: "Connect developments related to World War I to the onset of World War II. The test DOES NOT ask multiple choice questions such as: What was the treaty that ended World War I? It DOES ask questions such as: In what way did the Treaty of Versailles establish conditions that led to the outbreak of World War II?

FOURTH – Read the section focusing on the benchmark.

As you read you will find two types of information. One is background information that helps you understand the benchmark, but does not respond directly to it. The second is information that helps you respond to the benchmark. For example, in History Benchmark A the first two paragraphs provide basic information about the Enlightenment. The third paragraph and the list of Enlightenment thinkers and their ideas respond directly to the benchmark. Both are necessary to understand the benchmark.

FIFTH – Use the glossary.

If you find a word in the text that you do not understand and it is underlined, look it up in the glossary that follows that section. Most of the words that are underlined and explained are words that come directly from the State of Ohio's *Academic Content Standards K-12 Social Studies* or from earlier versions of the social studies tests of the OGT. For that reason, they are used in the text so that you can become familiar with words that might show up in the questions on the test that you take.

By understanding this material and using the section at the front of this book called "Test-Taking Tips and Strategies," you should be able to pass the social studies portion of the OGT and be 1/5 of the way to graduating. Don't rely on luck to pass the test. Rely on yourself. Use this book and study.

Test-Taking Tips and Strategies

Before the Test
1. Review practice tests or materials in the weeks before the test. Cramming may not help. It could make you more nervous about taking the test.
2. Attend tutoring sessions.
3. Review the sections below:
    a. *Hints for Short Answer or Extended Response Questions*
    b. *Hints for Multiple Choice Questions*
    c. *Important Performance Verbs*
4. Get plenty of rest for several nights before the test.
5. The night before, pack everything you need for the test (for example, 2 pencils, erasers, and a watch). Put these items together in one place where you are sure to remember to take them with you.
6. Plan to eat a good breakfast on the testing day.

On Test Day
1. Eat a good breakfast.
2. Arrive early with supplies (at least 2 sharpened pencils and erasers). If parts of the test are timed, bring a watch so you can see how you are doing with the time you have to work.
3. Make sure you go to the bathroom before the test begins.
4. Try to stay positive and relaxed. Take a few deep breaths if you need to.

During the Test
1. Listen carefully to directions.
2. Read all directions on the test carefully. Check the bottom of each test page for directions that will tell you whether to "go on to the next page" or "stop."
3. Read all of each question slowly and carefully. Don't just read the beginning and try to guess what the question is

asking. Find the key words and circle or underline them. They will tell you what you are being asked to do. You can write on the test document.
4. Answer all the questions. Answer the easier questions first. Don't spend too much time on the harder questions. Put a pencil mark near those questions that you want to come back to. Maybe there will be something in another part of the test that will help you with this answer. Don't forget to come back.
5. Don't worry if others seem to finish before you. Just concentrate on your own test.

When You Are Finished with the Test
1. Check again to be sure that you answered all the questions.
2. Read your answers again quietly to yourself.
3. Be sure to completely blacken in the space that matches the answer you chose.
4. Make sure you wrote what you meant to write. Add to or change an answer only if you are sure you made a careless mistake, or misunderstood the question, or left out something.
5. Correct errors in grammar, punctuation, and spelling.
6. Make sure that all erasures are neat, clean, and complete.

Hints for Multiple Choice Questions
1. Look over the questions quickly to find those you can answer most easily. Answer them first. If you don't know an answer, skip that question, mark it, and come back to it. Maybe there will be something in another part of the test that will help you with this answer. Don't forget to come back.
2. Read the whole question slowly and carefully. Decide what you are being asked. Read all the possible choices. Cross out the letter of the answer or answers that you know are wrong. Then concentrate on the ones that are left. Look at similar answers and decide how they are different.

Here are some questions you can ask yourself to help you decide if it is wrong.

- Is this response talking about a different topic? If you can say, "this answer has nothing to do with the question," then the answer is probably wrong.
- Does this response have words I have never heard of, even though I went to class and did my work? Then the answer is probably wrong.

3. Underline key words such as: always, never, none, except, most, least. Be suspicious of answers that include the words "always," "never," or "none." These are often wrong answers.
4. Choose the best answer, even if you are not sure, in case you don't have time to come back to it.
5. Don't change a multiple choice answer unless you are sure you misunderstood the question or overlooked something. The answer you chose first is often the correct one.
6. Make sure you completely blacken in the space that matches the answer you chose.
7. Make sure that all erasures are neat, clean, and complete.

Hints for Short Answer or Extended Response Questions

1. Look quickly over the questions to find those you can answer most easily. Answer those first. If you don't know an answer, skip it. Mark it and come back to it. Maybe there will be something in another part of the test that will help you with this answer.
2. Read the whole question slowly and carefully. Decide what you are being asked. Underline or circle words that tell you what to do, such as: define, compare, explain, describe.
3. After you read the question, write down helpful phrases, words, and definitions in the test booklet before you begin writing your answer.
4. For the short answers, write a topic sentence and at least two examples. Try to fill about one-half sheet of paper in the answer document. For the extended answers, write a topic sentence and three or four examples. Try to complete a full sheet in the answer document.
5. Answer clearly. Give only what is asked for. A short, correct answer is worth more than a long, rambling one that doesn't really answer the question.
6. Answer in complete sentences, not in individual words or

phrases. Include topic terms (for example, Industrial Revolution), and give specific information. Use the vocabulary that goes with the topic (for example, assembly line, union, mass production).
7. When appropriate, use connecting words such as: because, since, when, after, before, therefore. Use correct grammar and spelling.
8. Write or print legibly.
9. Make sure all your written responses are in the proper space in the answer document. Nothing that you have written in the test booklet will be scored.
10. Re-read your answers again quietly to yourself.

Important Performance Verbs

Performance verbs tell you what to do with a short answer or extended response question, which you must answer in your own words. Learn these terms so you can do what the performance verb asks you to do in a question.

Analyze	Write about the different parts of the problem or situation asked about in the question and come to a conclusion about them.
	Example: Analyze the effects of World War I, with emphasis on the global scope, outcomes, and human cost of the war.
Assess	Make a judgment about the value of some event or thing.
	Example: Assess the impact of the Depression on the lives of average Americans during the 1930s. (See also "Evaluate.")
Compare	Tell how two things are alike or different. Identify the main points mentioned in the question. Sometimes the question will give you the exact points to compare. Using the example below, find the ways the incentives are alike in the two economic systems.
	Example: Compare economic incentives in a market economy with those in a mixed economy.

Contrast	Tell how things are different. Identify the main points mentioned in the question. Using the example below, find the ways the two kinds of monarchy are different.
	Example: Contrast an absolute monarchy with a constitutional monarchy.
Critique	Discuss or comment on the positive and negative sides of something.
	Example: Critique evidence which suggests that the treaties at the end of World War I contributed to the start of World War II.
Demonstrate	Show or prove something clearly.
	Example: Demonstrate how Supreme Court decisions have strengthened individual civil rights.
Describe	Give the characteristics of something. A description can also tell how something changes over time.
	Example: Describe the process for making a new federal law.
Detect	Discover or investigate something.
	Example: Detect bias and propaganda in Stalin's speeches to the Russian people.
Determine	Decide or find out something.
	Example: Determine the major causes of World War I.
Discuss	Write about the topic in the question as if you were debating the pros and cons of the topic with someone.
	Example: Discuss the advantages and disadvantages of the growth of cities.
Evaluate	Evaluation questions ask you to make a judgment of the worth of something, based on particular standards or criteria.
	Example: A question might give a quote from a newspaper article and then ask you to

	evaluate whether the article is credible (believable) or biased (giving only one side or point of view).
Examine	Study or inspect something in detail. *Example:* Examine the social, economic, and political struggles resulting from colonialism and imperialism.
Explain	Tell how or why something happened. *Example:* Explain why Japanese-Americans were put into internment camps during World War II.
Identify	Name something or tell what something is. *Example:* Name a group that suffered from discrimination in the United States before the Civil War.
Infer	Draw a conclusion about an event. *Example:* If a government says it believes the state should own and run all business, what can you infer about that government?
Interpret	Use data (information) from maps, graphs, and charts to make comparisons. *Example:* Given a bar graph showing the infant mortality (death) rates in the United States, China, India, and France, interpret the data to show which countries have higher or lower death rates among infants.
List	Write down several items which the question asks for. *Example:* List at least three systems of government.
Refute	Give proofs to show that a statement is false. *Example:* Refute the claim of the Nazi Party during World War II that Jewish people are inferior.
Summarize	Restate information in a shorter form by stating only what is most important. *Example:* Summarize the major causes of the stock market crash of 1929.

Support	Give facts, examples, and other evidence to prove a conclusion, generalization, or point of view.
	Example: Give examples to support this statement: The Industrial Revolution changed the way people worked.
Trace	Describe a path or sequence, such as explaining the order of events.
	Example: Beginning with World War I, trace the events that led to the development of the United States as a world power.

History A

THE ENLIGHTENMENT

Explain connections between the ideas of the Enlightenment and changes in the relationships between citizens and their governments.

The <u>Enlightenment</u> was an <u>intellectual revolution</u> that took place in Europe between 1688 and 1787. This time is often called the Age of Reason. It was influenced by the scientific revolution that took place between approximately 1550 and 1700. Scientists used experiments, logic, and reason to study the physical world. One of the most important scientists was Sir Isaac Newton. He described the universe as a giant machine that ran on natural laws, such as <u>gravity</u>. He thought that people could use science and reason to discover the natural laws that run the universe. Scientists, such as Newton, were encouraging people to ask questions of the world around them.

Newton's view of the physical world convinced other thinkers that the political, economic, and social world also ran on natural laws. They believed that by discovering and understanding these natural laws, people could create a better world. Enlightenment thinkers questioned the <u>authority</u> of church leaders, <u>monarchs</u>, and <u>nobles</u>. These thinkers challenged ideas such as <u>divine right</u> and <u>hereditary monarchy</u>. They asked questions such as: "What is the best form of government? Why should bloodline determine the next king or queen? Are not education and talent more important characteristics? Why don't the people have a voice in who governs them? What natural rights do people have?"

Enlightenment ideas inspired the American Revolution. Thomas Jefferson, the principal author of the Declaration of Independence, is shown presenting his original draft to the committee. Left to right: Thomas Jefferson, Roger Sherman, Benjamin Franklin, Robert R. Livingston, and John Adams

The Enlightenment encouraged changes in the relationship between citizens and their governments. Enlightenment ideas inspired the American Revolution, the French Revolution, and the Latin American Wars for Independence. Slogans, such as "no taxation without representation" from the American Revolution and "liberty, equality, and fraternity" from the French Revolution, reflect Enlightenment thought. Enlightenment values can be found in the U.S. Declaration of Independence, Constitution, and Bill of Rights. Inspired by the writings of Enlightenment thinkers, Simon Bolivar organized and led military forces that won independence from Spain for six Latin American countries. Enlightenment thoughts, such as Thomas Jefferson's "all men are created equal," continue to inspire people today.

Enlightenment Thinkers and Ideas

John Locke (English)
- all people have certain natural rights
- government is created with the consent of the governed
- government should protect people's rights
- if government doesn't protect people's rights, the people have the right to create a new government

Jean Jacques Rousseau (French)
- people sacrifice some freedom for the good of the community
- direct democracy is the best form of government

Baron de Montesquieu (French)
- the best type of government has its powers divided among legislative, executive, and judicial branches
- this separation of powers creates checks and balances that allow each branch of government to check on the other branches so no one branch becomes too powerful

Voltaire (French)
- people should have the right to freedom of speech, expression, and thought
- people should have freedom of religion and practice religious toleration

Cesare Beccaria (Italian)
- people accused of a crime should have fair and speedy trials
- there should be no torture of witnesses or suspects

Adam Smith (Scottish)
- competition in the free market benefits society (free trade)
- government should not interfere in the economy (laissez faire)

Glossary

History A

authority – the right to do something or to tell someone what to do; the right to give orders; the person in command.

Bill of Rights – the first ten amendments to the U.S. Constitution. They guarantee basic rights that the government cannot take away.

checks and balances – a system in which each branch of government checks on the other branches, so that no one branch becomes too powerful. For example, the U.S. Congress can pass a law, but the president can veto that law, and the Supreme Court can declare the law unconstitutional.

direct democracy – a form of government in which citizens vote directly on all laws and public issues.

divine right – belief that a monarch (king, queen, or emperor) received the right to govern from God and not from the people.

Enlightenment – an intellectual movement of the 18th century in which the ordinary person rejected the authority of rulers and the church, and valued his own logic and ideas.

executive branch – the branch of government that is responsible for enforcing the laws. The president heads the executive branch of the federal government. The governor heads the executive branch of Ohio's state government. The mayor heads the executive branch of Cleveland's city government.

fraternity – a group helping one another like brothers, even though they are not related.

free trade – international exchange of goods and services without government taxes (tariffs).

gravity – the pull one object, such as the earth, has on another object, such as a pencil, when you drop it. As Sir Isaac Newton (1642-1727) discovered, everything pulls on everything else. The earth pulls on the pencil, and the pencil pulls on the earth. The earth is larger and has the greater pull, so the pencil falls to the ground.

hereditary monarchy (hereditary monarch) – a government run by a king or other ruler who inherited the office from another family member. (the ruler who heads a hereditary monarchy.)

intellectual – concerned with knowing and thinking.

judicial branch – the branch of the federal, state, or local government that interprets the law and decides the guilt or innocence of the accused. The Supreme Court is the highest federal court, made up of nine Justices. In the State of Ohio, the Ohio Supreme Court is the lead court. Cities, suburbs, and counties have local courts.

laissez faire – the principle that the economy works best when there is little government interference or regulation.

legislative branch – the branch of government that makes laws. The Congress (the Senate and the House of Representatives) is the legislative branch for the federal government. The legislative branch for Ohio is the Ohio General Assembly, and for Cleveland it is the City Council.

liberty – freedom from control by others.

monarchy (monarch) – a form of government in which the ruler (monarch) is a king, queen, emperor, or empress. A monarch usually inherits the title and holds power for life.

noble – person who has a high rank or title which is inherited. Lords, knights, and dukes are examples.

religious toleration – willing to put up with someone's right to believe and worship in a different way than you do.

revolution – a dramatic or violent change. It could be political, economic, social, cultural, or intellectual.

separation of powers – a plan of government, used in the United States, which divides the power of government among three branches: the legislative branch makes the laws; the executive branch enforces the laws; and the judicial branch interprets the laws.

History B

INDUSTRIALIZATION

Explain the social, political, and economic effects of industrialization.

Industrialization is the change from an economy dominated by agriculture (farming) to one dominated by manufacturing with machines in factories in urban areas. The results of industrialization are dramatic social, political, and economic changes. The long-term impact of industrialization is so great that historians also refer to it as an Industrial Revolution. As you read the selection below, concentrate on how industrialization, or the Industrial Revolution, changed peoples' lives.

The Industrial Revolution began in England in the textile industry in the mid-1700s. During the 1800s, the Industrial Revolution spread from England to other European countries, the United States, and Japan. Since 1900 the Industrial Revolution has spread to Africa and Asia.

Before the Industrial Revolution, most people earned a living as farmers. Until then manufacturing was all done by hand and took a long time. Merchants delivered raw material to workers' homes. In their homes workers spun thread and wove cloth by hand. This was called cottage or domestic industry. Then came a big change.

During the mid-1700s, machines that spin and weave cloth were invented. These machines helped people

The spinning jenny, invented in 1764 by James Hargreaves, a weaver in the northwest of England, allowed a worker to produce eight (later, as many as eighty) spools of yarn all at once. Before this invention, several spinners were needed to produce enough yarn for just one weaver.

make cloth faster and in greater quantities than before. The introduction of machines that run with waterpower and steam engines moved manufacturing from homes to separate buildings called factories. Manufacturers needed many workers to run the machines. Workers moved from farms to towns and cities, so they could live near their new jobs.

New methods of production developed during the Industrial Revolution. In 1798 inventor, Eli Whitney, decided to build machines to make interchangeable parts for rifles. The use of <u>interchangeable parts</u> led to the assembly line and mass production. Because of mass production, the number of goods for sale increased and prices for products decreased. The modern <u>assembly line</u> and <u>mass production</u> were developed by the Ford Motor Company in the early 1900s. Industrialization made more goods available and affordable for more people.

Industrialization caused major economic changes. It led to a transportation revolution, including the development of the steamboat, improved roads, and the railroads. It led to the growth of the coal and iron industries. New industries, such as oil and steel, developed. By the late 1800s, electricity and gasoline became new sources of energy. Small businesses began to disappear as large, powerful <u>corporations</u> grew. In the United States, millionaire businessmen, such as Andrew Carnegie, John D. Rockefeller, and John Pierpont Morgan, became household names. By 1900 the United States was the greatest economic power in the world.

Industrialization changed the way people worked. Since work was done inside, time was measured by the clock, not by the weather or the seasons. At the beginning of the Industrial Revolution, workers had no control over their <u>wages</u>, hours, or working conditions. Wages were so low that women and children often worked to help support the family. Safety was not an important issue because unskilled workers were easy to replace. A boss could fire a worker at any time and for any reason.

In the 1800s workers in many countries struggled to form <u>unions</u>. They wanted to pressure businesses and corporations to improve wages, hours, and working conditions. Progress was slow and for some too slow. Karl Marx and Frederick Engels wrote the *Communist Manifesto* in 1848. They called for a workers' revolution to solve the problems workers were facing in Europe. The solution: communism should replace capitalism. A communist revolution was not successful until the Russian Revolution in 1917.

In the United States, some workers formed unions, such as the Knights of Labor and the American Federation of Labor. Instead of revolution, they preferred collective bargaining. Sometimes they went on strike and some strikes, such as the Homestead Strike and the Pullman Strike, were violent. Many Americans did not support unions, but began to see the need to help workers and the poor. Reform movements such as the Populist Movement of the 1890s and the Progressive Movement of the early 1900s called for laws to set a minimum wage, set maximum hours for women, and end child labor.

Industrialization changed the way people lived. It led to urbanization. Large numbers of immigrants and migrants moved to the cities in search of jobs. Cities grew rapidly and without plans for city services, such as garbage pick-up and sewage. Some neighborhoods became slums. Many of the rich and middle class moved from the center of the cities to suburbs or small towns. In the United States, reformers of the Progressive Movement called for many needed improvements: building codes, departments of public health, and zoning regulations. They urged election reforms giving ordinary people the right to use initiative and referendum to get new laws on the ballot. Another election reform was the secret ballot. Many reformers supported prohibition, outlawing the making, transporting, or sale of liquor anywhere in the United States.

The social class system changed because of industrialization. It created an industrial middle class (white-collar workers) and an industrial working class (blue-collar workers). The new industrial middle class included accountants, supervisors, managers, clerks, and salesmen. The new industrial working class included skilled and unskilled workers. Skilled workers were carpenters, machinists, plumbers, printers, bakers, and tailors. Unskilled workers included construction workers, janitors, and factory workers. Most good-paying jobs were closed to women. Middle-class women were expected to marry, stay home, and raise a family. It was acceptable for a woman to be a secretary, sales clerk, telephone operator, teacher, nurse, or social worker until she had children. Working-class women often had to work to help support the family. They were factory workers, cooks, seamstresses, or servants. Working-class children often worked, as well.

Working class women and their children often had to work to help support their families. It is estimated that one in six children worked full time in 1900. This young girl removes excess fabric from garments in a knitting mill.

Industrialization changed the population of many countries. So many workers were needed in the United States that businesses recruited people. Between 1880 and 1920, large numbers of immigrants came from southern and central Europe. They came to the United States in search of economic opportunity and to escape political and religious persecution. Most of these new immigrants were different from the old immigrants that came before 1880. The new immigrants were usually non-English speaking, Catholics or Jews, illiterate, unskilled, and poor. They moved to cities, settling in ethnic neighborhoods, where they could be surrounded by their language and culture. Between 1900 and 1920, a revolution in Mexico and economic opportunity in the United States led to a large increase in Mexican immigrants. During the same time, African Americans from the South began moving north in search of jobs and a better life. By 1920 the population of the United States was 50% urban, and the urban population was made up of many different peoples.

Glossary
History B

agriculture – farming; the science of growing crops and raising farm animals.

American Federation of Labor (AFL) – a group of labor unions, which first joined together in 1886 to fight for better job conditions. In 1955 another labor group, the Congress of Industrial Organizations, joined with the AFL to form the AFL-CIO.

assembly line – a line of factory workers and machines in which each worker puts together one part of a product, such as a car. When everyone has finished his job, the final product is ready to sell. Also called a "production line."

blue-collar worker – someone from the working class, often a factory worker or a person who does heavy work or works with his/her hands.

capitalism (capitalist) – an economic system in which businesses have private owners who make or sell goods for their own profit or for the profit of their shareholders.

collective bargaining – negotiations or talks between a company and a union concerning wages, hours, and working conditions.

communism (communist) – an economic system in which the businesses are owned and operated by the government. The government decides the type, quantity, and price of goods produced. They also decide what workers will make. Communism says it will provide for everyone's needs and get rid of social classes.

corporation – a business owned by stockholders who invest in the business and share in the profits.

cottage industry (domestic industry) – manufacturing goods in the home.

culture (cultural, culturally) – the way of life of a group of people, which includes their ideas, beliefs, customs, language, and traditions.

ethnic (ethnicity, ethnically) – having to do with a group of people who share a common culture, language, nationality, race, or religion. For example, new Chinese immigrants settled in a part of the city called China Town, so they could live with their own ethnic group.

illiterate – unable to read and write.

immigrant (immigration) – a person who enters a country and makes it his home, often becoming a citizen of his new country.

initiative – the right for citizens to propose a new law or get rid of an existing law through a vote. It is usually based on a petition.

interchangeable parts – two or more items that can be used in place of each other. One can replace the other because they are the same.

Knights of Labor – an early labor union (1869), which allowed African Americans, unskilled workers, and women into its group. It is also responsible for starting "Labor Day."

mass production – the making of goods in large amounts, often using an assembly line.

middle class – all the people who are not rich or poor. Most have a comfortable standard of living.

migrant – a person who moves. Often it is used to describe people who move within their own country.

persecution (persecuted) – constant mistreatment, especially because of race, religion, sex, or political beliefs.

Populist Movement – a political movement in the United States during the 1890s. It called for reforms that would help farmers and workers and formed a political party, the Populist Party.

Progressive Movement – an urban, middle-class reform movement from 1890 to 1917 that wanted to solve the problems caused by the Industrial Revolution.

prohibition – the outlawing of the making, selling, and transporting of alcoholic beverages. The 18th Amendment established prohibition in the United States in 1919. This amendment was repealed in 1933.

raw material(s) – unprocessed natural thing(s) like wood and metal that are used to manufacture products.

referendum – the process by which laws or constitutional amendments are submitted directly to the voters for approval or rejection.

reform (reformer) – to improve or change something that is wrong or unsatisfactory.

revolution – a dramatic or violent change. It could be political, economic, social, cultural, or intellectual.

seamstress – a woman whose occupation is sewing. In the early part of the 19th century, women often worked at sewing machines in a large factory.

secret ballot – a type of voting where each person's vote is kept secret, but the total results of the election are made public.

strike – refusing to work, in order to achieve a goal such as higher pay or better working conditions.

suburb; suburban (suburbanite) – a community or land near a city, with easy access to the city. (a person who lives in the suburbs.)

textile – a fabric or cloth that has been woven or knitted.

union – a number of persons joined together for a common purpose, such as better pay and better working conditions. They may use negotiation, picketing, and going on strike in order to get what they want from their employer.

urban – having to do with cities or towns.

urbanization – the development or growth of cities or towns.

wages – money that is paid to a worker for work or services done.

white-collar worker – usually someone from the middle class who has a clerical, business, or professional job.

working class – the people whose work is manual. They may be skilled or unskilled labor.

zoning – dividing an area from other areas for a special purpose. Some areas are zoned for residential housing, and others are zoned for industry or parks.

History C

IMPERIALISM

Analyze the reasons that countries gained control of territory through imperialism and the impact on people living in the territory that was controlled.

Imperialism is the policy of extending control over other countries or <u>territories</u>. The goal of imperialism is to build an <u>empire</u>. This can be done by military <u>conquest</u>. Alexander the Great conquered most of the known world in ten years. Adolf Hitler conquered much of Europe and called his rule the <u>Third Reich</u>. Both men sought world domination (control).

Another example of imperialism is <u>colonization</u>. A <u>colony</u> is a group of people who settle in a distant land, but maintain ties with their mother country. If other people are already living on the land, the new settlers and mother country work to take political control. The original people do not have equal rights. In the sixteenth century, Spain created an empire in the Americas that included present day South America, Central America, Mexico, and the Southwestern United States. The native people, or Indians, experienced great suffering. Civilizations such as the Aztec and Inca were destroyed. Native Americans were killed, <u>enslaved</u>, <u>deprived</u> of their land, and forced to accept a foreign <u>culture</u>. At the same time, Spain became the richest and most powerful country in the world.

In the seventeenth century, France, Great Britain, and several other European countries competed with Spain by establishing colonies in the Americas. The thirteen colonies which later became the United States of America were a part of the British Empire. In the early 1800s, Latin American wars for independence weakened the power of Spain. By the nineteenth century, Great Britain was the most powerful country in the world. It created an empire that included countries on every <u>continent</u>, except Antarctica. Great Britain claimed with pride that the sun never set on the British Empire.

By 1880 European countries decided to compete for colonies once again. Historians call this the "new imperialism." Newly formed countries, such as Belgium, Germany, and Italy, led the way. Older European countries, such as France and Great Britain, sought more colonies. This was the beginning of an empire-building race in Africa and Asia. By 1914, there were only two independent African countries, Ethiopia and Liberia. All the other African countries were colonies. Most Asian countries had a similar experience. India and the East Indies (Indonesia), Cambodia, Laos, and Vietnam were colonies. China was divided into trading zones called spheres of influence.

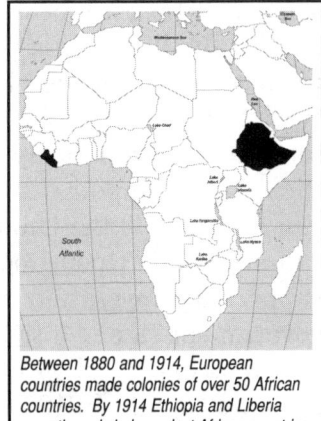
Between 1880 and 1914, European countries made colonies of over 50 African countries. By 1914 Ethiopia and Liberia were the only independent African countries.

Japan, however, had a different experience. It became Asia's first modern imperial power. For several hundred years, Japan chose to be a closed society isolated from most of the world. In 1853 Commodore Matthew Perry sailed U.S. warships into Tokyo Harbor with a letter from President Pierce, asking that Japanese ports be opened for trade. Recognizing the economic and military strength of the United States, Japan decided to open its ports. It also decided to learn from Western powers and modernize. Japan built factories and railroads, created a public education system, and developed a modern army and navy. Japan's desire to build an empire led to wars with China and Russia. By 1905 Japan was a world power with an empire that included Taiwan and Korea.

China was unable to defend itself from the major world powers and was divided into spheres of influence. Seen here dividing up the China pie are, from left to right, England, Germany, Russia, France, and Japan (French cartoon from the late 1800s).

The United States entered the race for an empire, as well.

The United States focused on the Far East, islands in the South Pacific, the West Indies, and Central America. In 1898 the United States <u>annex</u>ed Hawaii. After the Spanish-American War (1898), the United States took control of most of Spain's colonies. It temporarily controlled Cuba, and annexed Puerto Rico, the Philippines, and islands in the South Pacific, including Guam. In 1899 the United States claimed trading rights in China with its <u>Open Door Policy</u>. In 1903 the United States supported a <u>revolution</u> in Panama. The new Panama government signed a <u>treaty</u> giving the United States control over a strip of land on which the United States built the Panama Canal. In 1904 the Roosevelt <u>Corollary</u> to the <u>Monroe Doctrine</u> stated that the United States would use its army and navy in the nations of the Western Hemisphere whenever necessary.

Why did some countries seek to annex or control other countries and territories between 1880 and 1920? The reasons were economic, social, and political. The economic reasons were that countries wanted <u>raw materials</u> and a <u>market</u> for manufactured goods. For example, South Africa was rich in gold and diamonds. Hawaii produced sugar and pineapples. Europe and the United States wanted these things. Because of the Industrial Revolution, Europe and the United States had many manufactured products to sell. Colonies could provide buyers for their cloth, tools, machinery, and other products.

The political reasons for imperialism were tied to <u>nationalism</u>. <u>Colonizing</u> countries wanted power. They wanted other countries to look up to them. Only the most powerful nations have and hold colonies. Powerful countries can use colonies as sites for military and naval bases. A colony might supply a powerful country with an important natural resource, such as oil. It might help the powerful country fight its wars.

A major social reason for imperialism is <u>racism</u>. <u>Colonizers</u> said they were bringing civilization and religion to the people living there. Many believed the native people were <u>primitive</u> and inferior. The colonizing country claimed it could improve the lives of the natives by bringing them modern technology, education, and medicine. They felt the natives would be saved from hell by becoming Christians. According to the powerful countries, colonization was actually good for the poorer, dark-skinned people of the world. British poet Rudyard Kipling called this help the "white man's burden."

What was the impact of imperialism on those who were colonized? It is true that native people who were colonized learned about the modern world and its riches from the colonizing country. It is also true that there were many negative effects. These countries and territories were occupied. The local rulers lost power. A conquering country would set up new boundaries and new laws for its own benefit. It often ignored the customs or traditions of the native people. It took the natural resources, mineral wealth, and agricultural products out of the colony without giving fair prices for these items. Many native people were forced to work as slaves or low-paid workers on plantations, in mines, and for businesses owned by Europeans and Americans. Native people were denied equal rights and treated as inferiors. There was little respect for their local languages, traditions, and religions. These changes weakened the native families and local governments.

There are few colonies now. After World War II, most colonies became independent. Today's empires are made and kept by controlling another country indirectly, mainly through economics. For example, a more powerful country might promise money or threaten to take away trade rights and grants of money. A powerful country might threaten a weaker or smaller country with war or the loss of military protection. By these methods, one country can control another country's decisions without occupying it.

Glossary

History C

annex – to add; to add land to an existing country or state. For example, the state of Texas belonged to Mexico, but the United States annexed Texas in 1845.

colonialism (colonial, colonized, colonists) – the policy of establishing a colony. For example, the European nations colonized Africa.

colonization – a powerful government's sending of some of its citizens to claim and control a weaker country's land, resources, and people.

colonize – to start a colony.

colonizer (colonized) – people or a country that sets up a colony.

colony (colonies, colonists) – a settlement of people in a new land who maintain ties with their mother country. The original thirteen colonies of the United States received their independence from Great Britain after the Revolutionary War.

conquest – taking over by force.

continent – one of the seven large land masses of the world. The United States is located on the North American continent. The other continents are South America, Europe, Asia, Africa, Australia, and Antarctica.

corollary – a small addition to another accepted statement; a natural consequence or result.

culture (cultural, culturally) – the way of life of a group of people, which includes their ideas, beliefs, customs, language, and traditions.

deprive – to take something away from someone and not let that person have it back; often refers to property, possessions, and privileges.

empire – a group of countries and territories under the control of one ruler or government.

enslave – to make someone a slave (a human being who is owned as property).

market – a place to buy or sell something.

Monroe Doctrine – the 1823 speech delivered by President James Monroe to Congress, warning European powers not to interfere in the affairs of independent nations in the Western Hemisphere. He also stated that the American continents were no longer open to European colonization.

nationalism (nationalist) – loyalty to one's own nation or country; especially putting one nation above all others, with major emphasis on promotion of its culture and interests.

Open Door Policy – Secretary of State John Hay's 1899 proposal to allow all trading nations access to the Chinese market.

primitive – simple; belonging to earlier times.

racism (racist) – the belief that one race is naturally superior to others; discrimination and prejudice against a group of people because of their race.

raw material(s) – unprocessed natural thing(s) like wood and metal that are used to manufacture products.

revolution – a dramatic or violent change. It could be political, economic, social, cultural, or intellectual.

sphere of influence – an area or a nation over which a more powerful nation has control; one country's controls over another country's area or territory.

territory (territories) – land belonging to a country or under the control of a government.

Third Reich – Germany under the rule of Adolf Hitler from 1933 to 1945. Reich is German for the word empire.

treaty – a formal agreement between two or more rulers or nations.

History D

TWENTIETH CENTURY CONFLICT: WORLD WAR I TO WORLD WAR II

Connect developments related to World War I to the onset of World War II.

World War I: Causes and Effects

On June 28, 1914, a nineteen-year-old Bosnian Serb assassinated the heir to the throne of Austria-Hungary. By August 4, 1914, Europe was at war. Great Britain, France, and Russia were the Allied Powers. Germany and Austria-Hungary were the Central Powers. By 1915 Japan and Italy joined the Allied Powers, and the Ottoman Empire and Bulgaria joined the Central Powers. Fighting took place on three continents. Laborers and troops came from six continents. How could an assassination lead to such a world war? Well, the assassination was the spark, not the cause, of the Great War or World War I. The major causes of World War I were nationalism, imperialism, militarism, and alliances.

Nationalism spread throughout Europe in the nineteenth century. It led to the creation of two new nations; Italy united in 1870 and Germany in 1871. Nationalism encouraged ethnic groups, such as the Czechs, Hungarians, Serbs, and Slovaks of the Austro-Hungarian Empire, and the Armenians of the Ottoman Empire to call for independence. Nationalism encouraged national competition and the development of imperialism, militarism, and alliances. Those historical forces created a climate for war.

World War I was a total war. The war was fought not only on the front lines, but on the home front. Both were targets because both contributed to the war effort. Almost 9 million soldiers died and about 21 million soldiers were wounded, and estimates of civilian deaths are 7 to 9 million. The war cost almost $338 billion (in 1918 dollars); destroyed cities, towns, villages, farms, factories, railroads, bridges, and roads; and disrupted most nations' economies.

Why was World War I so destructive? One reason was the impact of new weapons. Larger <u>artillery</u>, an improved machine gun, poison gas, the tank, airplanes, and the submarine caused the death of millions of soldiers and civilians. By 1915 these new weapons led to a <u>stalemate</u> on the Western Front. Both sides dug a system of <u>trench</u>es from which to attack and defend. Trench warfare with its emphasis on sending troops "over the top" and across "no-man's land" in the face of new weapons led to large numbers of <u>casualties</u>. Each side hoped to exhaust the other side's personnel and resources first. The United States entered the war in 1917 on the side of the Allied Powers. This additional military support led Germany to agree to a <u>cease-fire</u> on November 11, 1918.

Whole networks of trenches were dug on the Western Front, primarily in France, that eventually stretched for hundreds of miles. Soldiers experienced long periods of boredom followed by the terror of heavy artillery shelling and infantry attacks. Soldiers also had to fight lice and rats that feasted on the dead. One British soldier on guard duty and four others sleeping can be found in the photograph.

The Paris Peace Conference in 1919 was composed of 32 nations, but only the leaders of France, Great Britain, Italy, and the United States, known as the Big Four, made the final decisions. President Wilson called for a "peace without victory," but the other leaders had different ideas. They wanted to gain or regain territory, ensure their national security, and punish Germany. The <u>Treaty of Versailles</u> placed all guilt for the war on Germany, demanded $33 billion of <u>reparations</u>, limited the size of the German army, <u>prohibit</u>ed the making or purchasing of weapons or war materials, and prohibited having submarines or an air force. Germany was also forced to return land to France and surrender all its <u>colonies</u>. The Treaty of Versailles did create an international peace organization, the <u>League of Nations</u>, but Germany was <u>excluded</u> from membership, and the United States did not join.

The Treaty of Versailles and the treaties with the other Central Power members created a victory without peace. Germany was angry and bitter, especially concerning the war guilt clause. The Austro-Hungarian Empire and the Ottoman Empire were <u>disbanded</u>. Russia and other nations had territory taken away. Italy and Japan felt cheated because they gained little territory. Lebanon, Iraq, Palestine, and Syria had their borders drawn by Europeans and were treated as colonies. The enormous loss of life and destruction caused by the civilized world left many people disillusioned, especially those who fought in the war. Some artists and writers of the time called themselves the "lost generation."

The United States as a World Power

In 1914 most Americans were against participating in World War I. There were large numbers of Americans with Austrian, German, or Irish background who were anti-British. However, most Americans favored the Allied Powers because of the country's historical background, English language, and trade relationships. U.S. newspaper stories often made Germans look brutal, savage, and uncivilized. Some of the stories were exaggerated, and some were British propaganda.

President Woodrow Wilson formally announced that the United States would be neutral. However, several dramatic events led the United States down the road to war with Germany. The first event was the sinking of a British passenger ship, the *Lusitania*, in 1915. This German attack killed 1,198 people including 128 Americans and almost 100 children. In response to American anger, Germany promised not to attack passenger ships or sink merchant ships without stopping and searching them first. However, in 1917 they announced a return to unrestricted submarine warfare.

The second event was the publishing of the Zimmermann note in March 1917. German foreign minister Arthur Zimmermann sent a telegram suggesting Mexico become a German ally and attack the United States. In return, Mexico would receive the land it lost to the United States during the Mexican War (1846-1848). Americans were shocked and angry. Later that month German submarines sank five unarmed U.S. merchant ships. President Wilson asked for, and received, a declaration of war from Congress April 6, 1917.

President Wilson wanted World War I to be the "war to end all wars." In a 1918 speech, he listed his goals for the war, which became known as the Fourteen Points. Eight points were aimed at solving specific problems, such as trade barriers, freedom of the seas, and <u>self-determination</u>. The other six sought to prevent future wars. His last point called for "a general association of nations" to maintain world peace.

President Wilson decided to personally attend the Paris Peace Conference in 1919. He hoped his Fourteen Points would become the basis of future world peace. The other nations were interested in gaining or regaining territory, their national security, and punishing Germany. Only his last point, the League of Nations, was included in the Treaty of Versailles.

Many Americans and members of the Senate were unhappy with the Treaty of Versailles. They did not support joining a League of Nations which might draw the United States into another foreign war. President Wilson traveled throughout the nation seeking support from the public to pressure the Senate to <u>ratify</u> the treaty. He exhausted himself and suffered a stroke. After a bitter fight in the Senate, the Treaty of Versailles was rejected, forcing the United States to <u>negotiate</u> a separate treaty with Germany and its allies.

The Russian Revolution: Causes and Consequences

In 1900 Russia was an industrial and military power, yet it was not a modern nation. Most European nations had <u>parliament</u>s and citizens could vote. Russia was ruled by a <u>czar</u>, an <u>absolute monarch</u> who inherited the throne. The czars made and enforced the laws. They did not hesitate to use force to crush <u>dissent</u>. Freedom of speech and press were severely limited. Laws <u>discriminate</u>d against some ethnic and religious groups, especially Jews.

Russia had many social and economic problems too. About 85 percent of the Russian people were <u>peasant</u> farmers, and most lived in extreme poverty. Meanwhile, the <u>noble</u>s were less than two percent of the population and owned the best land. The industrial workers worked an average of 65 hours a week. Factory conditions were worse than in other European countries. <u>Strike</u>s and <u>union</u>s were illegal.

In the early 1900s Russia experienced a series of poor

harvests which led to an economic depression. Food shortages and rising prices caused an outbreak of revolts, strikes, and protests. In 1905 the Russo-Japanese War ended with a humiliating loss for Russia. Popular discontent erupted and led to the 1905 Revolution. Strikes spread throughout the country and student walkouts closed universities. In October Czar Nicholas agreed to the creation of a parliament (Duma) to advise him. In practice, he ignored any demands. Because of several years of good harvests, most people were content and did not complain.

World War I reawakened popular discontent. At first the people of Russia united behind the war effort with patriotic enthusiasm. But the army was poorly equipped and led. By 1917 military losses, high casualty rates, and food and fuel shortages on the home front revealed the failure of the government. Protests and riots broke out. Soldiers ignored orders and deserted. Czar Nicolas II was unable to maintain control. The time was ripe for revolution.

The 1917 Russian Revolution occurred in two stages, the March Revolution and the November Revolution. The March Revolution forced the czar to abdicate. The new government leaders continued the failing war effort, were unable to solve the nation's problems, and plotted against each other. The result was anarchy and the November Revolution. Vladimir I. Lenin was the leader of the Bolsheviks, a small communist party. His promise of "Peace, Land, and Bread" had grown increasingly popular. He seized power with little resistance. Russia became the world's first communist nation.

Lenin moved quickly. He signed a peace treaty with Germany. The treaty forced Russia to give Germany a lot of territory, but it ended Russia's participation in World War I. Lenin also seized large estates, gave the land to peasants, and took control of some industries. Czar Nicholas and his family and all other leaders who opposed Lenin were executed. With support from the United States and some other Allied Powers, those who opposed the Bolsheviks formed the White Army. Between 1918 and 1921, a civil war raged and took almost 15 million lives. The Bolshevik's Red Army was victorious.

Russia became the Union of Soviet Socialist Republics (USSR) or Soviet Union in 1922, and Moscow became the capital. The new government was a communist dictatorship. The Communist Party was the only political party permitted. When Lenin died in 1924, Joseph Stalin, the head of the Communist Party, became the new head of the government.

Stalin was a ruthless and brutal dictator who sought absolute power by creating a totalitarian state. He demanded total obedience and personal sacrifice for the good of the state. To win public support, Stalin used propaganda to indoctrinate people. The government owned all newspapers, publishing houses, radio stations, and film production companies. Censorship was used to control Soviet composers, writers, and artists. Because the USSR was officially atheist, people of all religions were persecuted.

When Stalin died in 1953, the USSR had become the second greatest economic and military power in the world, but at great personal cost. Those who resisted Stalin's rule were classified as enemies of the state and were terrorized, imprisoned, sent to labor camps, or executed. To find traitors the secret police listened to phone calls, opened mail, and planted informers everywhere. Children were taught to report any disloyal comments heard at home. In 1934 Stalin used terror tactics on his Communist Party and sought to eliminate any threats to his power. The Great Purge was a series of trials and executions of thousands of political and military leaders. It is estimated that between 10 and 20 million people were killed for political reasons during Stalin's rule.

Post-World War I Turmoil

World War I and the Treaty of Versailles left many problems unresolved and created new ones. One major problem was how to prevent another war. Many people hoped the League of Nations would use nonviolent methods such as negotiation and economic sanctions to prevent future wars. Although the United States did not join the League of Nations, in 1921 it organized the Washington Disarmament Conference. The United States, France, Great Britain, Italy, and Japan agreed to reduce their number of battleships and build no additional ones for ten years. In 1928 the United States and France proposed an agreement to outlaw war as an instrument to solve international problems. Eventually, 64 nations signed the Kellogg-Briand Pact. These attempts to prevent another war would prove difficult to enforce.

Colonial rebellion was another major problem. In the early 1900s, there were organized groups in colonies who wanted independence. The treaties of World War I forced Germany to surrender all colonies and brought an end to the Austro-Hungarian Empire and the Ottoman Empire. This encouraged the spread of nationalism, more calls for independence, and colonial rebellions. Most colonial rebellions between 1914 and 1939 were crushed.

Some colonies did win independence. Between 1919 and 1921, Irish rebels fought against British military forces. After much bloodshed, the Treaty of 1921 created the Irish Free State from 26 southern counties. Six northern counties remained with England, Scotland, and Wales as a part of the United Kingdom. Rather than fight another war in 1919, the British granted Afghanistan independence. Faced with a nationalist revolt, the British granted Egypt independence in 1922, but insisted on the right to keep troops stationed there. Growing nationalism in Iraq led to independence from the United Kingdom in 1932. After the 1919 Amritsar Massacre, the Indian independence movement grew. Mahatma Gandhi became the new leader. Beginning in 1920 he and his followers organized large protests using nonviolence and civil disobedience. In 1935 the United Kingdom decided to grant India some independence.

Another major problem was economic recovery. World War I left many nations with huge war debts. England and France owed the United States over $10 billion. Germany owed $33 billion in reparations. Nations also had to rebuild their economies and adjust to peacetime production. Many nations chose to print extra money, which led to inflation. Germany printed so much paper money it became worthless and the economy collapsed.

The United States, however, prospered during and after the war. New consumer products, advertising, and installment credit created a growing demand for consumer products, such as automobiles and radios. Business profits rose and so did stock prices. Hoping to make quick profits, more people began to speculate in the stock market.

The economy grew during the 1920s, especially manufacturing. However, this was not true for all sectors of the economy. Farmers and workers did not do well. The distribution of wealth became increasingly unequal. In 1929 industrial production declined, and in October the stock market crashed. People panicked and lost confidence in the economy. Consumer spending decreased, production fell, unemployment increased, and many farms, businesses, and banks failed. The failure of the U.S. economy had a global impact. The decrease in the U.S. demand for foreign products and the increase in interest rates and tariffs hurt world trade. The Great Depression soon became a global depression.

The Great Depression brought economic crisis, political turmoil, and social unrest. Different nations responded differently to the Great Depression. The United States and most European nations created government programs to provide assistance for people in need. They passed laws to revive and reform the economy, but remained democratic governments. Other nations, such as Germany, Italy, and Japan, accepted dictators who promised to provide economic recovery and restore national pride. This led to the rise of militarist and totalitarian states.

In Japan military leaders criticized the government, supported the popular Emperor Hirohito, and promised economic recovery. They promised that new territories would provide Japan with natural resources and guaranteed markets. In 1931 the army invaded Manchuria, a province of China. Nationalist groups at home threatened those who did not support the army. In 1932 members of the military assassinated the prime minister. Soon military leaders had control of the government. In 1937 Japan invaded China again. This began the Second Sino-Japanese War and led to the slaughter of millions of Chinese civilians. In 1940 Japan invaded French Indochina. That same year Japan formed an alliance with Germany and Italy.

In Italy, strikes and riots occurred shortly after World War I. Many Italians were angry with the government because of the poor economy and the World War I treaties that gave Italy far less territory than expected. In 1921 Benito Mussolini organized his Fascist Party which promised to give strong leadership, to revive the economy, and to restore national pride. He criticized the government and used his Fascist "Blackshirts" to attack and terrorize anti-Fascist groups. By 1922 economic conditions were worse and the Blackshirts marched on Rome, demanding that the king appoint Mussolini prime minister. Once in power, Mussolini gave himself the title "Il Duce," the leader. By 1925 he was a dictator. All other political parties were outlawed, secret police jailed those who opposed him, and radio, newspapers, and other publications were censored. He strengthened his army and invaded Ethiopia in 1935 and Albania in 1939.

In Germany a new government, the Weimar Republic, formed in 1919. That same year the Nazi Party began to form. Nazism was German fascism. Adolf Hitler joined and soon became their leader, Der Führer. He wanted to be like Mussolini. So, when the German economy collapsed because of inflation, Hitler and his Brownshirts attempted a coup. This attempt to take over the government failed, and he was sent to prison. While in prison for treason, Hitler wrote *Mein Kampf* (My Struggle) which described his beliefs and goals. In 1924 he returned as party leader and worked toward taking over the country peacefully. He believed that true Germans were members of a master race called "Aryans" and blamed all of Germany's problems on the Communists and Jews. He promised to ignore the hated Treaty of Versailles, rebuild the army and navy, regain Germany's lost territories, and create an empire. He said his Third Reich would last a thousand years.

Few people paid much attention to Hitler and the Nazi Party until the Great Depression struck. His dynamic, emotional speeches moved people longing for security and strong leadership. By 1932 the Nazi Party was the largest political party in Germany. In an attempt to control him, President von Hindenburg appointed Hitler chancellor (prime minister) in 1933. Hitler moved to outlaw freedom of the press, labor unions, and all other political parties. Laws were passed denying Jews most of their rights. Criticism of Hitler or the Nazi Party was not allowed. Children were taught at school to report any disloyal comments made at home. A protection squad (SS) and secret police (Gestapo) were used to arrest and eliminate all opponents. Like Stalin, he moved to create a totalitarian society by controlling pubic opinion. Radio, newspapers, publishing houses, art, literature, and film became propaganda tools.

Hitler seized control of the economy and put millions of people to work or in the military. Expanding the military violated the Treaty of Versailles. Hitler was preparing for war. He invaded the Rhineland and formed an alliance with Mussolini in 1936. He invaded Austria in 1938 and Czechoslovakia in 1939. Other nations protested, but not one was willing to go to war. However, France and Great Britain did promise to come to Poland's defense if necessary.

Causes of World War II

On September 1, 1939, Germany invaded Poland. Two days later Great Britain and France declared war on Germany. The German war machine conquered most of Europe by 1940 leaving only Great Britain secure. Germany, Italy, and Japan formed an alliance called the Axis. Great Britain, China, the Soviet Union, and eventually the United States formed the Allied Powers. Over 50 nations participated by the end of the war.

World War II was the most destructive war in the history of the world. It is estimated there were over 50 million deaths, and over half were civilians. Approximately 50 million people were displaced from their homes. The cost for the United States alone was approximately $300 billion. How could another world war happen?

One of the major causes of World War II was the failure of the Treaty of Versailles. The treaty left the winners dissatisfied and the losers bitter and humiliated. It did not address the issues that caused the war: nationalism, imperialism, militarism, and alliances. Those unresolved issues helped cause World War II. The Axis Powers appealed to their citizens'

Here, dictators Benito Mussolini (Italy, left) and Adolf Hitler (Germany, right) stand reviewing the troops. They planned to conquer the world.

national pride, created empires, expanded the size and power of their armed forces, and allied themselves with one another.

Another cause of World War II was the rise of dictatorships. Economic distress caused by World War I and by the Great Depression led the people of Germany, Italy, and Japan to accept dictatorships. These dictators eliminated any opposition and invaded other nations in a quest for power, glory, and economic security.

The failure of the League of Nations to respond to German, Italian, and Japanese aggression helped cause World War II. It could only ask member nations to apply economic sanctions and volunteer to send troops. The League of Nations had no international peacekeeping force. For example, when Italy invaded Ethiopia in 1935; the League of Nations condemned the attack. However, no member nation was willing to take military action.

The policy of appeasement is also a cause of World War II. World War I had been so devastating that most nations wanted to avoid another war at almost any cost. They adopted a policy of appeasement toward aggressor nations in order to preserve peace. This lack of action only encouraged more aggression. When Germany marched troops into the Rhineland and annexed Austria, the powers of Europe did nothing. Next, Hitler demanded the Sudetenland, a part of Czechoslovakia with many German-speaking people. Rather than risk war, Great Britain and France agreed to let Germany take the Sudetenland. In 1939 Germany took all of Czechoslovakia and demanded Poland give them Danzig, formerly a German port. Great Britain and France promised to come to the aid of Poland, but because of their policy of appeasement, Hitler did not believe he had cause to worry.

The United States Participation in World War II

By 1919 the United States was the greatest economic and military power in the world. However, most Americans did not want their country to play a major role in world affairs, especially in Europe. The United States suffered 116,000 casualties in World War I. Most Americans wanted to avoid any alliances that might lead to involvement in another war. Trade with Europe was good, but otherwise most Americans wanted a return to a foreign policy of isolationism. As tensions increased in Europe, most Americans sided with their old allies, but did not want to be involved. Between 1935 and 1937, Congress passed Neutrality Acts that made it illegal to sell arms or lend money to nations at war.

In 1939 World War II began in Europe with Germany's invasion of Poland. President Franklin D. Roosevelt formally announced that the United States would be neutral. Yet, President Roosevelt wanted to aid the Allies. The president and other interventionists feared that the defeat of the Allies would leave the United States surrounded by the Axis Powers. Roosevelt convinced Congress to amend the Neutrality Act and permit any nation to buy arms on a "cash and carry" basis. He called his policy "armed neutrality."

By the end of 1940, most of Europe had been conquered by Germany and the only major power left was Great Britain. British prime minister Winston Churchill appealed to U.S. president Roosevelt for help. In 1941 the Lend-Lease Act was passed which allowed the president to lend or lease weapons, food, or supplies to nations who were important to the security of the United States. The president began sending destroyers to escort cargo ships from those nations and signed a bill for the first peacetime draft. President Roosevelt called the United States an "arsenal for democracy." In August of 1941, President Roosevelt and Prime Minister Churchill met for the first time on a destroyer in the North Atlantic to sign the Atlantic Charter. Like the Fourteen Points, it was a vision of a world of freedom and peace for all nations and people.

Although President Roosevelt believed the United States would have to enter the war, public opinion was strongly against direct intervention. That would change on December 7, 1941. The Japanese surprise attack on Pearl Harbor, Hawaii killed over 2,300, wounded more than 1,000, and almost destroyed the entire U.S. Pacific fleet. Calling it "a date which will live in infamy," President Roosevelt asked for and received a declaration of war from Congress the very next day. The United States was attacked and the public overwhelmingly supported the call for war. On December 11, Germany and Italy declared war on the United States.

The entry of the United States into World War II made it a global conflict. The war was fought in Africa, Asia, and Europe and in both the Atlantic and Pacific Oceans. Like World War I, it was a total war. Nations mobilized on the home front to support the front lines. The United States gave the Allies new hope. It brought more men, money, and supplies to the Allied cause. In 1942 the United States defeated Japanese forces in the Battle of Midway, gaining control of the Pacific Ocean. In 1943 invading German forces surrendered to the Soviet Union at Stalingrad, Axis forces were defeated in North Africa, Italy was invaded, and Mussolini fell from power. Then, on June 6, 1944, known as D-Day, the Allies invaded occupied France on the beaches of Normandy. This was the beginning of the liberation of Europe. Germany surrendered to the Allies on May 8, 1945, V-E day (Victory in Europe Day). Japan was retreating, but refused to surrender. On August 6, 1945, the United States dropped an atomic bomb on the Japanese city of Hiroshima. The entire city was destroyed. Three days later an atomic bomb was dropped on Nagasaki. Japan officially surrendered September 2, 1945, V-J Day (Victory in Japan Day). World War II was over.

War bonds and stamps were used to raise money and to involve the whole country in the war effort. They were also propaganda. Note the evil-looking drawings of Axis powers, from left, Italy, Germany, and Japan.

Glossary
History D

abdicate – formally giving up an important office of power or authority.

absolute monarchy (absolute monarch) – a form of monarchy whose power is not limited by law or a legislature. (the ruler of an absolute monarchy.)

aggressor (aggression) – the person, group, or nation that is the first to attack another person, group, or nation.

alliance (alliances) – a partnership; an association of groups with a common goal.

amend – to change.

anarchy (anarchist) – absence of government or law. (someone who feels that governments are unnecessary and should be abolished.)

annex – to add; to add land to an existing country or state. For example, the state of Texas belonged to Mexico, but the United States annexed Texas in 1845.

appeasement – the act of bringing to a state of peace, contentment, or calm; buying off an aggressor by giving in.

arsenal – a storehouse or place where something can be found; also a place to make or store arms and military equipment.

artillery – large guns usually mounted (attached) to another item of war, such as a missile launcher.

assassination (assassinate) – killing or murdering someone by surprise, especially a political leader or other public figure.

atheist – someone who does not believe that God exists.

Bolshevik – Russia's revolutionary group led by Lenin. They started the Russian Revolution that led to communism in Russia. By 1918 they were known as the Communist Party.

casualty (casualties) – a person injured or killed in war or a disaster.

cease-fire – an agreement to stop fighting.

censorship (censor) – the practice of removing parts of books, plays, films, etc. thought to be harmful to the interests of the organization or government or offensive to the public; in times of war, removal of items thought to support or be of interest to the enemy.

civil disobedience – a method of nonviolent protest. It is a deliberate and public refusal to obey a law and often leads to people being arrested.

civil war – war between different political groups in one country.

civilian – a person not on active duty in the military, police, or firefighting forces.

colonial rebellion – attempts by colonies to free themselves, usually by force.

colony (colonies, colonists) – a settlement of people in a new land who maintain ties with their mother country. The original thirteen colonies of the United States received their independence from Great Britain after the Revolutionary War.

communism (communist) – an economic system in which the businesses are owned and operated by the government. The government decides the type, quantity, and price of goods produced. They also decide what workers will make. Communism says it will provide for everyone's needs and get rid of social classes.

competition – a rivalry where two or more people, countries, or businesses are trying to get the same thing.

continent – one of the seven large land masses of the world. The United States is located on the North American continent. The other continents are South America, Europe, Asia, Africa, Australia, and Antarctica.

coup (coup d'état) – a sudden, often violent, overthrow of a government by a small group.

czar – the title of any of the emperors who ruled Russia before 1917; comes from the Latin word caesar.

declaration – a formal announcement.

declare – to state formally.

depression – a time when businesses do badly and many people lose their jobs. The stock market crash of October 1929 was the beginning of the Great Depression. The effects of the Great Depression were partly responsible for World War II.

Der Führer – "the leader," the name by which Adolf Hitler was known.

dictatorship (dictator) – a form of government in which the ruler (dictator) or ruler's power is not limited by citizens or a legislature. A dictator has absolute power that is enforced by an army and secret police.

disarmament – to give up or reduce the number of weapons.

disbanded – broken up or dissolved. A group or organization disbands when its work is finished or when there is no longer a need for it to continue to operate.

discontent – dissatisfaction; feeling the need for improvement.

discrimination (discriminate) – unfair treatment by a government or individual citizens, usually because of race, religion, nationality, sex, or certain disabilities; prejudice.

dissent – difference of opinion; disagreement.

draft (to draft) – a system which requires citizens to join their country's armed forces. (to call citizens to serve in the armed forces.)

economic sanctions – actions which limit the buying and/or selling of products in order to convince a country to change its policies.

empire – a group of countries and territories under the control of one ruler or government.

ethnic group – a group of people who share the same national origin, religion, race, or other group characteristics.

exclude – to leave out of something, usually on purpose.

fascism (Fascist) – a system of government ruled by a dictator, who restricts individual rights and places strong controls on the economy. It places nation and race above the individual and uses terror and censorship against anyone who opposes the government. Mussolini in Italy founded the Fascist Party.

front lines – where the soldiers are fighting.

global (globalization, globalism) – worldwide, referring to the whole world.

Great Depression – global depression of the 1930s when businesses, banks, and the stock market failed, and many people lost their jobs. It was the longest and most severe depression ever experienced by the industrialized Western world.

heir – someone who inherits (or is entitled to receive) the property, position, or title of another simply because he or she is related to that person (often a parent or grandparent).

home front – civilian support of the war; for example, working in a factory that makes tanks or uniforms.

imperialism – the policy of extending control over other countries or territories; to build an empire.

indoctrinate – to teach a specific idea or practice.

infamy – an extreme, evil act that is known to everyone.

inflation – a general increase in prices when the money supply increases and the supply of goods and services does not; a decrease in the purchasing power of money.

installment credit – making a fixed number of payments.

intervention (interventionist) – interfering in another country's affairs, usually by force or threat of force. (a person who thinks his country should interfere in the affairs of another country.)

isolationism (isolationist) – national policy of avoiding political or military agreements with other countries. (someone who supports such a policy.)

League of Nations – an international alliance formed after World War I to preserve world peace. It existed from 1920 to 1946 and was replaced by the United Nations.

liberation (liberate) – setting someone or something free.

market – a place to buy or sell something.

Mein Kampf – book written by Adolf Hitler in which he explained his beliefs about race, that Germans were the superior race and had the right to dominate all lesser races. The greatest evils of the world were Judaism (Jews) and Communism and they must be destroyed.

militarism (militarist) – a policy of glorifying military power, ideas, and values.

mobilize – to get an army ready for war.

nationalism (nationalist) – loyalty to one's own nation or country; especially putting one nation above all others, with major emphasis on promotion of its culture and interests.

Nazism (Nazi) – the beliefs and practices of Adolf Hitler's National Socialist German Workers' Party including racial superiority, government control of society and the economy, and loyalty to one's nation or people above all else.

negotiation (negotiate) – a discussion to find a solution to a disagreement. Using negotiation, opposing parties talk and compromise, instead of fighting, to find a solution to a problem.

neutrality (neutral) – choosing to not take sides in a war or dispute.

noble – person who has a high rank or title which is inherited. Lords, knights, and dukes are examples.

nonviolence (nonviolent) – the belief and practice of working actively for political and social change without using violence.

Mahatma Gandhi and Dr. Martin Luther King, Jr. were both strong supporters of the philosophy of nonviolence.

opposition – challengers; people who provide resistance.

Ottoman Empire – an area stretching from present day Turkey to southern Europe and from the Middle East to North Africa. The Ottoman Empire (1299 to 1922) was ruled by the imperial power, Turkey.

pact – agreement between two or more nations, groups, or persons.

parliament – the legislature or law-making body of countries such as Canada, the United Kingdom, and Israel.

patriotic (patriotism) – loving, defending, and supporting one's country and its interests.

peasant – an agricultural laborer or small farmer, often uneducated.

persecution (persecuted) – constant mistreatment, especially because of race, religion, sex, or political beliefs.

prime minister – the chief executive in a parliamentary system of government.

prohibit – prevent or forbid.

propaganda – selective facts, ideas, or information used to win support for a cause or a person. It usually has a strong emotional appeal.

prosper – to gain economic success.

protest – to strongly express objection to or disapproval of something; strong disapproval or objection.

quest – a long or difficult search for something.

ratify (ratified) – to confirm or approve, usually by a vote.

reparations – the debts a nation must pay for the harm done during a war.

resistance – opposition.

revolt – to rebel against an authority such as a leader or government; a rebellion or uprising.

revolution – a dramatic or violent change. It could be political, economic, social, cultural, or intellectual.

sector – portion, part.

seized – taken possession or control of by force.

self-determination – the right of people to choose their own government. Self-determination was one of President Wilson's Fourteen Points.

speculate (speculation) – to buy with plans of selling for a profit because of an increase in price.

stalemate – a position or situation in which no action can be taken.

strike – refusing to work, in order to achieve a goal such as higher pay or better working conditions.

tariff – a tax on products that come from another country.

Third Reich – Germany under the rule of Adolf Hitler from 1933 to 1945. Reich is German for the word empire.

total war – a war which involves all the resources of a nation including the armed forces and the civilian population. Farms, factories, and civilian populations, as well as armed forces are targets.

totalitarian – governed by a system which wants absolute control over all aspects of a person's private and public life. Individual freedoms must be sacrificed for the good of the state.

treason (traitor) – betraying of one's own country. A traitor is a person who betrays his/her own country.

Treaty of Versailles – the agreement signed at the end of World War I between Germany and the Allies. For damages to the Allies during the war, Germany was required to make large financial payments (reparations). The United States did not sign the treaty.

trench – a long, narrow ditch with earth piled in front that is used to protect soldiers in battle.

turmoil – confusion, disorder, and unrest.

union – a number of persons joined together for a common purpose, such as better pay and better working conditions. They may use negotiation, picketing, and going on strike in order to get what they want from their employer.

unrestricted submarine warfare – attacks on any ships, including battleships, merchant ships, and passenger ships that might support the enemy. Germany's attacks on American ships (merchant and passenger) was one reason that the United States entered World War I.

History E

TWENTIETH CENTURY CONFLICT: THE COLD WAR AND CONTEMPORARY CONFLICTS

Analyze connections between World War II, the Cold War, and contemporary conflicts.

World War II: Consequences

World War II had a dramatic impact on the postwar world. As the most destructive war in the history of the world, it has affected people and political policies from 1945 to the present day. The war cost the world one trillion dollars. At least 50 million people died due to the war, and over half of the dead were civilians. Russia lost approximately 20 million people. China lost about 10 million people. Approximately 11 million people were killed in concentration and work camps. About 418,000 Americans died due to the war.

Like World War I, World War II was a total war. Cities were bombed. Many lay in ruins. Factories, farms, and transportation systems were destroyed. Poverty was widespread. Approximately 50 million people in Asia and Europe had to leave their homes and become refugees. These refugees were orphans, prisoners of war, survivors of concentration and work camps, civilians running from invading armies, and homeless people whose neighborhoods had been destroyed. To provide food, shelter, and medicine for those in need, the International Red Cross and other organizations set up refugee camps. Some refugees eventually returned to their communities and others emigrated to other countries, such as the United States and Canada.

As the Allied forces freed Europe from Nazi control, they liberated concentration camps. Soldiers were stunned by horrible sights, such as piles of dead bodies and survivors that looked like living skeletons. The Nazis used these camps for slave labor and for <u>extermination</u> of those groups the Nazis considered "inferior." They murdered approximately six million Jews, two-thirds of the Jews living in Europe at that time. Many men, women, and children died in gas chambers. Then their bodies were burned or buried in mass graves. The Nazis called their plan for the total destruction of the Jewish people the "Final Solution to the Jewish Question." Today that state-sponsored <u>genocide</u> is called The <u>Holocaust</u>.

Soldiers found bodies piled against a building, waiting burial, at the concentration camp at Buchenwald, Germany.

Although the Jewish people were the Nazis' main target, they also <u>systematically</u> murdered Gypsies, Slavs, Jehovah's Witnesses, homosexuals, the mentally and physically handicapped, political opponents, and others. Historians estimate that 11 million people were murdered by the Nazis. After the war the <u>Allies</u> brought some Nazi leaders to trial for those deaths and for other war crimes. There were 13 trials held in Nuremberg (Nürnberg), Germany between 1945 and 1949 known as the Nuremberg Trials. Between 1946 and 1948, Japanese war crimes trials were held in Tokyo, Japan.

Even during World War II, the Allies were thinking about peace. Allied leaders discussed their vision of a postwar world at several conferences. In April 1945, representatives of the Allied nations met in San Francisco to draft a plan for the United Nations, an organization to promote peace and help prevent future wars. Fifty nations signed the Charter of the United Nations in June 1945. UN headquarters were located in New York City. Today, there are over 190 member nations.

One of the earliest threats to peace after World War II was the Arab-Israeli War of 1948. The horror of the Holocaust led to strong demands for the creation of a Jewish state, a safe place in the world for Jewish people to call home. In 1947 the United

Nations approved the creation of an Arab state and a Jewish state in Palestine, located in the Middle East. Arabs rejected the plan, but the Jews accepted it. Fighting between Jews and Palestinians began immediately.

Israel declared itself a state in May 1948. Arab states refused to recognize the right of Israel to exist. The armies of five Arab states invaded Israel. By 1949 Israel had defeated those Arab states and increased the amount of land under their control. Palestinian Arabs were forced to live under Israeli control or become refugees in Arab states. The Arab-Israeli conflict continues today.

The world entered the <u>Atomic Age</u> in 1945 when the United States dropped the first atomic bomb on Hiroshima, Japan. That one bomb killed or severely wounded 160,000 civilians and completely destroyed an area of 4.7 square miles. Dropping of the atomic bomb led to the ending of World War II. Only the United States had the technology to build and use this terrible and powerful weapon. This made the United States the most powerful military nation in the world. The United States was a <u>superpower</u>. Then, in 1949, the Soviet Union exploded an atomic bomb. Suddenly there were two superpowers. In 1952 the U.S. exploded the first <u>hydrogen bomb</u>, which was many times more powerful than the atomic bomb. In 1955 the Soviet Union exploded a hydrogen bomb. The United States and the Soviet Union were locked in an <u>arms race</u>, with each country trying to make bigger and more destructive weapons.

The Cold War: Conflicting Ideologies

After World War II, there were two major powers, the United States and the Soviet Union. Each had a different <u>ideology</u> and a different <u>worldview</u>. The United States was a <u>democracy</u> with a <u>capitalist</u> economic system. Except for the attack on Pearl Harbor, World War II was not fought on U.S. soil. American goals were to spread democracy and <u>free trade</u> to ensure future prosperity and security. The Soviet Union was a <u>communist dictatorship</u>. Both World War I and World War II were fought on Soviet soil, with enormous human and economic costs. Soviet goals were to spread <u>communism</u>, especially in neighboring countries, to ensure future prosperity and security. These conflicting ideologies and different worldviews led these two large countries to fear and mistrust each other, which spread to the rest of the world.

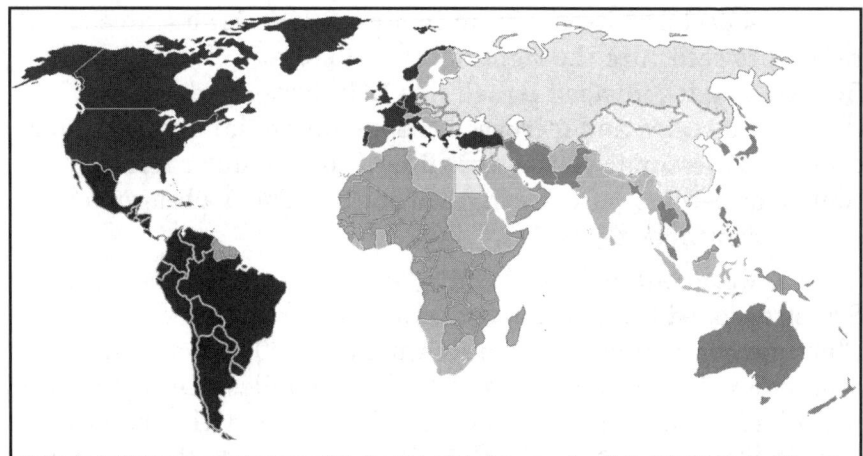

During the Cold War, some countries became U.S. allies (dark color); others were allies with the USSR (light colors). The rest of the world, the so called Third World, avoided alliances and tried to stay neutral.

Both the United States and the Soviet Union claimed that the other side wanted to rule the world. Neither, however, wanted to fight another direct war, especially one that might cause nuclear destruction. They began an intense global competition known as the Cold War. Cold War competition included an arms race, a space race, propaganda campaigns, and spying missions. Each superpower supported opposing sides in other countries' civil wars and conflicts, such as Korea and Vietnam. The Cold War lasted until the collapse of the Soviet Union in 1991.

The Cold War Conflicts

The first major conflict was over Soviet-occupied Eastern Europe, just after World War II. At the 1945 Yalta Conference, Soviet dictator, Stalin, promised free elections in Eastern Europe. The Soviets held elections, but made sure local Communists were put into positions of power in all Eastern European countries. Only then did Stalin withdraw his troops. The Communist countries of Eastern Europe followed Soviet policies, becoming Soviet satellites.

In 1946 Stalin declared communism and capitalism could not exist together, and that there would be war. Stalin ended most communication and trade between Eastern and Western Europe. British prime minister Winston Churchill warned that the Soviet Union's influence in Eastern European nations had created an "iron curtain" across the continent of Europe. Once again, the world was dividing into two armed, dangerous camps: the Soviet Union and Eastern Europe and the United States and Western Europe.

The next major conflict was over Germany. At the 1945 Yalta Conference, the Allies agreed to divide Germany into four occupation zones, each to be controlled by one of the Allies. They also divided Berlin, the capital city. In 1948 the United Kingdom, France, and the United States began to withdraw from their occupation zones. They pressured the Soviet Union to permit Germany to reunify. The Soviet Union responded by blocking all rail and road routes to Berlin, which was in the Soviet zone. Western Allies decided not to use force. Instead, they sponsored a massive airlift of supplies to the isolated people of Berlin. The airlift lasted almost a year. In 1949 the Soviet Union ended the Berlin blockade, but Germany and Berlin remained divided East and West.

Also in 1949, the North Atlantic Treaty Organization (NATO) was formed. The United States, Canada, and ten Western European nations formed a military alliance for collective security. They promised that an attack on any one member was an attack on all. The Soviet Union responded by forming its own military alliance with seven Eastern European nations in 1955 called the Warsaw Pact. Europe was formally divided into two opposing camps, an eastern communist bloc and a western non-communist bloc.

When World War II ended in 1945, the civil war between the Communists and the Nationalists of China started again. The Communists, led by Mao Zedong, won the civil war in 1949 and set up the People's Republic of China, the world's second communist nation. (The Soviet Union was the first.) The People's Republic of China, or Red China, established a one-party communist dictatorship. The Nationalist forces, who were not Communists, retreated from the mainland to the small island of Taiwan, which they called Nationalist China. The world now had two Chinas. The Soviet Union supported the People's Republic of China, and the United States supported Nationalist China. Communism was spreading.

The Cold War and U.S. Foreign Policy

The Cold War dominated United States foreign policy for over forty years. The fear of communism and nuclear war influenced the way American citizens viewed the world and the decisions their politicians made about U.S. foreign policy. Communists were the new enemy. Neither Democrats nor Republicans wanted to be accused of being a "Red," a "commie," or "soft on communism." U.S. foreign policy would no longer be isolationist. Cold War foreign policy, called containment, focused on preventing the spread of communism to other countries. Containment policy meant the United States would be involved in international affairs. It meant providing economic aid and using military strength around the globe to stop communism.

The United States began practicing a containment policy in 1946 when President Truman asked Congress for $400 billion for Greece and Turkey to help them resist communist pressure from rebels and neighboring countries. Truman said that the United States must be the leader in supporting the free peoples of the world, an idea known as the Truman Doctrine. Then, in 1947 Secretary of State George Marshall suggested that the United States provide money to help to rebuild war-torn Europe so that it could resist communism. Between 1948 and 1952, the Marshall Plan sent about $17 billion of assistance, with an additional $80 billion over the next fifteen years.

United States foreign policy continued to focus on containment. The goal of the Berlin airlift in 1948 was to keep West Berlin from becoming communist controlled. In 1953 the United States supported a coup in Iran that helped put a dictator, the Shah, in power because he would be our ally. For similar reasons, in 1954 the United States equipped and trained Guatemalan rebels for a successful coup in their country. In 1961 the United States failed to properly support the Bay of Pigs

<u>invasion</u> in Cuba to overthrow Cuban communist dictator Fidel Castro.

Containment policy led the United States into limited warfare and the threat of nuclear war several times. The first time was in 1950, during the Korean War. Communist North Korea invaded non-communist South Korea. The United States asked the United Nations to help South Korea. Although 41 nations sent some type of aid, the United States provided about 90 percent of the troops and military aid. China fought on the side of North Korea, and the Soviet Union provided North Korea with military equipment and supplies. The United States and China faced the possibility of war. Both sides chose not to expand the war outside of Korea. In 1953 North Korea and South Korea signed an <u>armistice</u>. They never signed a peace <u>treaty</u>, so Korea remains divided at the <u>38th parallel</u>.

United Nations forces withdraw from Pyongyang, the North Korean capital, after Chinese enter the war in 1950. The 38th Parallel is still the dividing line between North and South Korea.

A nuclear war between the United States and the Soviet Union almost happened in October 1962 because of an event known as the Cuban Missile Crisis. Photographs taken by <u>satellites</u> showed Soviet <u>missiles</u> installed in Cuba, only 90 miles from Florida. President Kennedy organized a naval blockade of Cuba. He demanded that Soviet <u>premier</u> Khrushchev remove the missiles. Khrushchev demanded that Kennedy remove U.S. missiles from Turkey and promise not to invade Cuba. The world watched and waited. After a week, both sides agreed to each other's demands. Later that year a <u>hot line</u> was set up directly connecting the president of the United States and the premier of the Soviet Union. Its purpose was to reduce the possibility of an accidental war.

The next major threat to turn the Cold War into a hot war was the Vietnam War. As in the Korean War, the United States supported South Vietnam, and the Soviet Union and China supported communist North Vietnam. As in Korea, the United States feared a victory for North Vietnam would lead to the spread of communism into surrounding Asian countries. At first, the United States sent military advisors, then some troops. Gradually the United States sent more and more troops.

The war became hotter in 1965 when the United States started bombing North Vietnam. Soon bombing spread to neighboring Cambodia and Laos. In 1968, with 500,000 U.S. troops in Vietnam and no end of the war in sight, the two sides began peace talks. The United States withdrew its troops and turned the war over to South Vietnam. North Vietnam defeated South Vietnam in 1975 and in 1976 formed the Socialist Republic of Vietnam.

Social, Economic, and Political Struggles: Asia and Africa

After World War II, Africa and Asia experienced social, economic, and political struggles, as a result of colonialism and imperialism. More and more colonized people demanded the right of self-government. Growing nationalism led to independence movements. The first colony to become independent was the Philippines. It was granted independence without a struggle by the United States in 1946. Other colonies experienced bitter conflict and war. For example, Nationalists in Indonesia declared independence from the Dutch after World War II. The Dutch resisted. There were four years of fighting before Indonesia gained independence in 1949. Some former colonies, such as the Philippines, became democracies. Others, such as Indonesia, became dictatorships. By 1965 most colonies in Africa and Asia were independent countries. The European colonial empires were gone.

India had one of the biggest struggles for independence. In 1935, Great Britain granted India the right to local self-government, but kept control of India's national government. Many Indians continued to call for complete independence during World War II. In 1942 Mahatma Gandhi called for nonviolent civil disobedience in his Quit India Movement. This led to widespread protests, demonstrations, and strikes. Some turned violent. Great Britain responded with fines and mass arrests of many people, including Gandhi and all the leaders of the Indian National Congress.

Great Britain realized that Indian nationalism could not be contained. Negotiations for independence began immediately at the end of World War II. The Hindu and Muslim political leaders could not agree on what type of government they wanted. Many Muslims living in India wanted their own country. They feared the Hindu majority would ignore Muslim interests. Muslims organized nationwide demonstrations to demand an independent Muslim state, Pakistan. Hindus and Muslims fought and rioted. In Calcutta, a large city in India, over 5,000 people were killed and 15,000 injured.

In 1947 leaders from Great Britain and India agreed to partition (divide) India into two independent nations, a secular India and a Muslim Pakistan. Over 500 Indian princes had to immediately decide which nation they and their people would join. Hindus living in Pakistan and Muslims living in India had to decide whether or not they should move. Over 10 million people became refugees, displaced from one country to the other. Violence erupted. Hindus attacked Muslims moving to Pakistan, and Muslims attacked Hindus and Sikhs moving to India. Hundreds of thousands of people were killed. Mahatma Gandhi, the leader of the independence movement, urged people to use nonviolence and to tolerate all religions. A Hindu who disagreed with Gandhi assassinated him. Violence between Hindus and Muslims continued. From 1947 to 1949, India and Pakistan fought a war over the region of Kashmir, which is on the border of both countries. They fought again in 1965, 1971, and 1999.

There were also struggles for independence in Indochina, a region, which included the present-day Cambodia, Laos, and Vietnam. Before World War II, France controlled Indochina. However, during the war Japan invaded and occupied Indochina. After Japan's defeat, France wanted control again. Cambodia and Laos became self-governing, but remained under French control. In 1953 Cambodia and Laos became independent nations. Both countries then experienced <u>unstable</u> government and civil war. Today, Laos is a communist state and Cambodia has a <u>constitutional monarchy</u>.

Vietnam's experience was different. Immediately after World War II, the communist leader Ho Chi Minh declared independence for the new Democratic Republic of Vietnam. Talks with France failed, and between 1946 and 1954 France and Vietnam fought a bitter war. Fearing the spread of communism, the United States gave France money to fight the war. China and the Soviet Union supported Ho Chi Minh. In 1954 the French were defeated at Dien Bien Phu. They signed an armistice, the Geneva Accords, which temporarily split Vietnam at the <u>17th parallel</u> into North and South Vietnam. An election was planned for 1956 to decide who would rule a united Vietnam. Because they feared a Ho Chi Minh victory, South Vietnam never agreed to hold the election. In 1957 communist-supported rebels <u>revolt</u>ed against the corrupt government of South Vietnam. The United States began giving South Vietnam military aid and assistance. This was the beginning of the War in Vietnam. Today Vietnam is a communist state.

In 1914 there were two independent African countries. By 1945 there were four. After World War II, colonial powers had neither the money, nor the will to keep their colonies in Africa. Africans who had participated in World War II and its fight for freedom demanded freedom in their homelands. In 1951 Libya was the first country in North Africa to win independence. In 1957 the Ivory Coast became the first African country south of the Sahara Desert to win its independence. Today it is called Ghana. Independence spread throughout the African continent. Today there are over 50 independent African countries.

Independence did not bring peace and prosperity to Africa. Colonial powers had taken the <u>raw materials</u> they wanted or needed. They had not developed the African economies. Since the colonists used low-paid, unskilled workers on farms or in mines, there was a very small <u>middle class</u> in most African countries. Many Africans were <u>illiterate</u> because educating workers was not important to colonial bosses. Most countries used borders drawn by their former colonial rulers. Creating national unity was difficult because African ethnic groups within those borders had different cultures. This led to ethnic conflicts and civil wars. Colonial powers had given Africans little experience in self-government. They were unprepared to build democratic governments. In some countries dictators seized power. These problems continue today in countries such as the Congo, Rwanda, and Sudan.

Fall of the Soviet Union and the end of the Cold War: Causes and Consequences

The Cold War was expensive for the United States and the Soviet Union, especially the arms race. It cost a lot of money to keep a large peacetime military force, develop new weapons, and support allies. Despite these costs, the U.S. market economy continued to grow, providing Americans with a wide selection of goods, services, and many new products invented for the space program. However, the Soviet command economy struggled. The government of the Soviet Union decided how many cars to make as well as how many tanks. The government's main concern was military strength, not consumer products. Most citizens waited years to buy a new car. There were even shortages in food and housing. Shortages led to long lines, waiting lists, inflation, a black market, and very unhappy citizens.

Cold War tensions grew worse during the late 1970s after the Soviet Union invaded Afghanistan. In the 1980s President Ronald Reagan referred to the Soviet Union as an "evil empire." He dramatically increased U.S. military spending. In 1985 when Mikhail Gorbachev became the new leader of the Soviet Union, he wanted to make the Soviet Union stronger without increasing military spending. President Gorbachev signed a treaty with the United States agreeing to destroy some missiles. Gorbachev also withdrew Soviet troops from Afghanistan. His policy of "glasnost," or openness, gave Russians more freedom of speech and expression. Non-Communists could now run for office. Another policy, "perestroika" or restructuring, was introduced to make the economy stronger.

Gorbachev encouraged political and economic reforms in the nations of Eastern Europe attached to the Soviet Union. These reforms eventually led to the collapse of communism in Eastern Europe. In 1989 a series of revolutions took place. Most were nonviolent. In Poland members of Solidarity, a labor union, threatened to strike unless elections were held. The government finally agreed to hold free elections. In 1989 the Communist Party lost control of the Polish parliament. Lech Walesa, a founder and leader of Solidarity, was elected president of Poland in 1990.

Other Eastern European countries such as Hungary, Czechoslovakia, and Romania held free elections and rejected communism, too. The East German government tried to avoid reforms, but the people demonstrated until free elections were held. The new prime minister permitted free travel between East and West Germany and opened the Berlin Wall. Thousands of East Germans crossed the wall and met West Germans. During the following weeks, the public began destroying sections of the concrete wall. The destruction of the Berlin Wall was the beginning of the end of the Cold War. In 1990 East and West Germany reunited.

Gorbachev's reforms also led to the collapse of the Soviet Union in 1991. The Soviet Union consisted of 15 republics; the largest was Russia. Some republics such as Latvia, Estonia, and Lithuania demanded control over their own territory. Feelings of nationalism spread in other republics such as Ukraine, Belarus, and Georgia. The once all-powerful Communist Party complained that Gorbachev's reforms had gone too far. Others, such as Russian president Boris Yeltsin, complained the reforms had not gone far enough.

In 1991 a small group within the Communist Party kidnapped Gorbachev and attempted a coup. Russian citizens did not support the coup. There were mass demonstrations. Gorbachev was freed, but had little power or influence left. The presidents of Russia, Ukraine, and Belarus declared the Soviet Union dissolved. There were now fifteen newly independent nations. Eleven former Soviet republics created a new voluntary association known as the Commonwealth of Independent States.

Suddenly the Soviet Union no longer existed. The Cold War was over. Only five communist nations were left in the world: China, Cuba, Laos, North Korea, and Vietnam.

Regional and Ethnic Conflict

The end of the Cold War did not bring world peace. Regional and ethnic conflicts in Europe, Africa, and Asia became new threats to peace and stability in the world.

African nations struggled with regional and ethnic conflicts. From 1948 until 1993, the white government of South Africa strictly enforced a policy of apartheid, racial segregation. Apartheid laws divided the country into different areas for different races to live and segregated public services, including hospitals, restaurants, schools, and transportation. Although they were the majority of the population, black South Africans were second-class citizens. Most lived in poverty, and none could vote. Years of protest and violence ended in 1993 when South Africa held its first democratic elections. The people elected a multiracial government, including a black president, Nelson Mandela.

Ethnic conflict in Africa during the 1990s led to charges of ethnic cleansing and genocide. In 1994 civil war and ethnic conflict in Rwanda and Burundi between the Hutu and the Tutsi caused the deaths of over one million people and made more than two million homeless. Since 1998, almost four million people have died in ethnic conflicts in the Congo. In the Darfur region of Sudan, over 200,000 Africans have been massacred. Over two million are homeless there, and many have fled to neighboring Chad.

Europe had its share of violent ethnic conflict. In 1991, Yugoslavia began to break apart when Croatia and Slovenia declared independence. When Bosnia-Herzegovina and Macedonia declared independence in 1992, Serbia was against the break up. Serbian president Slobodan Milosevic supported the policy of ethnic cleansing of Muslims and Croats in Serbian-controlled areas. When the province of Kosovo declared independence from Serbia, Milosevic continued his policy of ethnic cleansing of the Albanian Muslims living there.

There have been continuing ethnic conflicts between Arabs and Israelis since the creation of the State of Israel in 1948. The Arab nations refused to recognize Israel's right to exist. Wars between Israel and surrounding Arab nations broke out in 1948, 1956, 1967, and 1973. In 1977 the world was surprised when Egyptian president Anwar Sadat offered to negotiate a peace with Israel. United States president Jimmy Carter invited President Sadat and Israeli prime minister Menachem Begin to the United States to discuss terms for peace. The result was the Camp David Accords, which traded land for peace. In 1979 Egypt officially recognized the State of Israel, and Israel returned the Sinai Peninsula to Egypt. Two years later, President Sadat was assassinated by Muslim extremists.

The Camp David Accords made the other Arab nations angry. The agreement did not mention the issue of the Palestinian people. Most Palestinians were either living under Israel's political rule in the occupied territories of the Gaza Strip and the West Bank, or they were refugees living in Lebanon, Jordan, and Syria. Increasingly, Palestinians supported the Palestine Liberation Organization (PLO), which made armed attacks and raids against Israel. Israel struck back with attacks and raids of their own. They also continued building Jewish settlements in the occupied territories, driving out the Palestinians.

In 1987 the Palestinians expressed their growing frustrations in a series of boycotts, demonstrations, riots, and strikes. Israel responded with military force, and young Palestinians threw rocks at Israeli soldiers. This uprising was called the "intifada." In 1993 the PLO and Israel tried to end the Israeli-Palestinian conflict by signing agreements known as the Oslo Accords. The Palestinian Authority was created and given limited government control in the West Bank and the Gaza Strip in 1994. Israel withdrew most of its troops from those areas, and the Palestinians began taking control. In 1996 Palestinians elected a legislature and a president, PLO leader Yasir Arafat.

In 2000 Palestinian self-rule was still not complete. Another intifada began. These armed attacks included suicide bombers and caused the deaths of hundreds of Israelis. Israel struck back, killing thousands of Palestinians. In 2002 Israel built a huge wall to separate Israel from the West Bank. To reduce tensions and violence, Israeli prime minister Ariel Sharon decided to evacuate all Israeli settlers from the Gaza Strip and the West Bank. Many settlers refused to leave their homes and were forcibly removed by Israeli soldiers.

In 2004 Yasir Arafat died. Hamas, a radical Muslim group involved in terrorist activities, won control of the Palestinian parliament. In 2006 Palestinians still do not have their own nation, and radical Palestinian groups continue to use suicide bombers.

Other areas of the Middle East also saw regional conflicts. During the Lebanese Civil War, started in 1975, Christian groups fought against Muslim groups, including the PLO. Both Syria and Israel were involved. Although the civil war is over, Lebanon remains divided and unstable. In 1980 the Iran-Iraq war began. This eight-year war bankrupted both nations and caused a very high number of casualties for both sides. In 1990 Iraq invaded Kuwait. United States president George H. W. Bush worked through the United Nations and created a coalition of thirty-nine nations. They demanded that Iraqi president Saddam Hussein withdraw his forces from Kuwait. He refused. In January 1991 the Persian Gulf War began. Bombing raids were followed by an invasion of coalition forces. On February 28, 1991 the war ended. A defeated and weakened Saddam Hussein remained in power. Both Iraq and Kuwait suffered large losses of life and property.

Most Muslims were glad that Saddam Hussein's power was limited, but some Muslims were unhappy about U.S. troops stationed in Saudi Arabia. Some saw the West, especially the United States, as the enemy of Islam. Radical Muslim Osama bin Laden and his terrorist group, al-Qaeda, attacked the United States on September 11, 2001. Four commercial jetliners hijacked by 19 terrorists were used as weapons. Two were crashed into the Twin Towers of the World Trade Center in New York City, one into the Pentagon building in Washington D.C., and one crashed in rural Pennsylvania after passengers revolted. Over 3,000 people were killed in these suicide attacks.

United States President George W. Bush declared a "war on terrorism." The president demanded that Afghanistan's rulers, the Taliban, turn over bin Laden. When they refused, the United States and allies attacked Afghanistan. The Taliban was overthrown, but Osama bin Laden was not captured. In 2003 President Bush accused Saddam Hussein of protecting terrorists and possessing weapons of mass destruction. Unable to convince the United Nations to take military action to force Iraq to disarm, President Bush formed a coalition of nations and invaded Iraq. The Iraq War lasted two months. The Iraqi people were freed from a cruel dictator, but no weapons of mass destruction were found. In 2006 there is still no peace in the country.

Terrorist attacks around the world have continued. In 2004 terrorists bombed commuter trains in Madrid, Spain, killing 192 people. In July 2005 four Muslim extremists coordinated terrorist bombings in London, England at three subway stops and on one bus, killing 56 people. In October 2005, bombings in Bali, Indonesia by a terrorist group linked to al-Qaeda killed 23 people. In November 2005 al-Qaeda coordinated bombings in three hotels in Amman, Jordan, killing 60 people. In 2006 Muslim extremists continued attacks, suicide bombings, executions, and assassinations in Iraq.

Glossary
History E

17th parallel – the latitude north of the equator that divided North and South Vietnam in 1954.

38th parallel – the latitude north of the equator that divided North and South Korea in 1945.

airlift – a way to transport people or cargo by air in an emergency. The Berlin airlift was one of the more famous airlifts.

alliance (alliances) – a partnership; an association of groups with a common goal.

Allies (Allied Powers) – name of the group of countries that opposed the Central Powers during World War I and the Axis Powers during World War II.

allies (ally) – friends, supporters; a group of countries joined together with a common purpose.

armistice – an agreement to stop fighting temporarily; a truce or cease-fire.

arms race – competition to have more and more powerful weapons than your opponent.

atomic (Atomic Age) – related to atoms, atomic energy, or atomic bombs (atom bombs); capable of doing much damage; splitting atoms into smaller parts which gives off extreme power and energy.

bankrupted – made unable to pay debts.

Bay of Pigs – an area on the southern coast of Cuba. A U.S. sponsored force of Cuban exiles landed there in 1961 to overthrow Fidel Castro. Almost all of them were killed or captured by Castro's well-prepared armed forces.

black market – an illegal system of buying and selling officially-controlled goods.

bloc – a group or groups joined together for a particular purpose.

blockade – the closing off of an area to keep people or supplies from going in or out.

capitalism (capitalist) – an economic system in which businesses have private owners who make or sell goods for their own profit or for the profit of their shareholders.

casualty (casualties) – a person injured or killed in war or a disaster.

civil disobedience – a method of nonviolent protest. It is a deliberate and public refusal to obey a law and often leads to people being arrested.

civil war – war between different political groups in one country.

civilian – a person not on active duty in the military, police, or firefighting forces.

coalition – a temporary alliance of different persons or groups with a common goal.

Cold War – the global struggle for power and influence between the United States and the Soviet Union following World War II. There was no direct fighting or military combat.

collective – shared.

colonialism (colonial, colonized, colonists) – the policy of establishing a colony. For example, the European nations colonized Africa.

colony (colonies, colonists) – a settlement of people in a new land who maintain ties with their mother country. The original thirteen colonies of the United States received their independence from Great Britain after the Revolutionary War.

command economy – In a command economy, the government or ruler decides what should be produced, who should make it, and who should receive what is made.

communism (communist) – an economic system in which the businesses are owned and operated by the government. The government decides the type, quantity, and price of goods produced. They also decide what workers will make. Communism says it will provide for everyone's needs and get rid of social classes.

concentration camp – a guarded place where persons (prisoners of war, political prisoners, and refugees) are housed; used especially by the Nazis during World War II to confine, punish, and kill large numbers of Jews.

constitutional monarchy – a type of monarchy in which the powers of the king or queen are limited by a constitution and a legislature elected by the citizens.

contain (containment) – to keep under control or to restrict the spreading of the influence of an enemy.

coup (coup d'état) – a sudden, often violent, overthrow of a government by a small group.

culture (cultural, culturally) – the way of life of a group of people, which includes their ideas, beliefs, customs, language, and traditions.

democracy – a form of government in which citizens are the source of power. Government is created and maintained with the consent of the people.

democratic – allowing more people to participate in the decision-making processes of institutions such as government, colleges, or universities. For example, during the 1960s some students wanted to participate in the decisions to set student policies such as curfews and political activities.

dictatorship (dictator) – a form of government in which the ruler (dictator) or ruler's power is not limited by citizens or a legislature. A dictator has absolute power that is enforced by an army and secret police.

emigrate (emigrant) – to leave one's country to live elsewhere. (a person who leaves his country to live elsewhere.)

empire – a group of countries and territories under the control of one ruler or government.

ethnic (ethnicity, ethnically) – having to do with a group of people who share a common culture, language, nationality, race, or religion. For example, new Chinese immigrants settled in a part of the city called China Town, so they could live with their own ethnic group.

ethnic cleansing – removing an ethnic group or groups from an area using force. It could include forced emigration and genocide.

evacuate – to make everyone leave a place.

extermination – killing off all the people.

extremist (extremism) – someone having extreme political or religious opinions.

free trade – international exchange of goods and services without government taxes (tariffs).

genocide – the planned elimination of an ethnic group.

Hamas – Islamic Palestinian organization that supports and is involved in violently resisting Israel in the Israeli-occupied territories.

hijack – to seize a vehicle, like an airplane or bus.

Hinduism (Hindu) – 4,000-year-old religion followed by most of the people of India.

holocaust – slaughter or sacrifice. The mass murder of European Jews and other victims by Adolf Hitler and his followers is called "the Holocaust."

hot line – direct telephone line, always kept open, between two top leaders like the President of the United States and the Premier of Russia.

hydrogen bomb – a bomb that explodes with violent energy, stronger than an atom bomb.

ideology – an organized set of ideas and opinions.

illiterate – unable to read and write.

imperialism – the policy of extending control over other countries or territories; to build an empire.

invade (invasion) – to enter and attempt to conquer or take over a country using force.

Islam – a religion based on a single god, Allah, and on the word of God as revealed to Muhammad during the 17th century and written in the Qur'an (Koran).

isolationism (isolationist) – national policy of avoiding political or military agreements with other countries. (someone who supports such a policy.)

liberation (liberate) – setting someone or something free.

market economy – in a market economy, individuals make their own decisions about what goods to produce and to sell at a profit, with limited governmental interference.

massacre – to cruelly kill or slaughter people.

middle class – all the people who are not rich or poor. Most have a comfortable standard of living.

missile – rocket-propelled weapon.

monarchy (monarch) – a form of government in which the ruler (monarch) is a king, queen, emperor, or empress. A monarch usually inherits the title and holds power for life.

Muslim – a person who practices Islam.

nationalism (nationalist) – loyalty to one's own nation or country; especially putting one nation above all others, with major emphasis on promotion of its culture and interests.

Nazism (Nazi) – the beliefs and practices of Adolf Hitler's National Socialist German Workers' Party including racial superiority, government control of society and the economy, and loyalty to one's nation or people above all else.

negotiation (negotiate) – a discussion to find a solution to a disagreement. Using negotiation, opposing parties talk and compromise, instead of fighting, to find a solution to a problem.

nonviolence (nonviolent) – the belief and practice of working actively for political and social change without using violence. Mahatma Gandhi and Dr. Martin Luther King, Jr. were both strong supporters of the philosophy of nonviolence.

nuclear – involving atomic weapons and atomic energy.

occupied (occupation) – invaded and controlled.

Palestine Liberation Organization (PLO) – political and parliamentary organization of Palestinian Arabs dedicated to the establishment of an independent Palestinian state.

parliament – the legislature or law-making body of countries such as Canada, the United Kingdom, and Israel.

premier – prime minister.

prime minister – the chief executive in a parliamentary system of government.

propaganda – selective facts, ideas, or information used to win support for a cause or a person. It usually has a strong emotional appeal.

raw material(s) – unprocessed natural thing(s) like wood and metal that are used to manufacture products.

refugee – a person who runs away for safety, usually to another country.

region (regional) – a geographic area defined by some characteristics or features not found in surrounding areas. Northwest Ohio, the coal-mining region of Ohio, and the Arctic region are examples.

reunify (reunification) – to unite again; to join after being separated. East and West Germany were reunified after the 1989 fall of the Berlin Wall.

revolt – to rebel against an authority such as a leader or government; a rebellion or uprising.

rural – relating to or characteristic of the country, country people, or country life. An example of rural people is farmers.

satellite – (1) a smaller object that circles a larger object in the sky; (2) a country that is economically and politically controlled by a more powerful nation.

secular – worldly, not religious or spiritual.

segregation (segregate) – the law or practice of separating and isolating people by characteristics such as race, religion, or nationality.

Sikh – a person who believes in Sikhism, a religion from northern India.

space race – a competition between the United States and the Soviet Union that lasted over ten years. The space race began in 1957 when the Soviet Union launched the first artificial satellite, Sputnik.

stabile or stable (stability, stabilize) – not changing and not likely to change.

strike – refusing to work, in order to achieve a goal such as higher pay or better working conditions.

suicide bomber – someone who plans to destroy an important economic, military, political, or symbolic target, usually by attaching the bomb to his/her own body.

superpower – a country that is dominant in the world. During the Cold War, there were two: the United States and the Soviet Union; now it is just the United States.

systematically – plan or act methodically step by step.

Taliban – an Islamic fundamentalist group that controlled Afghanistan from 1996 to 2001. After the September 11, 2001 attacks, they refused to deliver Osama bin Laden and other Al-Qaeda leaders to the United States. A U.S.-led coalition invaded Afghanistan and drove the Taliban from power. Osama bin Laden was not captured.

terrorism (terrorist) – using fear and violence for political purposes.

tolerate (tolerance) – respecting the beliefs, customs, and physical differences of others.

total war – a war which involves all the resources of a nation including the armed forces and the civilian population. Farms, factories, and civilian populations, as well as armed forces are targets.

treaty – a formal agreement between two or more rulers or nations.

Truman Doctrine – a policy established by President Truman in 1947, stating that the United States would provide military and economic assistance to countries threatened by "outside pressures."

unstable – easily changed, not permanent.

weapons of mass destruction – nuclear, chemical, or biological weapons that can kill many people at one time.

work camps – the term used by the Nazis for their concentration camps where prisoners were used as slave labor.

worldview – a complete set of beliefs and views about the world and everyday life; a way of seeing and interpreting the world; a viewpoint.

Yalta Conference – a meeting between President Roosevelt, Prime Minister Churchill, and Premier Stalin at Yalta (a seaport in the Ukraine) February 4-12, 1945 in anticipation of the defeat of Germany.

HISTORY F

DOMESTIC AFFAIRS IN THE UNITED STATES DURING THE TWENTIETH CENTURY

Identify major historical patterns in the domestic affairs of the United States during the 20th century and explain their significance.

The Twenties: Major Political, Economic, and Social Developments

After the Russian Revolution of 1917, many Americans worried about a communist revolution in the United States. A radical union, the International Workers of the World (IWW), wanted to overthrow capitalism and create a socialist society. In 1919 a series of strikes, including the Boston police strike and the Seattle general strike, made other unions look radical. That same year 38 package bombs were mailed to a number of well-known Americans, including billionaire businessman John D. Rockefeller and U.S. attorney general A. Mitchell Palmer. Although no one was able to identify the bombers, public anger and fear were directed at anarchists, communists, and socialists. These fears grew quickly and became a national hysteria (panic) that historians call the Red Scare.

In response, Attorney General Palmer organized raids of communist, socialist, and labor union offices searching for radicals. The Palmer raids led to the arrest of over 10,000 people. Most were denied their constitutional rights. About 600 were deported. In 1920 Attorney General Palmer declared a communist revolution was planned for May 1, May Day. Nothing happened, but in September a huge bomb exploded on Wall Street killing over 30 and injuring over 300. When 1921 ended with no revolution, public opinion changed. The Red Scare was over. However, there would be another Red Scare after World War II.

World War I changed the attitudes of many Americans about women's suffrage. During World War I, women fought on the home front. Women took over traditional male jobs at home and the workplace. While men were away fighting, some women took industrial jobs and helped run businesses. In 1919 Congress passed the women's suffrage amendment to the Constitution. By 1920, two-thirds of the state legislatures had ratified the Nineteenth Amendment, which guaranteed women the right to vote in all national, state, and local elections.

In 1900 about 90 percent of African Americans lived in the South. Most lived in rural areas. In the early 1900s, some African Americans migrated north to escape segregation, discrimination, and violence and in search of job opportunities. Then, a shortage of workers during World War I encouraged hundreds of thousands of African Americans to migrate to northern cities such as New York, Philadelphia, Cleveland, and Chicago. African American newspapers such as Robert Abbott's *The Chicago Defender* reported on the opportunities for a better life in the North. Migrants sent letters home to family and friends, telling them about their new lives. About 1,500,000 African Americans migrated north in search of the "Promised Land" between 1900 and 1930.

African American migrants soon discovered new problems in northern cities. Although wages were higher, lack of education and discrimination kept many in low-paying jobs as laborers and servants. Housing was segregated, overcrowded, and run down. Competition for jobs and expanding black neighborhoods increased racial tension. There were 25 race riots in 1919. About 100 people died, and many more were injured. A second Ku Klux Klan (KKK) had formed in Georgia in 1915 and quickly spread to northern states such as Indiana and Ohio. By 1925 the KKK claimed 5,000,000 members. Meanwhile, Marcus Garvey's Universal Negro Improvement Association (UNIA) attracted black members. Garvey believed that the United States would never solve its racial problems. While instilling black pride through his weekly newspaper, speeches, and parades, Garvey supported black separatism and a back-to-Africa movement.

A rally of the second Ku Klux Klan in 1922. The Klan used scare tactics, such as cross burning, lynching, and other acts of violence against anybody who was "different." Targets included African Americans, foreigners, Catholics, and Jews.

As racism increased during the 1920s, so did nativism. The Ku Klux Klan directed its hatred not only to blacks, but also to Communists, Catholics, Jews, and immigrants. Congress passed immigration laws, which reflected nativist attitudes. These laws established quotas for immigrant groups, favoring immigrants from Northern and Western Europe and discriminating against immigrants from Asia and from southern and eastern Europe. One example of the power of nativism is the 1921 Sacco-Vanzetti trial. Two Italian immigrants were found guilty of robbery and murder despite a lack of hard evidence. Many people, including the judge, assumed their guilt because they were active in the anarchist movement. Despite appeals and international attention, they were executed in 1927.

After World War I, Americans wanted to return to "normalcy." But Americans could not agree on what was normal. A dramatic clash of values took place. Some people, often the young, urban, and rebellious, just wanted to let loose. They saw themselves as the new and modern generation. For the modernists, the 1920s were the "Roaring Twenties," a decade of wild parties, bootleg liquor, speakeasies, jazz, flappers, and the Charleston. The modernists were materialistic, spending their money on automobiles, radios, and the new household appliances, such as vacuum cleaners. They wanted to go to professional baseball games and maybe see Babe Ruth; to see movies starring Rudolph Valentino, the "Latin Lover," or Clara Bow, the "It Girl;" or to swim at the beach wearing the newest style, a daring one-piece bathing suit.

To other Americans "normalcy" meant a return to the pre-war traditional values. These traditionalists saw the new modern attitudes and urban life style as immoral and pleasure seeking. Many were rural and small town Christian fundamentalists. Instead of listening to jazz, they listened to evangelists, such as Billy Sunday, preach about the evils of drinking, dancing, and gambling. They supported the Eighteenth Amendment, that established prohibition. They were against teaching evolution in the public schools. The 1925 court case *Tennessee v. John Scopes*, the so-called "Scopes Monkey Trial," highlighted this clash between rural traditionalists and urban modernists.

Literature of the twenties rejected the values of the pre-war generation and the fundamentalists. World War I left many young writers <u>disillusioned</u> and <u>alienated</u>. They rejected the traditional values of their parents' generation and the shallow materialism of the new modern generation. Writers such as F. Scott Fitzgerald and Ernest Hemingway spent time in Europe looking for inspiration. Gertrude Stein called these young writers members of the "Lost Generation."

African American writers had a different experience. Harlem in the 1920s was the cultural capital of the United States for African Americans. Writers such as Langston Hughes, Zora Neale Hurston, and Claude McKay were a part of the Harlem <u>Renaissance</u>. Their creative works defined a new proud, strong, assertive identity. The same positive themes were reflected by African American artists, musicians, and entertainers such as Aaron Douglas, Duke Ellington, and Josephine Baker. These African Americans insisted on defining and redefining themselves by their standards.

The 1920s ended with a crash, the Stock Market Crash of 1929. During the twenties more Americans than ever before invested in the <u>stock market</u> and <u>real estate</u>. People and businesses began <u>speculating</u> in search of quick profits and "get rich quick" schemes. Speculation drove up the price of <u>stocks</u> and real estate. People also began "buying on margin," which means putting a small amount of money down on a stock or property purchase. Eventually people began to realize their stocks were not worth what they paid for them. On October 24, 1929, Black Thursday, so many people sold their stocks that prices dropped dramatically. On October 29, Black Tuesday, there were not enough buyers for all who wanted to sell. Suddenly people and businesses found themselves holding stocks that were worthless. Those who had bought on margin still owed lenders. The market had gone from <u>boom to bust</u>.

The Thirties: Major Political, Economic, and Social Developments

The <u>Great Depression</u> began with The Stock Market Crash. What caused the Great Depression? Economists and historians list several causes. Here are six of them.

- Unequal distribution of wealth: During the 1920s, the top 5% of the people earned a lot of money. They took in 33% of the

country's wealth. The incomes of farmers and ordinary workers did not increase.
- Overproduction of goods: Most people could not afford to buy all the goods being made. Factories had to cut back on production and lay off workers.
- Easy credit: Many people bought on credit and could not make their payments when the Great Depression came.
- Speculation: People and businesses speculated in the stock market, often "buying on margin." When the stock market crashed, they lost all they had invested and borrowed and still owed their lenders.
- <u>Tariff</u>s: The U.S. government passed The Smoot-Hawley Tariff to protect some American businesses. It increased tariffs on <u>imported</u> goods. Other countries responded by raising tariffs on U.S. goods going into their countries. American businesses sold less to those foreign countries, and business profits went down.
- Restricted money supply: The Federal Reserve Board lowered the amount of money in use. People and businesses could not easily borrow money to pay debts and improve their businesses.

How terrible was the Great Depression? As the economy continued to fail, people panicked. <u>Consumer</u>s lost confidence in the economy. They bought less. Factories and businesses cut back on production and laid off workers. By 1933 about 25% of the workforce was unemployed. Those with jobs earned less or worked fewer hours. People who could not pay their debts lost their homes, farms, businesses, cars, and other possessions. The Depression was a time of standing in long lines—bread lines, soup lines, and job lines. Some businessmen, now poor and jobless, sold apples on the street for a nickel. <u>Hobo</u>s rode the rails (trains) from town to town looking for work. Young people left their homes looking for food. Homeless camps appeared in major cities. Gangsters, such as Bonnie and Clyde, robbed banks. Protests about the lack of jobs, such as the Bonus Army March on Washington, D.C. in 1932, turned violent. People were afraid.

In 1931 another disaster hit the United States. It stopped raining in much of the <u>Great Plains</u>. By 1936 only a few drops of rain had fallen. Winds as strong as 50 miles an hour blew topsoil into the air creating a dust bowl in parts of Oklahoma, Kansas, Colorado, New Mexico, and Texas. Many poor farmers from this area, called "Okies," lost their farms. Many decided to pack up their few belongings and migrate to California to find jobs as fruit and vegetable pickers. Over 350,000 traveled nearly 2,000 miles only to discover there were few jobs. Many settled in hastily set up government farm labor camps where they experienced sickness and starvation. John Steinbeck wrote a novel, *The Grapes of Wrath*, in 1939 to tell the world about the suffering of the Okies.

YEARS OF DUST

RESETTLEMENT ADMINISTRATION
Rescues Victims
Restores Land to Proper Use
No rain, no crop, no livelihood, and for many no hope.

President Herbert Hoover tried to restore confidence in the economy by saying that things would improve soon. But things got worse. Hoover thought that state and local governments and private charities should give public relief. He didn't want people to depend on the federal government to solve their problems. By the time he saw the need for more direct government action, his policies gave too little help, too late.

In 1932 voters decided it was time for a change. They elected Democratic candidate Franklin Delano Roosevelt. Roosevelt's campaign song was "Happy Days Are Here Again." He promised the American people a "new deal." On Inauguration Day he declared, "The only thing we have to fear is fear itself." The very next day, he stopped the bank panic by declaring a bank holiday, closing all banks until order and confidence in the banking system were restored. Several days later, he began his "fireside chats" on the radio to explain his policies and to restore confidence in the economy.

What was this "new deal" that President Roosevelt promised the American people? At first, no one was sure. President Roosevelt had no concrete programs, but he was willing to experiment. He asked his advisors and a group of university professors called the "Brain Trust" for fresh ideas and new programs. The New Deal became a series of programs and agencies designed to provide the American people with relief, reform, and recovery.

Relief, Reform, & Recovery Programs of the New Deal

Program	Services
Agriculture Adjustment Administration (AAA)	Paid farmers to grow less in order to raise crop prices (Such payments are called subsidies.)
Federal Emergency Relief Administration (FERA)	Federal money to help the state and local jobless and homeless
Public Works Administration (PWA) Civil Works Administration (CWA) Works Progress Administration (WPA)	Federal money for jobs on projects such as roads, bridges, public buildings, and the arts
Civilian Conservation Corps (CCC) National Youth Administration	Education, training, and jobs for youth
Federal Deposit Insurance Corporation (FDIC)	Bank deposits guaranteed up to $5,000
Federal Housing Administration (FHA)	Loans insured for building or repairing houses
National Labor Relations Act	Unions guaranteed the right to organize and workers guaranteed the right to join a union
Fair Labor Standards Act	A minimum wage, maximum hours, no child labor
Social Security Act	An old-age insurance plan, unemployment compensation, assistance for the disabled, and some aid for dependent children

Although President Roosevelt was elected four times, he had many critics. Some said his New Deal was making government too big and strong. The Supreme Court seemed to agree when it said two of his major reform programs were unconstitutional.

Roosevelt responded by asking Congress to pass a bill that permitted the president to add one federal judge for each judge over the age of 70. Under this bill, President Roosevelt would have been able to appoint six new Supreme Court justices. His nominees would, of course, agree with his ideas. Critics called the bill "court-packing."

Democrats and Republicans in Congress and the public overwhelmingly opposed this bill. They said President Roosevelt was trying to destroy the U.S. Constitution's system of checks and balances. Some accused him of wanting to become a dictator.

The New Deal put the federal government in charge of promoting a healthy economy and social justice in the country. These new responsibilities made the federal government bigger, especially the executive branch. The New Deal did not, however, end the Great Depression. There was some economic improvement, but not an economic recovery. When World War II began, the federal government began spending billions of dollars for weapons and supplies. Suddenly factories needed workers, and unemployment dropped. This massive amount of government spending to support the war effort ended the Great Depression.

World War II: The Home Front

World War II, like World War I, was a total war. It had a major effect on the lives of all people: soldiers and civilians, men and women, and even children. It affected the economy and the media, including radio, movies, and comic books. It offered new opportunities and challenges to African Americans, Japanese Americans, Mexican Americans, and women.

After the bombing of Pearl Harbor, President Roosevelt created the War Production Board (WPB). It decided which companies needed to become wartime industries and made sure they received the raw materials needed. The WPB promised those industries would get a generous profit for their products. Automobile assembly lines began making tanks instead of cars. Battleships, submarines, bombers, bombs, M-1 rifles, ammunition, uniforms, bandages, and other war material became necessities.

U.S. companies <u>armed</u> and equipped military forces for the fight in Europe and Asia and gave assistance to U.S. <u>allies</u>. To pay for the war, the federal government raised income taxes and sold <u>war bonds</u>. For the first time most American citizens paid income taxes and had them automatically deducted from their paychecks.

Wartime production created jobs, but it also created shortages of consumer products and the threat of <u>inflation</u>. Government agencies were formed to help the economy adjust. The Office of Price Administration (OPA) had the power to freeze prices and rents. It <u>ration</u>ed products needed for the war effort. Civilians received coupons limiting their purchases of products such as tires, gasoline, fuel oil, sugar, coffee, meats, and nylon. The National War Labor Board (NWLB) had the power to set wages and hours and oversee working conditions in important national industries, such as airlines, automobiles, shipping, and mining. Unions agreed not to strike during the war and to bring their wage and hour complaints to the NWLB.

War information was always in the newspapers and on the radio. The Office of War Information (OWI) was created to control the release of war news. However, the media usually supported the government's official view of the war voluntarily. The goal was to keep up public <u>morale</u> and support for the war effort. <u>Propaganda</u> was everywhere. The OWI produced radio programs such as *This is Our Enemy* and hundreds of newsreels shown in theaters before the main feature. A series of <u>documentary</u> films were made by Hollywood directors for the government to explain American involvement in the war to soldiers and civilians. Patriotic movies such as *So Proudly We Hail* and songs such as *God Bless America* and *White Christmas* were popular. War posters in factories, public buildings, schools, and storefront windows called on Americans to "Buy War Bonds," "Produce for Victory," "Train to Be a Nurse's Aide," and "Remember Pearl Harbor." Comic book superheroes such as Captain Marvel and Captain America fought Axis Power supervillains.

World War II changed the U.S. workforce. Most able-bodied men were either in the armed forces or working by 1943. The government encouraged women to get jobs. "Rosie the <u>Riveter</u>" became the symbol of women who accepted their patriotic duty and went to work. About six million women worked in shipyards, on assembly lines, and in defense plants. Most, however, held jobs as secretaries and clerks. They were all paid less than men and were expected to return to their primary responsibilities of home and family after the war.

During World War II, many African Americans and Mexican Americans got jobs. In 1941 President Roosevelt, under pressure from civil rights leaders such as A. Philip Randolph, issued the Fair Employment Act. It banned discrimination based on race, creed, color, or national origin in all federal agencies and private defense industries. Over one million African Americans migrated north and west to take advantage of job opportunities. Racial tension increased in northern cities. In 1943 riots broke out in Harlem and Detroit. Racial tensions also increased in urban areas of the Southwest, when Mexican Americans also took advantage of new wartime jobs. The government let Mexican farm workers enter the United States as temporary workers, called "braceros." Tensions due to this sudden increase in Mexicans led to the Zoot Suit Riots in Los Angeles, California, in 1943.

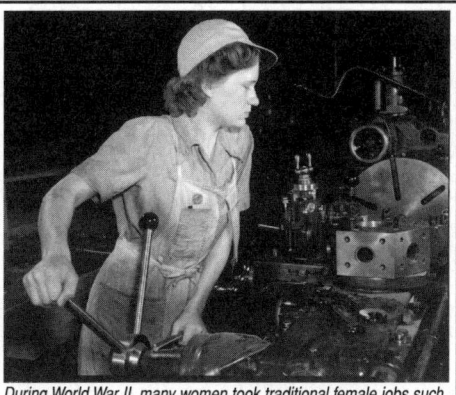

During World War II, many women took traditional female jobs such as secretary and clerk. However, some took traditional male jobs such as electrician, mechanic, and welder. The woman in the photograph is operating a lathe.

World War II changed the U.S. workforce. The war effort brought defense jobs not only to women, but to women of all races.

After the Japanese bombing of Pearl Harbor, Japanese Americans were suspected of being spies and traitors. Anti-Japanese hysteria gripped the

West Coast. In 1942 President Roosevelt issued an executive order that forced over 110,000 Japanese and Japanese Americans to leave their homes and live in internment camps located in remote desert areas in western states. They brought only what they could carry. People lost their homes, businesses, farms, most of their possessions, and much of their pride. The camps were fenced, patrolled by guards, and had primitive living conditions. German and Italian Americans experienced some prejudice during the war, but only Japanese Americans experienced internment and loss of civil liberties.

Major Domestic Developments After 1945

After World War II, many people worried about a return to economic hard times. Instead, the U.S. economy entered one of the longest periods of continued expansion in its history. The gross national product grew from about $200 billion in 1945 to almost $970 billion in 1970. Per capita personal income grew from about $1,200 in 1945 to almost $4,000 in 1970. By 1970 almost 60 percent of all families were members of the middle class.

Many factors caused this economic boom. With few consumer goods available during the war, many Americans put their money in savings accounts. Now they longed to spend money, especially on houses and cars. Business and industry rushed to change to a peacetime economy. Real wages were higher which meant consumers had more money to spend. In addition, the GI Bill of 1944 gave veterans the opportunity to go to college at government expense and to take out low-interest, long-term loans to buy houses, farms, and businesses. Returning servicemen wanted to marry and start families. The result was a baby boom. Between 1945 and 1964 about 78 million babies were born. This, of course, increased the demand for consumer products.

The United States turned into a consumer culture. People saw cars as status symbols, television as our major source of entertainment, appliances as necessities, and gadgets as adult toys. The American economy depended on consumption.

Companies continually introduced new and improved products. They hired advertising agencies to persuade consumers that conveniences were necessities, wants were needs, and consumption brings happiness. Despite pockets of poverty, the United States became an <u>affluent society</u>.

The government continued to play an active role in the postwar economy. Fighting the <u>Cold War</u> was expensive, but most Americans supported massive military spending to stop <u>communism</u>. About half of the federal budget went to the military. Military spending especially helped the aviation and electronic industries grow. The relationship between business and government grew stronger.

The postwar economic boom caused major shifts in the population as more people could afford to move to the <u>suburb</u>s. Builder William J. Levitt, one of the pioneers who mass-produced low-priced homes, helped make suburban living affordable. <u>Suburbanization</u> meant the population of major cities declined. With white Americans moving to the suburbs, the central cities increasingly became the home of poor nonwhites. Businesses followed their customers and built shopping centers to meet the needs of middle class <u>suburbanite</u>s. The Interstate Highway Act of 1956 built 42,000 miles of federal highways, connecting major cities and making it even easier to move away from the city centers. By 1970 almost 38 percent of the population lived in the suburbs.

People also moved from the Frost Belt (colder northern states) and into the Sun Belt (southern states between Florida and California). The population especially grew in the West and Southwest. A warmer climate and more job opportunities in defense industries and service industries encouraged this migration. In 1963 California passed New York to become the state with the largest population. Political power also shifted to the Sun Belt. Of the nine presidents elected between 1960 and 2004, seven were from the Sun Belt.

The African American migration continued. Between 1940 and 1970, about four million African Americans moved to northern and western cities in search of opportunities. African American families living in the North and West earned more money and had a higher standard of living than southern blacks. More families owned their homes and saw their children graduate from high school. However, frustration with continued discrimination, segregation, and the slow progress of the civil rights movement led to riots in major cities during the 1960s. In Cleveland there were riots in the Hough area in 1966 and in the Glenville area in 1968. The riots encouraged many white American and middle-class African American families to move to the suburbs.

The United States experienced a second Red Scare after World War II. When the war ended, national security was still a major concern. The developing Cold War only increased fears of communist conspiracies. In 1947 President Truman's Loyalty Review Board began investigating the backgrounds of all federal employees. Thousands were fired or resigned. The House of Representatives Un-American Activities Committee (HUAC) began searching for Communists. In 1947 the HUAC investigated the motion picture industry. Those who refused to testify were held in contempt of court. Others found themselves blacklisted by employers. The imprisonment of former Assistant Secretary of State Alger Hiss in 1949 for perjury about charges of espionage convinced many Americans that communism was an immediate threat. That same year Julius and Ethel Rosenberg were accused of turning over atomic secrets to the Soviets. They were tried for treason, found guilty, and executed.

Into this tense atmosphere came Senator Joseph McCarthy. In 1950 he claimed he had a list of 205 known Communists working in the U.S. State Department. When questioned by the media, he refused to release any evidence. Instead, he made highly emotional, vicious attacks on public officials, private citizens, and anyone who dared attack him. Many people responded positively to his call to root out Communists in the United States. Senator McCarthy found himself riding a wave of anti-communist hysteria. His communist "witch hunt" made him one of the most powerful men in the country. Even Presidents Truman and Eisenhower were afraid to speak out against him. In 1954 McCarthy's hearings about possible Communists in the U.S. were televised. When viewers saw

Senator McCarthy make false claims and <u>bully</u> witnesses, he lost much of his public support and his political power. By the end of 1954, the U.S. Senate found the courage to <u>censure</u> him. <u>McCarthyism</u> was over.

In 1957 a new Cold War challenge occurred. The Soviet Union launched Sputnik, the first man-made <u>satellite</u> to circle the globe. Americans were shocked. Had the United States fallen behind the Soviet Union in science and technology? In 1958 the U.S. launched its first satellite, Explorer 1. That same year the U.S. Congress and President Eisenhower created the National Aeronautics and Space Administration (NASA) to focus on missile development and space exploration. The space race had begun.

Space Race Highlights

1959	The Soviet Union launched the first space <u>probe</u> to escape the pull of the Earth's gravity.
1961	Yuri Gagarin of the Soviet Union became the first person to orbit the earth.
1961	Alan Shepard became the first American launched into space.
1962	John Glenn of Ohio became the first American to orbit the earth.
1963	Valentina Tereshkova of the Soviet Union became the first woman in space.
1965	Soviet Union cosmonauts completed the world's first space walk.
1965	The Americans completed their first space walk.
1968	The United States launched the first manned space mission to orbit the moon.
1969	Americans Neil Armstrong and Buzz Aldrin became the first humans to land on the moon.
1970	After 1970 the United States and the Soviet Union began cooperating more on space programs. Space scientists proposed space stations, reusable space shuttles, and unmanned probes to land on or fly close to other planets.

The changes in immigration patterns after World War II had a dramatic effect on the United States. The Immigration and Nationality Act of 1965 ended quotas based on national origin. The eastern hemisphere received a quota of 170,000 and the western hemisphere's quota was 120,000. In addition, wives, husbands, parents, and minor children of citizens were permitted to enter without being counted as part of the quota. The result was more immigration from Asia and Latin American and less from Europe and Canada.

Between 2000 and 2004, Mexico, China, India, the Philippines, and Vietnam accounted for the largest number of legal immigrants. There were also about 12 million illegal immigrants, about 80 percent of them from Mexico. Hispanics are now the largest minority ethnic group in the United States. The largest Hispanic ethnic groups are Mexican, Cuban, and Puerto Rican. Their Hispanic culture has influenced our food, music, and sports.

The Civil Rights Movement

Throughout the 20th century, groups such as the National Association for the Advancement of Colored People (NAACP), the Urban League, the Nation of Islam, and the Congress of Racial Equality (CORE) fought for equality for African Americans. But it was after World War II that the modern civil rights movement really began. During the war many African Americans rallied behind the "Double V" campaign, which stood for victory at home and victory abroad. Over one million African American men and women in the armed forces had fought against the Nazis, a racist enemy. They returned home where segregation was the enemy and wanted victory there, too.

Immediately after the war, some changes did take place. African Americans were increasingly visible in the sports and entertainment industries. In 1947 Jackie Robinson joined the Brooklyn Dodgers, breaking the color barrier in baseball. He went on to be the National League Rookie of the Year. That same year Larry Doby joined the Cleveland Indians. In 1948 President Truman ended segregation in the armed forces. Rock 'n' Roll music of the 1950s introduced Chuck Berry, Fats

Domino, Little Richard, and other black rhythm and blues singers to white audiences.

The fight to end segregation continued. In 1954 the U.S. Supreme Court ruled unanimously in *Brown v. Board of Education* that "separate educational facilities are <u>inherently</u> unequal." The Brown decision overturned the 1896 *Plessy v. Ferguson* decision. All states were ordered to <u>desegregate</u> their schools. Many states and communities organized resistance, including closing schools and encouraging newly formed private, segregated schools. In 1957 President Eisenhower had to use federal troops to ensure the peaceful <u>integration</u> of nine black students at Central High School in Little Rock, Arkansas.

The next legal challenge to segregation focused on public transportation. In 1955 Rosa Parks, a black woman, was arrested for refusing to give up her seat to a white man on a public bus in Montgomery, Alabama. Outrage about her arrest led to the call for a <u>boycott</u> and the appearance of a new civil rights leader, Dr. Martin Luther King, Jr. For 382 days African American residents of Montgomery refused to ride the buses. In 1956 the U.S. Supreme Court ruled that segregation on public transportation was unconstitutional. This victory gave Dr. King national attention.

Dr. King was a Baptist minister influenced by the <u>nonviolent</u> ideas of India's Mahatma Gandhi. He preached a philosophy of nonviolent resistance in the face of injustice. He helped form the Southern Christian Leadership Conference (SCLC) to organize nonviolent protests. Soon students practiced King's nonviolent direct action by organizing <u>sit-in</u> <u>demonstration</u>s and being <u>freedom riders</u>. Televised reactions to these protests showed the American public the hatred and violence of Southern white racists.

At the 1963 March on Washington, Dr. King gave his inspirational "I Have a Dream"

About 250,000 Americans, black and white, participated in the 1963 civil rights march on Washington. This photograph shows Dr. Martin Luther King, Jr. delivering his famous "I Have a Dream" speech on the steps of the Lincoln Memorial.

speech, appealing to the conscience of the country. Increasing numbers of white Americans supported his call for equality and justice. One year later President Lyndon B. Johnson signed the Civil Rights Act of 1964. It banned discrimination by race, color, religion, sex, or national origin in public facilities and employment. Encouraged by another protest, the March on Selma, Congress passed the Voting Rights Act of 1965. It outlawed the use of <u>literacy tests</u> and <u>poll taxes</u> as requirements for voting registration and provided federal registration of voters when necessary. <u>Jim Crow</u> laws were abolished and the number of black registered voters increased dramatically.

Despite signs of progress, frustration with the slow pace of change was growing. Some black leaders called for a more <u>militant</u> approach. Nation of Islam minister Malcolm X preached black separatism and <u>nationalism</u>. He said African Americans must control their own communities. His answer was not nonviolence. Racism must be fought and freedom won "by any means necessary." Other black militant groups such as the Student Nonviolent Coordinating Committee (SNCC) and the Black Panthers called for "Black Power." Between 1964 and 1968, anger and frustration in black neighborhoods led to rioting in cities such as New York, Los Angeles, Cleveland, Detroit, and Newark. In 1968 Dr. Martin Luther King, Jr. was assassinated, and riots erupted in every major city across the nation.

The modern civil rights movement ended legal segregation, made <u>racial discrimination</u> illegal, and destroyed barriers preventing African Americans from voting. Many of the movement's major gains were political. African Americans were elected to the House of Representatives and the Senate, appointed to presidential cabinets and the Supreme Court, and elected and appointed as state and local officials. The size of the African American middle class grew and so did the number of blacks graduating from high school and college. However, major problems surrounding poverty remain unsolved.

The modern civil rights movement inspired other minority groups. Native Americans became more assertive and organized. Most still lived on <u>reservations</u> and were not interested in integration. They wanted more land, stolen land returned, and <u>self-determination</u>. In 1968 the American Indian Movement (AIM) formed to fight for the rights of Native Americans and to revive the importance of cultural traditions.

Like other minority groups, Mexican Americans wanted equality. They, too, lived with too much poverty, segregation, and discrimination. In 1962, Cesar Chavez founded the United Farm Workers Association (FWA) to organize farm workers into a union. The FWA used nonviolent methods, such as strikes and boycotts, to win improvements in wages and working conditions. The <u>Chicano</u> Movement of the mid-1960s wanted to separate Mexican Americans from the <u>Anglo</u> population and to preserve their cultural identity. The members called for boycotts of schools that discriminated against their culture. Student groups held protests, demonstrations, and walkouts. One militant group, the Brown Berets, patterned itself after the Black Panthers.

Social Unrest, Protest, and Change

Inspired by the civil rights movement, groups, such as college students, <u>antiwar</u> protesters, and women, organized and called for changes. Among the protesting groups in the early 1960s was the Students for a Democratic Society (SDS). The SDS demanded colleges and universities become more <u>democratic</u>. They felt students should participate in the decisions that directly affected their lives. One protest at the University of California in Berkeley in 1964 was called the Free Speech Movement. Through this protest Berkeley students demanded an end to the ban on political activities on campus. Many of the student protesters had been active in civil rights demonstrations, so they organized sit-ins. One sit-in led to 800 arrests. Students in other colleges and universities began to protest campus rules and regulations, including dorm hours and visitors.

U.S. involvement in the war in Vietnam increased. By 1965 the U.S. government was <u>draft</u>ing young men to fight in Vietnam. Americans protested. Student groups in colleges and universities held antiwar rallies. The SDS organized the first national antiwar demonstration in Washington DC in 1965. As more and more Americans were killed or injured, the antiwar movement grew. Mothers, doctors, ministers, college professors, and even some Vietnam veterans protested U.S. involvement in the war. Around 300,000 people joined an antiwar march in New York City in 1967. Nightly news reports brought depressing images of suffering, death, and destruction in Vietnam; angry protesters; and daily body counts into American homes. Although most Americans and most students were not <u>activists</u>, by 1968 many Americans were questioning U.S. participation in the war in Vietnam.

In 1968 U.S. soldiers were told to destroy the My Lai village enemy soldiers and sympathizers. When the killing stopped, more than 350 apparently unarmed women and children had been massacred. Images like this one provoked world outrage and helped turn U.S. public opinion and that of Congress against the country's involvement in the war.

As the war continued, some antiwar protesters became more militant. Protesters occupied buildings, shouted swear words, burned their draft cards, poured blood on draft records, and fought with police. The most radical group, the Weathermen, bombed buildings and started riots. In 1970 protesters demonstrated on college campuses across the United States. At Kent State University in Ohio, National Guardsmen, ordered by the governor to restore order, shot and killed four students and injured nine. Ten days later at Jackson State in Mississippi, two black students were killed, and 12 were injured. Student strikes and the fear of more violence closed hundreds of colleges, universities, and high schools.

The antiwar movement continued until the United States and Vietnam signed a <u>cease-fire</u> in 1973. U.S. casualties included over 58,000 American soldiers killed, 153,000 wounded, and over 14,000 missing in action (MIA). Vietnamese casualties included about five million Vietnamese soldiers and two to four million civilians killed. The last U.S. military forces left Saigon, Vietnam, on April 30, 1975. Vietnam became a communist state.

Because of the civil rights movement and the Vietnam War, many young Americans questioned authority and tradition. Their new viewpoints led to a general youth rebellion. Beginning in the 1950s, people saw signs of youth rebellion in the writing of the Beats, or Beatniks, and Rock 'n' Roll music. During the 1960s, more young people joined the youth rebellion. Some blamed their parents' generation for problems such as war, racism, and poverty. They rejected traditional American values, saying these values were shallow and materialistic. They called for a world of peace, love, and harmony. Under the symbols of "flower power," they chanted, "Make love not war." Some chose to experiment with new lifestyles and created a counterculture. A few experimented with living in communes, using drugs such as marijuana or LSD, and having "free sex." Many used very different fashion and music from those of their parents to show their rebellion. Long hair, jeans, bell-bottoms, T-shirts, peasant blouses, dashikis, headscarves, long beaded necklaces, and sandals became the style. Music styles such as folk, rock 'n' roll, psychedelic rock, soul, and funk became very popular.

The term "hippie" was used to describe rebellious young people of that time. However, more young people copied hippie fashions and styles than were actually hippies. Many runaways and college dropouts gathered in the Haight-Ashbury district in San Francisco. Soon this area was known as the center of hippie culture. Hippie culture reached its peak in 1969 at Woodstock, a three-day rock concert. By 1972 the youth rebellion was disappearing. As the years passed, the baby boomers and the Woodstock generation found themselves with more traditional goals, such as getting jobs, raising families, and voting.

During World War II, about six million women worked outside the home. After the war the number of working women temporarily dropped, but by 1947 that number was greater than during the war. More women also went to college, and by 1960 over half of women college graduates were working outside the home. More middle-class married women were taking jobs. Families with two incomes could afford a better life style.

The traditional American family was changing with the

changing role of women. However, women faced discrimination. They were often limited to lower-paying domestic and clerical work. Women who were doing jobs similar to men were earning less money. Many professions and executive positions were closed to women. Even women involved in the civil rights movement experienced discrimination. They made posters, marched in demonstrations, handed out flyers, and made coffee, but were excluded from leadership roles.

Some women claimed society's narrow definition of "feminine" meant they were second-class citizens. In 1963 Betty Friedan's book, *The Feminine Mystique*, declared that society only thought of women as wives and mothers. However, the Civil Rights Act of 1964 declared that discrimination in jobs or public accommodations based on race, color, national origin, religion, and gender was illegal. Suddenly women had legal support to challenge sex discrimination. More women than African Americans filed discrimination complaints.

A new women's movement began with the formation of NOW, the National Organization for Women, in 1966. NOW wanted full and equal participation for women in American society. They called for equal opportunity, fair pay, and more democratic marriages. Men and women who supported these demands were called feminists. They staged marches, demonstrations, and rallies calling for "women's liberation." Some radical feminists called for an end to all traditional gender and family roles. Feminists wanted an end to sexism. They supported passage of the Equal Rights Amendment (ERA) to guarantee full political, economic, and social equality to women. Congress approved the Equal Rights Amendment in 1972. However, not enough states voted to ratify the amendment. By 1982 ERA was dead.

Not all women supported the women's movement. Some believed women should keep their traditional roles. They felt there was nothing wrong with staying at home and raising children. Other women were too busy working and raising a family to worry about women's liberation. Many African American women believed issues of race and color were more important. Many men, fearing they would lose their place as head of the family, resented any changes to traditional roles.

Men and women were especially divided over the 1973 Supreme Court decision of *Roe v. Wade*, which legalized abortion. Many feminists claimed abortion was a woman's choice because it involved her own body. Others claimed abortion was murder. This emotional issue divided, and continues to divide, men and women across the country.

The women's movement has changed the status of women dramatically. Today, more women than men graduate from college. Women face fewer job barriers. More women than ever before earn professional degrees, hold executive positions, are elected and appointed to political offices, and play professional sports.

Glossary

History F

accommodation – a service which satisfies a need, such as a room, food, or a seat on a train or bus.

activist – someone who uses direct action to bring about change.

affluent society – a lot of material wealth owned by a lot of people.

alienated – feeling cut off from society.

allies (ally) – friends, supporters; a group of countries joined together with a common purpose.

anarchy (anarchist) – absence of government or law. (someone who feels that governments are unnecessary and should be abolished.)

Anglo – non-Hispanic white person.

antiwar – against war in general or a specific war.

armed – equipped with weapons.

authority – the right to do something or to tell someone what to do; the right to give orders; the person in command.

baby boom – large increase in the birthrate over a specific period of time.

baby boomers – name given to people born during the 18 years (1946-1964) after World War II.

ban – to stop, forbid, prohibit; a legal order prohibiting something.

blacklist (to blacklist) – a list of people or groups that are under suspicion or being punished. They are usually denied jobs or privileges.

boom – a rapid increase.

boom to bust – the economy goes from prosperity to depression.

bootleg – illegal.

boycott – an organized refusal to buy something or to participate in an event as a protest.

bully – to mistreat someone; to force.

bust – failure, bankruptcy, or economic depression.

capitalism (capitalist) – an economic system in which businesses have private owners who make or sell goods for their own profit or for the profit of their shareholders.

cease-fire – an agreement to stop fighting.

censure – officially condemn or blame for something.

Charleston – a popular dance of the 1920s.

checks and balances – a system in which each branch of government checks on the other branches, so that no one branch becomes too powerful. For example, the U.S. Congress can pass a law, but the president can veto that law, and the Supreme Court can declare the law unconstitutional.

Chicano – a Mexican American.

civil rights – the rights of every citizen to be treated the same under the law, including having the same opportunities as everyone else.

civil rights movement – movement (organized activities) to defeat legal racial segregation and discrimination.

civilian – a person not on active duty in the military, police, or firefighting forces.

Cold War – the global struggle for power and influence between the United States and the Soviet Union following World War II. There was no direct fighting or military combat.

commune – a group of people or families living together and sharing everything.

communism (communist) – an economic system in which the businesses are owned and operated by the government. The government decides the type, quantity, and price of goods produced. They also decide what workers will make. Communism says it will provide for everyone's needs and get rid of social classes.

competition – a rivalry where two or more people, countries, or businesses are trying to get the same thing.

conspiracy – a secret plot or plan.

constitution – the basic principles, laws, and structure of a government. It is usually a written document.

consumer – someone who buys and uses products and services for his own use and not for resale.

consumption – purchasing and using up goods and services by consumers.

contempt of court – disobedience or disrespect for the court system.

counterculture – culture with values opposite of the mainstream.

culture (cultural, culturally) – the way of life of a group of people, which includes their ideas, beliefs, customs, language, and traditions.

democratic – allowing more people to participate in the decision-making processes of institutions such as government, colleges, or universities. For example, during the 1960s some students wanted to participate in the decisions to set student policies such as curfews and political activities.

demonstration – a public display of group feelings about a cause.

deport – to force a foreigner to leave a country by legal means.

desegregate (desegregation) – to end segregation.

dictatorship (dictator) – a form of government in which the ruler (dictator) or ruler's power is not limited by citizens or a legislature. A dictator has absolute power that is enforced by an army and secret police.

disabled – physically or mentally challenged.

discrimination (discriminate) – unfair treatment by a government or individual citizens, usually because of race, religion, nationality, sex, or certain disabilities; prejudice.

disillusioned – having lost belief and hope in something or somebody.

documentary – factual, objective.

Double V Campaign – the call of black leaders for victory abroad and victory at home; fight the racist Axis powers and segregation and discrimination at home.

draft (to draft) – a system which requires citizens to join their country's armed forces. (to call citizens to serve in the armed forces.)

economic boom – a time of rapid economic growth and prosperity.

equality (equity) – having the same rights and opportunity as anyone else regardless of race, religion, gender, or social class.

espionage – spying to gather secret information.

ethnic group – a group of people who share the same national origin, religion, race, or other group characteristics.

evangelist – someone who tries to persuade others to become Christians.

evolution – the theory that all forms of life developed from other more simple forms of life.

execute – to kill someone according to a legal sentence, like the punishment given to someone who has been convicted of killing someone.

executive branch – the branch of government that is responsible for enforcing the laws. The president heads the executive branch of the federal government. The governor heads the executive branch of Ohio's state government. The mayor heads the executive branch of Cleveland's city government.

feminist (feminist movement) – someone who believes in and fights for women's rights.

flapper – a young woman of the 1920s who rejected traditional behavior and fashion. Flappers wore short skirts, cut their hair short, used make-up, drank alcohol, and smoked cigarettes.

freedom ride (freedom riders) – black and white activists riding interstate buses through segregated southern states in the 1960s to protest illegal racial segregation in bus stations.

fundamentalist – a person who believes in a literal interpretation of a doctrine.

gender – one's sex; being a male or female.

Great Depression – global depression of the 1930s when businesses, banks, and the stock market failed, and many people lost their jobs. It was the longest and most severe depression ever experienced by the industrialized Western world.

Great Plains – central North America from Canada to Texas (north to south) and Central Lowlands to the Rocky Mountains (east to west).

gross national product – the total value of the goods and services produced by the nation during a specific period of time, usually one year.

hemisphere – one-half of the earth, either north or south of the equator or east or west of the prime meridian.

hobo – homeless traveler who often rode illegally in railroad box cars to get from town to town.

home front – civilian support of the war; for example, working in a factory that makes tanks or uniforms.

immigrant (immigration) – a person who enters a country and makes it his home, often becoming a citizen of his new country.

imports (imported, importer) – products brought in from a foreign country.

industrial (industry) – the making and distributing of products using machinery; manufacturing.

inflation – a general increase in prices when the money supply increases and the supply of goods and services does not; a decrease in the purchasing power of money.

inherently – naturally built into; naturally forming an important part of something.

integration – the inclusion of all people as equals, regardless of color or national origin.

internment – imprisonment or confinement.

internment camp – a camp set up for those considered dangerous during times of war. Japanese Americans were forced to live in internment camps shortly after the 1941 Japanese bombing of Pearl Harbor in World War II.

Jim Crow – the term used for laws and practices that segregated (separated) blacks and whites in the United States.

Ku Klux Klan (KKK) – a secret terrorist organization in the United States opposed to blacks, Roman Catholics, Jews, foreigners, and organized labor. The KKK worked against civil rights in the South during the 1960s.

labor union – a group of workers organized to help improve wages, benefits, working hours, and working conditions.

liberation (liberate) – setting someone or something free.

literacy test – a reading and writing test. It was one of the voter registration procedures used to deny blacks in the South the right to vote.

materialism (materialistic) – concern for material things like cars, money, clothes, etc.

McCarthyism – mid-20th century attitude, named for Senator Joseph McCarthy, accusing people of planning to overthrow the government, of being communists, or supporting communists with little hard evidence.

media (mass media) – movies, newspapers, radio, television, and other forms of mass communication to the general public.

middle class – all the people who are not rich or poor. Most have a comfortable standard of living.

migrant – a person who moves. Often it is used to describe people who move within their own country.

migrate (migration) – to move from one location to another. It is often used to describe people who move within their own country.

militant – aggressive; combative; willing to fight for a cause.

minimum wage – according to the law, the amount of money which must be paid to a worker for each hour he/she works. An employer can pay more than the minimum wage but not less. Not all workers are covered by minimum wage laws.

minority (minorities) – smaller group(s) of people, as opposed to a large group, the majority. Women, Hispanics, and African Americans are often thought of as minorities.

modernist – someone who has the latest styles, practices, tastes, attitudes, and views; a person considered up-to-date.

morale – confidence; good spirits; sense of willingness.

nationalism (nationalist) – loyalty to one's own nation or country; especially putting one nation above all others, with major emphasis on promotion of its culture and interests.

nativism – policy of a nation to favor the interests of the people who were native born over the interests of immigrants.

nonviolence (nonviolent) – the belief and practice of working actively for political and social change without using violence. Mahatma Gandhi and Dr. Martin Luther King, Jr. were both strong supporters of the philosophy of nonviolence.

Pearl Harbor – a U.S. naval base on Oahu Island in Hawaii that was attacked by Japan in 1941. It was the center of the Pacific fleet of the U.S. Navy. This attack was the reason that the United States entered World War II.

per capita personal income – how much money each individual in a group has, based on the total income of the group divided by the number of people in that group.

perjury – telling lies under oath.

poll tax – a tax which must be paid in order to vote. Since the poll tax cost more than most poor whites and African Americans could pay, it kept many from voting.

prejudice – an unfair opinion about a person or thing, formed before learning the facts about the person or thing.

primitive – simple; belonging to earlier times.

probe – a device used to send back information from outer space; exploration or expedition.

prohibition – the outlawing of the making, selling, and transporting of alcoholic beverages. The 18th Amendment established prohibition in the United States in 1919. This amendment was repealed in 1933.

propaganda – selective facts, ideas, or information used to win support for a cause or a person. It usually has a strong emotional appeal.

psychedelic rock – music style of the 1960s in the United States and Great Britain counterculture influenced by drug usage. They wanted to recreate the effect of drugs in music and live performances.

quota – a number or percentage that is set as a maximum or minimum amount. For example, immigration laws often set limits on the number of immigrants from different countries allowed into the United States.

racial – based on race.

racial discrimination – unfair treatment in education, employment, voting, or social events of one racial group by a different racial group.

racism (racist) – the belief that one race is naturally superior to others; discrimination and prejudice against a group of people because of their race.

radical – a person, group, or idea that favors making extreme changes, usually political in nature.

raid – a surprise attack.

ratify (ratified) – to confirm or approve, usually by a vote.

ration (rationed) – to fix or limit the amount of something, especially food, given to a person or group from what is available.

raw material(s) – unprocessed natural thing(s) like wood and metal that are used to manufacture products.

real estate – land including all the property on it that cannot be moved.

recovery – economic upturn. It is an extended improvement in general business activity including employment, industrial production, wholesale and/or retail prices.

Red Scare – a widespread fear of communists in the United States and their secret plans for a communist revolution.

reform (reformer) – to improve or change something that is wrong or unsatisfactory.

relief – money or supplies provided by the government for the needy; welfare.

renaissance – rebirth or revival.

reservation – land set aside for a special purpose, especially in the United States for Native Americans (American Indians) to live on.

revolution – a dramatic or violent change. It could be political, economic, social, cultural, or intellectual.

riot – noisy, violent public disorder, usually by a group or crowd of people.

riveter – someone who works a machine to join metal plates together with rivets (short metal fasteners). "Rosie the Riveter" was often seen on posters to support the war effort and to show that women were helping keep things going at home while the men were at war.

rural – relating to or characteristic of the country, country people, or country life. An example of rural people is farmers.

satellite – (1) a smaller object that circles a larger object in the sky; (2) a country that is economically and politically controlled by a more powerful nation.

segregation (segregate) – the law or practice of separating and isolating people by characteristics such as race, religion, or nationality.

self-determination – the right of people to choose their own government. Self-determination was one of President Wilson's Fourteen Points.

separatism – belief in being separate.

sexism – treating people differently because of their sex (gender). This is most often directed at women in an unfavorable way.

sit-in – a type of demonstration in which a group of people protest against something by sitting down in a place and refusing to leave; a peaceful protest.

socialism (socialist) – any of various economic and political ideas that favor the government's ownership and administration of the means of production.

speakeasy – place to purchase and consume illegal liquor during Prohibition (1920-1933).

speculate (speculation) – to buy with plans of selling for a profit because of an increase in price.

standard of living – level of well-being of individuals or groups, based on characteristics such as education, income, healthcare, life expectancy, and available goods and services.

status symbols – signs of wealth like large homes and expensive cars.

stock (stock market) – share of ownership in a corporation. (the business of buying and selling stocks.)

strike – refusing to work, in order to achieve a goal such as higher pay or better working conditions.

suburb; suburban (suburbanite) – a community or land near a city, with easy access to the city. (a person who lives in the suburbs.)

suburbanization – growth of suburbs.

suffrage (suffragist) – the right to vote. (a person, male or female, who supports giving women the right to vote.)

tariff – a tax on products that come from another country.

total war – a war which involves all the resources of a nation including the armed forces and the civilian population. Farms, factories, and civilian populations, as well as armed forces are targets.

tradition (traditional, traditionalist) – inherited, established, or usual pattern of thought, action, or behavior.

treason (traitor) – betraying of one's own country. A traitor is a person who betrays his/her own country.

unconstitutional – not allowed by the Constitution; against the law.

urban – having to do with cities or towns.

wages – money that is paid to a worker for work or services done.

war bond – a form of savings bond that was used by many of the fighting countries to fund World War I and World War II.

women's movement (also referred to as the feminist movement and women's liberation) – groups that want to improve life for women. Present issues include abortion, domestic violence, maternity leave, equal pay, sexual harassment, and sexual violence.

People in Societies A

CULTURAL PERSPECTIVES

Analyze the influence of different cultural perspectives on the actions of groups.

The culture of a group of people is their way of life that includes their ideas, beliefs, customs, language, and <u>traditions</u>. Religion, political beliefs, and a common historical experience are important parts of culture. A person's perspective on a subject refers to how he or she views and understands that subject. Cultural differences lead to different perspectives, and differing perspectives affect the actions of groups of people worldwide. Below are four examples of how different cultures view events from different perspectives.

How Different Cultures View the Creation of the State of Israel

The Jewish community believes Abraham was the founder of the Jewish nation. According to the Bible, God gave land to Abraham and his descendants. Later that land was called the "Promised Land" and the "Land of Israel." It included the modern State of Israel and surrounding territory. The Land of Israel was conquered several times. Revolts against Roman rule led to the forced <u>migration</u> of most Jews from their <u>homeland</u>. The Land of Israel became known as Palestine, and Jews were eventually scattered around the world.

Jewish communities have a long history of <u>persecution</u> in many countries. In the 1800s growing <u>anti-Semitism</u> in Europe led to more instances of <u>discrimination</u> and violence. In the late 1800s some Jews began <u>emigrating</u> to Palestine and many purchased land from modern-day Palestinian owners. They claimed they simply wanted to live on their land at peace with their neighbors. However, some Jews called for Palestine to become an independent state. As Jewish <u>immigration</u> increased, so did tension between Jews and Palestine's Arab population. In 1947, following World War II, the United Nations voted to divide Palestine into an Arab and a Jewish state. The Jews accepted the plan, and the Arabs rejected it.

The Arabs did not accept the UN plan and went to war because their perspective was very different. In the centuries after the Jewish exile, Arabs in surrounding territories took ownership of Palestine. The Ottoman Empire, centered in modern day Turkey, ruled most Arabs for about 400 years. During World War I, Arabs revolted against the ruling Ottoman Empire and sided with the Allied powers in hope of establishing a single Arab state. However, the Ottoman Empire was divided and put under the temporary control of France and the United Kingdom. Slowly Arab states began to establish their independence and in 1945 formed the Arab League to work together concerning common problems. Those Arab nations were unhappy with increases in Jewish immigration and did not want the creation of a Jewish state in the middle of Arab and Muslim lands. They believed the United Nations' plan was unfair to the 67% of the Palestinians who were not Jewish and would leave a number of Arabs trapped inside a Jewish state.

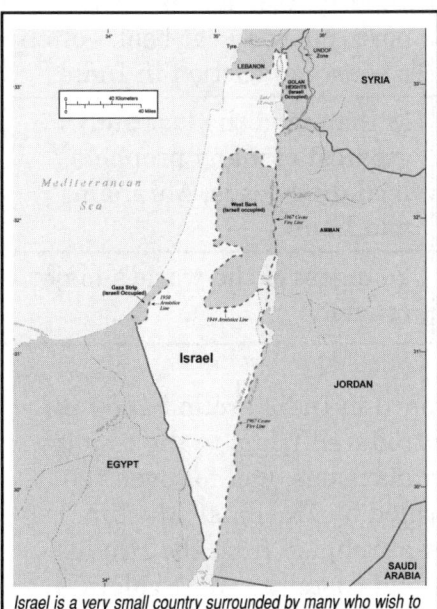

Some Arabs complained the plan gave the new Jewish state too much land and too much of the best land. Since the majority of Palestinians were Arabs, Palestine should be an Arab state.

As a result of these widely different perspectives, Jews and Arabs have found it difficult to live together in peace. Since the end of World War II, Jews and their Arab neighbors have fought six major wars. Israel won each war and seized additional land each time. Many Palestinians have been forced

Israel is a very small country surrounded by many who wish to eliminate it. Notice the three Israeli occupied territories.

THE NEW LITTLE BOOK   PEOPLE IN SOCIETIES A ■ 111

from their homes and now live in poverty as refugees in surrounding Arab countries such as Jordan, Lebanon, and Syria. The Palestinian organization Hamas has vowed to destroy Israel and replace it with an Islamic state.

How Different Cultures View the Partition of India and Pakistan

Differing perspectives on the partition of India and Pakistan have both religious and historical origins. During the 1940s about 75% of India was Hindu and about 25% was Muslim. There were major differences between the two religions that made mutual respect and tolerance difficult. Some of those differences are found in the chart below.

Hinduism	Islam
Belief in many gods	Belief in one and only one God, Allah
Does not seek converts	Actively seeks to convert people to Islam
Belief that cows are sacred and must not be killed or eaten	Dietary restrictions include pork, but may eat beef – often a source of friction in India
No particular founder or prophet	Muhammad the last and greatest of many prophets, including Jesus, Abraham, and Noah
Oldest of the world's major religions	Youngest of the world's major religions

Historically, Hinduism developed in India around 1500 BC. Around 700 AD Arab invaders introduced Islam to the country. For centuries there were Muslim invasions, and for over 500 years, most parts of India were ruled by Muslims. Muslim rulers not only practiced a different religion from the Hindus, but also had different languages and customs. Most rulers taxed Hindus heavily to support their wealthy lifestyle, discriminated against Hindus, and tried to force Hindus to convert to Islam. The result was mutual distrust, hatred, and violence that continued for centuries.

The British East India Tea Company began to control India in 1769, and by 1857 India was a British colony. Though they were far outnumbered by both Hindus and Muslims, the British were able for many years to take advantage of the differences between the two groups. Eventually Indians began to demand independence from England. The Indian National Congress (INC), a political party, was formed in 1885 to seek a larger role in government for educated Indians. When its efforts to participate were repeatedly opposed by the government, the INC became the leader of a freedom movement. Muslims were suspicious of the growing influence of the largely Hindu INC. In 1906 the Muslim League was formed to protect and advance Muslim interests. The League insisted that a separate country be set up for Indian Muslims. They did not wish to be controlled or dominated by the Hindus once the British left.

The two main spokespersons for Indian independence were Mahatma Gandhi and Muhammad Ali Jinnah, both British educated and trained lawyers. Gandhi was a Hindu, and Jinnah was a Muslim. Gandhi pushed for majority rule of India. Since there were many more Hindus than Muslims, Hindus would surely control the new government in a <u>democratic</u> election. Partly for this reason, Jinnah wanted a separate nation for Muslims.

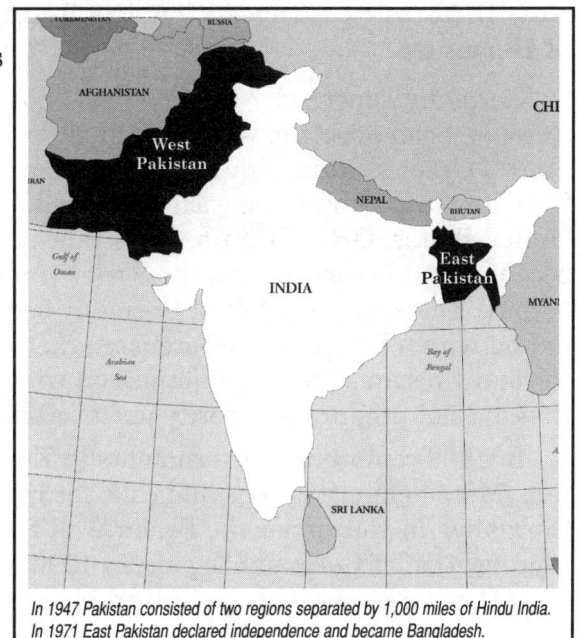

In 1947 Pakistan consisted of two regions separated by 1,000 miles of Hindu India. In 1971 East Pakistan declared independence and became Bangladesh.

In 1946 the British agreed to leave. Because the Hindu INC and the Muslim League could not settle their differences, India was partitioned in 1947. Borders were hastily drawn for Hindu India and the new Muslim state of Pakistan. As soon as the British departed, about 10 million Hindus, Muslims, and Sikhs found themselves in the wrong country according to their religion. Millions fled their homes, seeking safety on the other side. Hundreds of thousands were slaughtered in the riots that followed. Today India and Pakistan are still military rivals and have a great mistrust of one another. Both countries have nuclear weapons.

One of the largest migrations in history took place because of the partitioning of India and Pakistan. Emergency trains carried refugees to both India and Pakistan. Sometimes trains were attacked and passengers massacred. In this photograph, desperate refugees board trains with whatever they can carry. Notice where some were willing to sit.

How Different Cultures View the Reunification of Germany

Germany's surrender in May 1945 ended World War II in Europe. Soon after the war, the Allied Powers (the United States, Great Britain, France, and the Soviet Union) divided Germany into four zones, each controlled by one of them. The United States, Great Britain, and France controlled zones that became West Germany, and the Soviet Union controlled zone became East Germany. West Germany became a democratic nation with a free and prosperous market economy. East Germany became a communist nation with a controlled economy that did not produce prosperity for its citizens.

In 1989 communist governments in Eastern Europe began to fall. Mass demonstrations and calls for reform happened in East Germany. In November the Berlin Wall fell, and talks about the reunification of Germany began. In 1990 East Germany and West Germany reunited. Reunification affected various people and countries differently. Citizens of the former East Germany viewed reunification positively and eagerly embraced the idea of one Germany. So did many citizens of the former West Germany. Many West Germans had relatives and friends in the East.

Not everyone was happy. There were problems with Germans living on land taken from Poland by <u>Nazi</u> Germany. Much of this land had been returned to Poland after the war. Poland and the other previous owners forced some 2.3 million Germans living on that land to leave their homes and return to Germany. As part of the reunification agreement, Germany promised not to claim territories beyond their borders. This agreement destroyed the German refugees' hopes of returning to their homes, where many still had family and friends.

Another cultural problem with reunification arose from the vast difference in the economic systems of East and West Germany. West Germany had managed to repair much of the damage of war and build a strong market economy. Much of East Germany remained as Hitler had left it. The problem lay in the nature of the East German controlled economy. The government decided what should be produced and in which factories. The government also set wages and salaries. Workers were told what to do and how to do it. There was little or no opportunity to "get ahead" by working hard or suggesting new ways to do things. Thus, there was no <u>incentive</u> for workers to work hard or improve <u>productivity</u>. Many people believed the government's claims that it would take care of their needs and that only a controlling government could eliminate poverty.

In 1990 Helmut Kohl, the newly-elected, first chancellor of reunified Germany, promised that within four years East Germany's economy would be fully recovered and comparable with West Germany. This would be accomplished in part by using West German taxes to fund required reconstruction and <u>economic development</u> projects. Unfortunately, the East's recovery turned out to be much slower and more difficult than anybody had imagined. Even ten years later, after the German government had poured more that 1.3 trillion euros ($2,000,000,000,000) into economic redevelopment, the former East Germany had not fully recovered.

Both the East Germans and the West Germans were disappointed and disillusioned by these developments. West Germans tended to blame East Germans for being lazy and unwilling to work hard to improve their situation. Many East Germans accused West Germans of being arrogant and blamed them for failing to keep their promise of economic prosperity within four years.

How Different Cultures View the End of Apartheid in South Africa

Apartheid was a system of laws that established strict racial segregation and discrimination in South Africa from 1948 until the system began to fall apart in the late 1980s. From colonial times to the present day, whites have made up less than 12% of the total population of South Africa. The apartheid laws reflected the racist attitudes of the white minority. These laws were meant to increase racial separation and ensure that whites maintained firm control of the government and the economy. The result was that black South Africans, who were about 80% of the population, were second-class citizens and had a lower standard of living.

Segregation was imposed by apartheid laws. Signs, such as the one in the photograph, were bitter reminders of white racist attitudes.

Throughout the 20th century, opposition to apartheid grew from within and outside South Africa. By the 1980s, the international pressure of economic sanctions and growing violent and nonviolent protests at home made the government realize reform was necessary. In 1989 F.W. de Klerk was elected president of South Africa. Although he was white and privileged, de Klerk realized that apartheid must end. In 1992 the last white-only election took place. About 68% of the voters supported an end to apartheid.

In 1994 South Africa held its first free elections. African National Congress (ANC) <u>activist</u> Nelson Mandela, who had been imprisoned for 27 years, was elected president. In 1996 a new constitution was adopted. Apartheid was gone, but anger, hatred, and inequalities it created remained. Many black South Africans expected immediate improvements in areas such as education, employment, income, and healthcare. Many whites feared calls for revenge. How could the new government move forward?

In 1995 the new government established the Truth and <u>Reconciliation</u> Commission to investigate human rights abuses from 1960 to 1994. Those who committed abuses or were victims of abuse were encouraged to testify. The Commission had the power to grant <u>amnesty</u> to those who committed abuses and recommend assistance for victims. The purpose of the Commission was not to provide justice, but to uncover the truth so the process of forgiveness and healing could begin. Witnesses from both the former apartheid government and anti-apartheid groups such as the ANC testified. The Commission's final report condemned all who committed human rights abuses.

The ultimate goal of the Truth and Reconciliation Commission was to promote national unity and reconciliation after the end of apartheid. Reconciliation, however, is not complete. Tensions still exist between black and white communities, whose cultures, histories, and standard of living still differ dramatically.

CULTURE AND POLITICAL ACTION GROUPS

<u>Political action group</u>s within the United States and elsewhere often form to represent the perspectives of different cultural groups. These political action groups seek to advance their interests from their perspective. Here are a few examples.

National Association for the Advancement of Colored People (NAACP)

The National Association for the Advancement of Colored People (NAACP) was formed February 12, 1909, the one hundredth anniversary of Abraham Lincoln's birth, by a group of black and white intellectuals who were sympathetic with the plight of African Americans in the United States. Among the prominent founders of the association were Mary Ovington, W.E.B. Du Bois, Jane Addams, John Dewey, and Ida B. Wells. Their action followed the 1908 Springfield (Illinois) race riot in which two black men were lynched, five whites were killed, more than 40 homes were destroyed or damaged, and 24 businesses were forced to close at least temporarily.

The NAACP set out to address growing problems between blacks and whites and to promote equal rights for African Americans. The problems included not only mob violence and lynching of African Americans since the Civil War, but also Jim Crow laws found in every southern state. Jim Crow laws legalized racial discrimination and required segregation in all public facilities. Southern states also passed laws designed to prevent African American men from exercising their right to vote, such as requiring poll taxes and literacy tests.

To address those problems, the NAACP challenged Jim Crow laws and discrimination in the courts. There were many successes including *Brown v. Board of Education* (1954) that ruled segregation in public schools is unconstitutional. The NAACP remains active today with more than 500,000 members and a focus on voter issues, economic development, and educational programs for youth.

National Organization for Women (NOW)

The National Organization for Women (NOW) was formed in 1966. Although there are more women in the United States than men, women have suffered discrimination and have minority group status. Women were not allowed to vote until 1920 with the passage of the 19th Amendment to the U.S. Constitution. Women have traditionally not been paid as much as men for the same job. Even today, women are sometimes not allowed to join the same clubs as men. For example, women are not allowed to become members of the Augusta National Golf Club, the site of the annual Masters Golf Tournament. The purpose of NOW, according to its founder Betty Freidan, is "to take action to bring women into full participation in the mainstream of American society now, exercising all the privileges and responsibilities thereof in truly equal partnership with men."

NOW focuses on the rights and interests of women. Their issues center on eliminating discrimination by sex or gender and on areas concerning employment, including equal pay for equal work, an equal opportunity for promotions, and education that will help young women achieve their full potential. NOW also supports an equal rights amendment to the Constitution, abortion, gay rights, and ending sexual harassment and violence against women. Marches, pickets, voter registration drives, campaign contributions, lobbying, and civil disobedience have been used to address their issues.

However, some women do not support or even agree with NOW's goals. This has led to varying degrees of success. For example, in the 1970s, NOW and many other women's organizations campaigned to win enough support to ratify the Equal Rights Amendment, but they failed. On the other hand, its 1994 campaign helped pass the Violence Against Women Act. There are about 500,000 members of NOW today which includes both men and women.

American Indian Movement (AIM)

In the mid-1960s, a number of Indian groups began to question seriously why so many of their people seemed to be in prison or condemned to poverty, poor health, and despair. The American Indian Movement (AIM) grew out of a 1968 meeting of 200 members of the Indian community in Minnesota. They met to discuss a number of their immediate concerns including:

- police brutality
- housing
- 80% unemployment rate
- cultural insensitivity and a perceived lack of concern by the Minneapolis public schools toward Indian students
- racist and discriminatory policies of the Hennepin County welfare system

- failure of the federal government to honor its treaty commitments to Indian people.

AIM used the same protest methods as the NAACP, NOW, and other political action groups active at the time, such as marches, rallies, and sit-ins. Some early demonstrations used force, such as the 1973 Wounded Knee Incident in South Dakota that resulted in a 71-day occupation of the town and two deaths. They also helped Indians organize to defend themselves against police and judicial abuse and started job-training programs in cities and on reservations. Some of these programs have been successful and continue today.

AIM is concerned with preserving the cultural heritage (traditions) of its people. The organization believes that the strength of the Indian people lies in their spiritual heritage, traditional ways, and central relationship with the environment. They demand that rights guaranteed to Indian people by treaties and laws be upheld. They also conduct research, provide speakers, and offer educational programs for children and adults.

AIM has achieved some of its goals. In 1972 Congress provided financial support to local education authorities to improve educational opportunities for Indian children and adults. A 1975 law allowed Indians greater control over the education of their children and helped them to be able to preserve their culture. With the assistance of AIM, some tribes have successfully sued the federal government for treaty violations. The Inuit of Alaska sued and won nearly $1 billion. Though AIM has accomplished many of its initial goals set forth in 1972, Indians in American still do not fair as well economically, socially, or politically as the majority white population. Many Indians today choose to be a part of the greater American society, not part of an Indian-only society.

United Farm Workers

Large numbers of immigrants from Latin America came to the United States in the 1960s and 1970s. Like many other immigrants, they dreamed of a better life, free from persecution and poverty. Often these immigrants settled in the West and

Southwest, working as migrant farm workers. They moved from farm to farm on a seasonal basis, helping owners of large farms plant or harvest crops.

Many migrant farm workers believed their working and living conditions needed to be improved. The conditions in the fields and labor camps were often unhealthy and <u>unsanitary</u>. Workers put in long hours for very low pay. In 1965 grape pickers in the Southwest averaged $0.90 an hour. Imagine an adult making $9.00 per day before taxes! The federal minimum wage at the time was $1.25 per hour, but farm workers were not covered. The average wage for factory workers was about $2.50 per hour plus benefits. Due to the low wages paid to adults, children of migrant workers joined their parents in the fields. Children also worked long hours and were paid even less than the adults. Sometimes the children's duties or long working hours violated federal and state child labor laws. Adults who worked on farms lived shorter lives than adults who did not. Just as factory workers during the Industrial Revolution formed <u>labor unions</u> to protest low wages and poor working conditions while factory owners made large profits, farm workers in the 1960s and 1970s saw a need for organizations to help them achieve fair pay and decent working conditions.

The United Farm Workers of America (UFW) was formed in 1965 by the merger of two other organizations that were seeking to address the problems of migrant workers. The UFW adopted nonviolent protest methods like Mahatma Gandhi and Dr. Martin Luther King, Jr. The union struggled for five years, using <u>strikes</u> and <u>boycotts</u> of farm products such as grapes and lettuce. Sometimes union members did destroy property and use violence. Eventually they won a contract with the grape growers of California. This contract brought an end to certain unfair hiring practices. It protected workers from dangerous pesticides that were widely used in agriculture and provided medical insurance for the first time. There was an immediate increase in wages. Fresh water and toilets were provided in the fields. Even so, the UFW has faced ongoing resistance from farm owners and competition from other organizations such as the International Brotherhood of Teamsters. The UFW continues to struggle today to accomplish its mission.

AFRICAN AMERICAN, AMERICAN INDIAN, AND LATINO CULTURAL CONTRIBUTIONS

The perspective of African American, American Indian, and Latino art, music, literature, and media both reflect and help shape culture in the United States.

African American culture has strong African roots. For example, the African influence is found in food. The use of agricultural products such as rice, peanuts, and yams, and the development of soul food can be traced to Africa and the African American experience.

There is also a long history of story telling. During slavery, folk tales, story quilts and songs expressed hope and longing for freedom often by use of hidden meanings. This oral tradition continues today. It can be found in some rap lyrics and in literature such as Virginia Hamilton's popular collection of folktales, *The People Could Fly*.

African American art, music, and literature also reflect African culture and the African American experience. The Harlem Renaissance of the 1920s showcased African American cultural creativity and influenced the development of modern American culture. The art (paintings and murals) of Aaron Douglas, the novels of Zora Neal Hurston, the poetry of Langston Hughes, and the jazz of Duke Ellington reached into and beyond the borders of the African American community. For example, popular music such as rock 'n' roll and rap reflect the strong influence of the African American perspective in content and style, yet are an important part of mainstream American culture. The same is true of the impact of African Americans on the media including television talk show host Oprah Winfrey and movie stars Will Smith, Denzel Washington, and Cleveland's Halle Berry.

Today Native American perspectives also influence American culture. During the 19th and early 20th centuries, the majority population wanted American Indians, or Native Americans, to adopt traditional white American culture. Some children were sent to boarding schools where they were punished if they spoke anything except English. Today traditional customs, crafts, music, dance, language, and religion are being revived and taught to the young people. Community celebrations are often open to the larger population to educate the general community about Native American culture. Indian arts, especially the jewelry, pottery, and baskets of the Southwest, are popular. The creation of extremely profitable Indian tribe owned casinos and protests against the popular stereotypes such as the Cleveland Indians baseball mascot Chief Wahoo have made the larger community more aware of Native Americans and their culture. Books such as *House of Dawn* by American Indian author N. Scott Momaday present a different perspective. In addition, some movies such as *Dances with Wolves*, *Dreamkeeper* and *Last of the Mohicans* try to present accurate and realistic descriptions of American Indians and American Indian culture.

Hispanics are the largest minority group in the United States today. The largest Hispanic nationalities are Mexican, Puerto Rican, and Cuban. Although the majority live in Florida and the Southwest, their influence is everywhere. Popular Mexican and Central and South American restaurants are found, not only in the cities of Houston and Los Angeles, but even in Cleveland, Ohio. There are many Spanish language newspapers and magazines dedicated to those of Hispanic heritage, such as *Latina*. There are thousands of Spanish language radio stations and television networks, including Univision and Telemundo. Musicians such as Ricky Martin and Christina Aguilera make the top pop music charts, and tango and samba have become popular in many night spots, not just those catering to the Latino crowd. Recent Latino movie and television stars such as Jennifer Lopez and Jimmy Smits, movies such as *Real Women Have Curves*, and books such as Julia Álvarez's *How the García Girls Lost Their Accents* have mainstream appeal. Popular Latino rappers include B-real, Big Pun, Lloyd Banks, and Pitbull.

Glossary

People in Societies A

activist – someone who uses direct action to bring about change.

amnesty – a general pardon for a group of people, usually by a government.

anti-Semitism – prejudice against Jews.

boycott – an organized refusal to buy something or to participate in an event as a protest.

civil disobedience – a method of nonviolent protest. It is a deliberate and public refusal to obey a law and often leads to people being arrested.

communism (communist) – an economic system in which the businesses are owned and operated by the government. The government decides the type, quantity, and price of goods produced. They also decide what workers will make. Communism says it will provide for everyone's needs and get rid of social classes.

democratic – allowing more people to participate in the decision-making processes of institutions such as government, colleges, or universities. For example, during the 1960s some students wanted to participate in the decisions to set student policies such as curfews and political activities.

demonstration – a public display of group feelings about a cause.

discrimination (discriminate) – unfair treatment by a government or individual citizens, usually because of race, religion, nationality, sex, or certain disabilities; prejudice.

disillusioned – having lost belief and hope in something or somebody.

economic development – changing the way products are made by using technology to make more products and better products; using resources and people productively. Economic development is more than economic growth. The idea of economic development goes beyond increasing individual income to include things like health, education, safe environment, and freedom, in other words the quality of life.

economic sanctions – actions which limit the buying and/or selling of products in order to convince a country to change its policies.

emigrate (emigrant) – to leave one's country to live elsewhere. (a person who leaves his country to live elsewhere.)

homeland – a separate territory or country that a group of people can control and call their own.

immigrant (immigration) – a person who enters a country and makes it his home, often becoming a citizen of his new country.

incentive – motivation to action; an anticipation of a reward or a fear of a punishment.

Islam – a religion based on a single god, Allah, and on the word of God as revealed to Muhammad during the 17th century and written in the Qur'an (Koran).

Jim Crow – the term used for laws and practices that segregated (separated) blacks and whites in the United States.

labor union – a group of workers organized to help improve wages, benefits, working hours, and working conditions.

literacy test – a reading and writing test. It was one of the voter registration procedures used to deny blacks in the South the right to vote.

market economy – in a market economy, individuals make their own decisions about what goods to produce and to sell at a profit, with limited governmental interference.

migrate (migration) – to move from one location to another. It is often used to describe people who move within their own country.

minority (minorities) – smaller group(s) of people, as opposed to a large group, the majority. Women, Hispanics, and African Americans are often thought of as minorities.

Muslim – a person who practices Islam.

Nazism (Nazi) – the beliefs and practices of Adolf Hitler's National Socialist German Workers' Party including racial superiority, government control of society and the economy, and loyalty to one's nation or people above all else.

nonviolence (nonviolent) – the belief and practice of working actively for political and social change without using violence. Mahatma Gandhi and Dr. Martin Luther King, Jr. were both strong supporters of the philosophy of nonviolence.

opposition – challengers; people who provide resistance.

partition – division of a land area into smaller political and geographic units.

persecution (persecuted) – constant mistreatment, especially because of race, religion, sex, or political beliefs.

plight – a negative situation.

political action group – a group or organization that seeks to influence the election of public officials and the passage of laws.

poll tax – a tax which must be paid in order to vote. Since the poll tax cost more than most poor whites and African Americans could pay, it kept many from voting.

preserve – to keep safe; to not allow something to be lost, changed, or destroyed.

productivity – the amount produced by each person.

racism (racist) – the belief that one race is naturally superior to others; discrimination and prejudice against a group of people because of their race.

ratify (ratified) – to confirm or approve, usually by a vote.

reconciliation – the process of accepting and forgiving past injuries in order to build a closer relationship.

reform (reformer) – to improve or change something that is wrong or unsatisfactory.

refugee – a person who runs away for safety, usually to another country.

reservation – land set aside for a special purpose, especially in the United States for Native Americans (American Indians) to live on.

reunify (reunification) – to unite again; to join after being separated. East and West Germany were reunified after the 1989 fall of the Berlin Wall.

segregation (segregate) – the law or practice of separating and isolating people by characteristics such as race, religion, or nationality.

Sikh – a person who believes in Sikhism, a religion from northern India.

sit-in – a type of demonstration in which a group of people protest against something by sitting down in a place and refusing to leave; a peaceful protest.

standard of living – level of well-being of individuals or groups, based on characteristics such as education, income, healthcare, life expectancy, and available goods and services.

status – position or rank in comparison to others.

strike – refusing to work, in order to achieve a goal such as higher pay or better working conditions.

sympathetic – caring about the well-being of another person.

tolerate (tolerance) – respecting the beliefs, customs, and physical differences of others.

tradition (traditional, traditionalist) – inherited, established, or usual pattern of thought, action, or behavior.

treaty – a formal agreement between two or more rulers or nations.

unsanitary – not clean or healthy.

violate (violation) – to break or disregard the law. (the act of violating.)

People in Societies B

CULTURAL INTERACTION: OPPRESSION, DISCRIMINATION, CONFLICT

Analyze the consequences of oppression, discrimination, and conflict between cultures.

Although groups of people share common needs and ideas, we notice them by their differences, by their <u>diversity</u>. An Amish woman dressed in a long dress, white apron, white cape, a small white cap, and black shoes and stockings shopping in K-Mart captures our attention. So would two men standing in a checkout line speaking to one another in Vietnamese.

<u>Cultural</u> diversity includes differences in customs, dress, language, and religion. These cultural differences affect the way people and groups of people interact. People may find cultural differences interesting or irritating. They may ignore or respond to cultural differences. Sometimes nations respond to cultural differences. For example, as the Hispanic population has grown in the United States, so has the repeated call for a constitutional amendment to make English the national language.

Sociologists study how different cultural groups <u>interact</u>. Responses to cultural differences can result in <u>discrimination</u>, <u>oppression</u>, and <u>conflict</u> between cultures. Here are examples of conflict that sociologists study:

- In 2004 a law passed in France banned the wearing of religious symbols which included the headscarf some <u>Muslim</u>s consider a religious requirement for women. Many Muslims in France claim this law <u>discriminate</u>s against them.
- China seized control of Tibet in 1950. They established a <u>communist</u> government that controlled the economy and limited religious freedom. However, many Tibetans remain loyal to the Dalai Lama, the former spiritual and government leader. The Dalai Lama is living in India and says his people are oppressed.

- The conflict between Shiite and Sunni Muslims in Iraq led to violence and civil war. Each group claims to be the true followers of Mohammed and, therefore, the true followers of Islam.

The worst responses to cultural differences are political, economic, and social oppression which lead to the violation of human rights. Violating human rights means depriving someone, or a group of people, of their basic social, political, or economic rights such as life, liberty, or property. Examples of such terrible oppression include the exploitation of indigenous (native) people and genocide.

Exploitation of Indigenous People

From the 15th century to the mid-twentieth century, European nations colonized the Americas, Africa, the Middle East, and parts of Asia. Indigenous peoples were exploited by Europeans and Americans looking for raw materials or finished goods to trade. The result was conflict between cultures. Indigenous peoples experienced discrimination and oppression.

During the 19th century, Europeans and Americans changed the native culture in Hawaii by bringing manufactured goods, missionaries, and new diseases to the islands. Many Hawaiians abandoned their religion and customs, such as grass skirts and the hula, and became Christians. Hawaiians had no immunities to European and American diseases such as smallpox and so many died that their population decreased. Later as these outsiders developed sugar plantations, they needed native labor to grow the sugar cane. A shortage of workers led to a large number of Asian immigrants, especially Chinese, Japanese, and Filipinos. Today, Hawaii's population is 57% Asian, 41% white, and 22% Hawaiian or Pacific Islander.

Under pressures from trading partners, the ownership of private property was introduced to Hawaiians. Most Hawaiians lost their land. Wealthy businessmen pressured the Hawaiian ruler to accept a constitution that took away much of the Hawaiian monarch's powers and most Hawaiians' right to vote. When Queen Liliuokalani tried to return power to the monarchy, a small group of American and European businessmen organized a coup in 1893. Five years later the United States annexed Hawaii. In 1959 Hawaii became our 50th state. Since the 1970s, there has been a growing interest in rediscovering Hawaiian culture including language and history.

By 1840 almost all Native Americans in the eastern half of the United States had been forced to move west of the Mississippi River. About two-thirds of the Native American population lived on the Great Plains. With discovery of gold in California in 1848, miners followed by farmers, ranchers, and merchants moved west of the Mississippi River. Native Americans soon found their homelands and hunting grounds invaded by white settlers who claimed the land. In addition, the slaughter of the buffalo by hunters took away the major source of the Plains Indians' food, clothing, and housing. Culture conflict led to massacres and other atrocities. In 1867 the government demanded Native Americans move to reservations. Many younger leaders refused, which led to a series of Indian wars that lasted until 1890.

A major shift in U.S. policy in 1871 declared that the U.S. government no longer recognized any Indian nation or tribe as an independent power and would no longer negotiate treaties or make payments. The government began to administer the Indians' affairs by legislation of Congress through the Bureau of Indian Affairs (BIA). Private boarding schools and reservation schools opened to teach Native American children to assimilate into white society. They learned how to farm, dress, cook, keep house, and speak English. The Dawes Act of 1887 destroyed tribal ownership of reservation land by dividing it into family plots to be farmed. This took away the Indians' rights to continue their own government, economic system, social structure, and many cultural traditions. It attempted to impose white American culture on the Native Americans. By 1900 war, disease, and poverty reduced the Native American population to about 200,000.

The results of these human rights violations remain today and affect both cultural groups. Although the Indian population is about 3 million today, many Indians experience poverty, hold unskilled jobs, suffer from many health problems, and are without a good education. Some of those who moved to cities in search of opportunity returned to the reservation to maintain their culture. Today about 60% of Native Americans live in <u>urban</u> areas.

During the 20th century, Congress adopted legislation to encourage Indian self-government, reforms to allow loans for land purchase and educational assistance, and payment to some tribes for land claims. Some tribes operate businesses on reservations, such as gambling casinos, under their own rules, free of U.S. or state regulation. Native Americans fight for issues such as hunting and fishing rights, mineral rights, ownership of Indian remains and artifacts, and an end to sports mascots such as Cleveland Indians' Chief Wahoo.

Genocide and Ethnic Cleansing

Sometimes oppression and discrimination have led to genocide and <u>ethnic cleansing</u>. During World War II, <u>Nazi</u> Germany planned and carried out mass-killings in an attempt to eliminate European Jews. They also killed homosexuals, people with mental or physical disabilities, and many people from other cultural groups, namely Gypsies. More than six million Jews were killed, and many children orphaned. Those who were <u>liberate</u>d at the end of the war suffered from disease and <u>malnutrition</u>. All were homeless. This Nazi genocide is called "The Holocaust."

Many survivors <u>emigrate</u>d from Germany. Educated people – scientists, writers, and musicians – took their skills and education from Germany and used them to benefit their new countries. Many of them settled in the new State of Israel, the United States, and some South American and European countries. West Germany attempted to make financial <u>reparations</u> to the Jewish people. East Germany made a formal apology. The re-united German government has made payments to some families. Swiss bankers have attempted to face up to their role as bankers for the Nazis by repaying money and gold taken from Jewish victims. The art world still struggles to find out if some of the art they purchased after the war might rightfully belong to someone else.

Other instances of genocide and ethnic cleansing in Europe and Africa in the 20th century occurred due to ethnic conflicts. Ethnic conflict often occurred after ethnic groups were freed from living under a colonial government or a strong dictator. Some of the conflicts caused the loss of an entire culture.

- In the late 19th century, Armenians struggled to maintain their culture in the mainly Muslim Ottoman Empire ruled by Turkey. Armenia, whose people were mostly Christian, was located between the countries of Persia (now Iran), Russia, and Turkey. In 1894-95 and 1905, Turkey massacred Armenians in western Armenia. From 1915 to 1923, between 600,000 and 1.5 million Armenians were driven from their homes, massacred, or marched until they died. Tens of thousands emigrated to Russia, Lebanon, Syria, France, and the United States.

- The African countries of Rwanda and Burundi were at one time German colonies. After World War I, the lands were administered by Belgium. The two countries had very different governments, but Hutu and Tutsi peoples lived in each country. In Rwanda, the Hutus were the majority, but Tutsis controlled the government and discriminated against the Hutus. By 1962 when Rwanda became independent, the Hutus controlled the government and discriminated against the Tutsis. Many Tutsis fled to surrounding African countries such as Uganda and Burundi. In 1990 the rebel army of Tutsis from Uganda invaded and forced the Hutu government to agree to share power. However, the fighting continued.

  In 1994 a plane carrying the presidents of Rwanda and Burundi was shot down. Hutu extremists were accused of bringing down the plane. Those extremists began mass killings of Tutsis. About 800,000 men, women, and children were killed in only 100 days. The genocide ended when the rebel Tutsi army defeated the Hutu government forces. Fearing revenge, about 2 million Hutus fled to neighboring countries of Tanzania and Zaire (the Congo today). This large number of

refugees caused problems, which led to the First Congo War (1966-1997) and the Second Congo War (1998-2003). Almost 4 million died, mostly from malnutrition and disease. Millions were left homeless and in poverty. There were over 40,000 reported rapes.

- Bosnia experienced instability for hundreds of years under Ottoman rule. The Ottomans encouraged people to migrate from Serbia and Herzegovina to help resist surrounding enemies from Austria-Hungary and Venice. This migration created a mix of ethnic cultures within Bosnia. The three major ethnic groups were Bosniaks, Serbs, and Croats. Most Bosniaks were Muslim, most Serbs were Orthodox, and most Croats were Catholic. There was often tension and violence, especially over religious differences. After World War I (1914-1918), Bosnia became a part of Yugoslavia, however ethnic conflict continued. During World War II (1941-1945), Germany and her allies invaded Yugoslavia. A new independent state of Croatia was established and a pro-Nazi Croatian group was given control of the government. It soon targeted ethnic groups such as Jews, Gypsies, and Serbs for discrimination and genocide. Concentration camps were established. The result was a civil war. By the end of the war, over 300,000 people had been killed including most of Bosnia's 14,000 Jews and more than 100,000 Bosnian Serbs.

From 1945 to 1980 during the rule of the strong communist dictator, Tito, ethnic groups in Yugoslavia lived together fairly peacefully. After Tito's death ethnic conflict returned, and Yugoslavia began to fall apart. In 1992 Bosnia's parliament declared independence. Bosnian Serbs rejected independence and, with the military support of neighboring Serbia, responded with armed force including the mass shooting of civilians. The Serbs also began forcibly removing Muslims from the eastern portion of the country. Nearly half of the people of Bosnia became homeless victims of the war. This brutal treatment of a civilian population was called "ethnic cleansing." The term includes forced removal of an ethnic group including women, children, and the elderly—sometimes a march that causes many deaths on the way. More than 100,000 people were killed and almost 2,000,000 were refugees by 1995 when the Dayton Agreement established peace. The world community remained involved as Serbian leaders were tried for war crimes. In 2007 European Union forces and a small group of U.S. military personnel help keep the peace in Bosnia.

- Iraq is another country in which ethnic conflict has been severe. Arabs are about two-thirds of the population and Kurds are about one quarter. For hundreds of years the Kurds were nomads who moved from place to place. They lived in mountainous regions of modern Turkey, Iran, Syria, and Iraq. Although many Kurds are Sunni Muslims, they are culturally different from both the Arab Sunnis and the Shiites who live in Iraq. Since the end of World War I, Kurds have wanted their own state, but have not been able to gain it. Today, many live in urban areas of their oil-rich region. Saddam Hussein tried to extend his power into the Kurdish areas through threats, violence, and by forcing large numbers of Kurds to move. Many civilians were killed, and hundreds of thousands fled to Iran and Turkey. In 1988 Iraqi attacks used chemical weapons against civilians. Following the First Gulf War, the United States and its coalition partners set up a safe zone between the Arabs, to the south, and the Kurds in northern Iraq. In 2003 the government in Iraq included representatives of the Kurds.

Ethnic oppression, discrimination, and conflict have always existed and have always deprived people of a peaceful and productive life, the chance for education, and the liberty of choice. Countries that have experienced oppression, discrimination, and ethnic conflict nearly all fall into the United Nations' categories of low income or lower middle-income countries. These countries and their people

- Are dependent on food imports
- Have persistent hunger because of low export earnings that prevent them from importing food
- Have few people of working age, compared with those too young or too old to work
- Have high poverty
- Are dependent on aid and loans
- Are often totally dependent on selling their natural resources.

Legalized Discrimination in the United States: Jim Crow Laws

Thomas "Daddy" Rice was a white entertainer, a song and dance man. Around 1828 he saw a black man dancing for money on the street. He copied the dance and made it a part of his performance. He would blacken his face with burnt cork, dress in ragged clothes, and sing and dance. The chorus of his song, "Jump Jim Crow," was "Weel about and turn about and do jis so, Ebry time I weel about I jump Jim Crow." He acted out a popular stereotype of African Americans and it was a hit. The term "Jim Crow" eventually became attached to segregation laws.

Segregation laws appeared in northern states before the Civil War (1861-1865). African Americans experienced segregated railroad cars, steamboats, hotels, and restaurants. Some public facilities, such as libraries, were closed to African Americans. Black slaves in the southern states had their rights legally restricted by slave laws, and free blacks faced discrimination and segregation. After the Civil War, segregation laws in northern states began to disappear and southern slave laws were abolished. Southern states responded by passing laws called "black codes" to control ex-slaves. Many of these black codes were former slave laws. After the South was placed under military rule, the black codes were abolished.

By 1877 military rule ended and southern states began passing laws to keep races apart. For example, Southern state legislatures passed laws separating whites from "persons of colour" in public transportation. Anyone who looked black or was suspected of having black ancestors was considered a "person of colour." These segregation laws or Jim Crow laws, legalized discrimination on the basis of race. In 1891 a Louisiana civil rights group decided to challenge a law creating "separate but equal" railway cars for blacks and whites. In 1896 the U.S. Supreme Court ruled in *Plessy v. Ferguson* that "separate but equal" public facilities were constitutional. This decision encouraged more segregation laws.

Jim Crow laws spread throughout the South. Racial segregation was extended to all public facilities including schools, hospitals, parks, cemeteries, theaters, transportation, restaurants, restrooms, and water fountains. In practice, these facilities were separate, but rarely equal. Such legalized discrimination made African Americans second-class citizens. Jim Crow came to represent a way of life that included all the customs and laws that separated blacks and whites in the South.

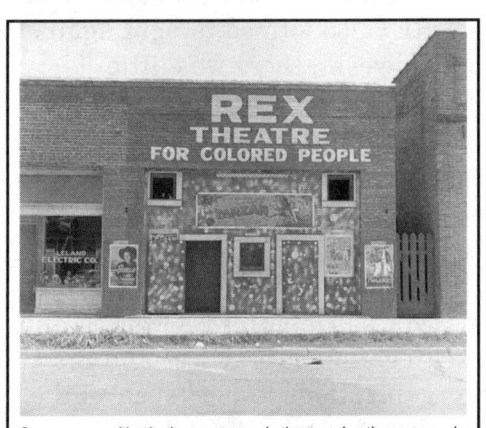

Some communities had separate movie theaters. In other communities, African Americans went to the same theater as whites, but had to sit in the balcony. Often there were separate entrances in the back of the theater. Ticket prices, however, were the same.

Struggles for Equality since the Late 19th Century: Race and Gender

Individual acts of resistance by African Americans to the rise of Jim Crow began immediately. Some protested or disobeyed Jim Crow laws and customs. They risked going to jail and the possibility of lynching. Others developed their own schools, colleges, social clubs, and other types of community groups. Local civil rights groups, such as the Citizens' Committee of

African Americans and Creoles in New Orleans that challenged Louisiana's Separate Car law in 1892, also organized.

The struggle to eliminate Jim Crow laws on a national level began in the early 20th century. The National Association for the Advancement of Colored People (NAACP) was founded in 1909 and challenged racial discrimination in the courts. Other civil rights organizations such as the National Urban League and the Congress of Racial Equality (CORE) also formed to fight against discrimination and segregation However, there was little success until after World War II.

In 1954 the NAACP successfully challenged the *Plessy v. Ferguson* decision. The Supreme Court ruled in *Brown v. Board of Education of Topeka* that "separate educational facilities are inherently unequal." The way was opened to end segregation. This historic court decision stimulated a mass civil rights movement, in which blacks and white sympathizers worked and protested together to end the segregationist practices and racial inequalities. New civil rights organizations formed such as the Southern Christian Leadership Conference (SCLC) and the Student Non-Violent Coordinating Committee (SNCC).

Congress eventually responded to the civil rights movement. Congress passed the Civil Rights Act of 1957, which established the Civil Rights Commission to investigate civil rights and voting rights abuses. The Civil Rights Act of 1964 made discrimination by race, color, religion, sex, or national origin in public facilities and employment illegal. The Voting Rights Act of 1965 provided African Americans federal support for voting registration and banned literacy tests and poll taxes as requirements for registration. Jim Crow laws were finally overturned by Supreme Court decisions and federal legislation.

Like African Americans, the women's struggle for equality began in the 19th century. Women wrote, spoke, and raised money for the abolition of slavery and voting rights for all. Women also fought for the rights of women in all states to own property, have a claim to their earnings, and have equal rights concerning the guardianship of their children. After the Civil War (1861-1865), women and blacks tried to work together for suffrage. In 1870, five years after slaves were freed, black men received the right to vote, but women did not. Women continued to organize and protest. In 1869 the National Woman Suffrage Association and the American Woman Suffrage Association were formed to fight for a constitutional amendment granting voting rights to women. Then they joined forces and formed the National American Woman Suffrage Association (NAWSA) in 1890. The National Association of Colored Women organized in 1896 to promote equality for African Americans, but also supported the struggles for women's suffrage. In 1913 the National Woman's Party was founded and organized more militant protests. Finally, the Nineteenth Amendment was ratified and women voted in the election of 1920.

Women on Strike. In 1909 immigrant women working in the ladies garment industry struck to protest low pay, strict supervision, and unsafe working conditions. The strikers won a few concessions – a 52-hour work week and a 12-15% raise – from 300 companies. But little was done about safety until after more strikes and the tragic Triangle Shirtwaist Factory fire two years later.

The right to vote did not end sex discrimination. In 1903 the National Women's Trade Union League was founded to fight for better wages and working conditions. The National Woman's Party worked to pass an Equal Rights Amendment. The National Council of Women was organized in 1935 to fight for civil rights for African Americans and women's rights. However, little changed concerning gender equality. Most Americans believed it was the man's responsibility to provide for the family and a woman's place was in the home raising a family. In addition, the sacrifices necessary during the Great Depression of the 1930s and World War II (1941-1945) put the issues of sex discrimination and women's rights in the background.

The civil rights movement of the 1950s and 1960s helped reawaken many to the struggle against sex discrimination and for women's rights. Also, increasing numbers of women were entering the workforce. In 1963, Congress passed the Equal Pay Act, requiring that men and women receive equal pay for equal work. The Civil Rights Act of 1964 banned discrimination by sex as well as race. In 1972 Title IX of the Federal Education Amendments barred discrimination in education programs on the basis of sex. It has received the most attention regarding funding for women's sports.

The National Organization for Women (NOW) was formed in 1966 to fight against sex discrimination and for full and equal participation for women in American society. In the 1970s NOW developed a nationwide campaign in support of the Equal Rights Amendment (ERA), which guaranteed equal rights to all Americans despite sex. ERA passed the House and the Senate by 1972, however was not ratified by enough states to become a part of the U.S. Constitution. NOW was successful on other issues, including its support of the Federal Education Amendments (1972) and the Violence Against Women Act (1994).

The most controversial change in women's' rights was the Supreme Court ruling in *Roe v. Wade* (1973). It prevents extreme state regulation of abortion. This ruling maintains that a woman can decide to end a pregnancy under certain conditions, based on the right to privacy. Many Americans, male and female, argue that abortion is taking a life and not an equal rights issue. They want a constitutional amendment to ban all or most abortions. Others, including NOW, argue that any additional limitations on abortion would be a step backward for women's struggle for equal rights.

The Status of Minorities and Women

The status of minorities and women changed slowly. During the 1960s the U.S. government began adopting and promoting affirmative action policies. They wanted to increase available opportunities and place some responsibility on institutions to actively recruit minorities and women. The goal was to increase the numbers of minorities and women by favoring them in areas of past discrimination such as college admissions, hiring and promotions, and government contracts for businesses. Critics claimed less-qualified or unqualified people were receiving opportunities rather than those who were most qualified. They called affirmative action a form of reverse discrimination that affected whites, especially white men. Several court cases eventually reached the U.S. Supreme Court. In *The Regents of the University of California v. Bakke* (1978), the Supreme Court ruled that the use of racial quotas is illegal, but race can be used as one of several factors in admissions decisions. Affirmative action remains a controversial issue.

In their quest for equality, African Americans and women have run into much opposition in this country. After World War II, African Americans and women were not given equality; they struggled to improve their status. This resulted in many laws and court decisions that supported their struggle for equal rights and led to dramatic changes in American society. Today African Americans and women vote and hold political offices such as governor, mayor, U.S. representative and U.S. senator, secretary of state, U.S. ambassador to the United Nations, and Supreme Court justice. Professions and jobs from firefighter to chief executive officer (CEO) were opened to qualified candidates regardless of race or sex. Since 1940 the percentages of African Americans and women who graduate from high school and college have increased dramatically. In fact, since 1979 the majority of college students are women.

The following graph shows the change in education attainment by race in Ohio from 1940 to 2000. Notice the difference between the percent of whites with a high school diploma or more and the percent of blacks. What was the difference in percentage between blacks and whites in 1940? What was the difference in 2000? How has that difference changed from 1940 to 2000?

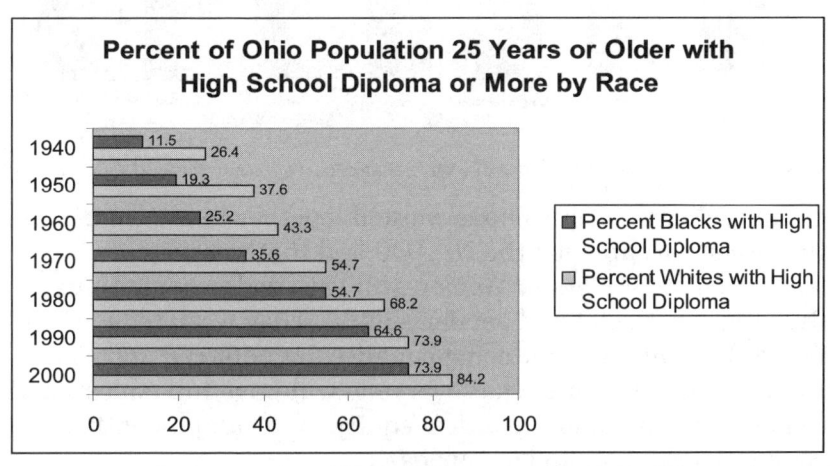

Percent of Ohio Population 25 Years or Older with High School Diploma or More by Race

Year	Percent Blacks with High School Diploma	Percent Whites with High School Diploma
1940	11.5	26.4
1950	19.3	37.6
1960	25.2	43.3
1970	35.6	54.7
1980	54.7	68.2
1990	64.6	73.9
2000	73.9	84.2

Source: U.S. Census Bureau, *Education 1940-2000_OH*

The struggle for racial and gender equality continues. Today African Americans and women do play a greater role in business and in government, yet they still fall behind the nation as a whole. Discrimination blocks career advancement for African Americans and women, especially to positions of power and authority. Surveys of major companies show that over 90% of senior-level managers are men, and over 90% of those men are white. Also, African American men and women earn less than white men and women. Women earn only three-quarters as much as men.

The following chart presents the 2004 <u>median</u> income of full time workers who are 16 years old and older. What is the difference in the median income of men and women? Which group has the highest median earnings? Which group has the lowest? What is the difference between black and white median earnings for males and females?

Income
Median earnings of year-round, full-time workers, 16 years and older, by sex, race and ethnic origin, 2005

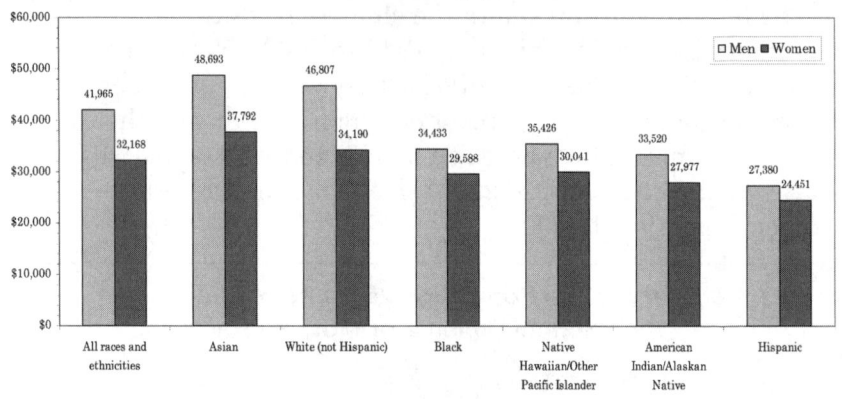

Group	Men	Women
All races and ethnicities	41,965	32,168
Asian	48,693	37,792
White (not Hispanic)	46,807	34,190
Black	34,433	29,588
Native Hawaiian/Other Pacific Islander	35,426	30,041
American Indian/Alaskan Native	33,520	27,977
Hispanic	27,380	24,451

Source: Income, Earnings, and Poverty Data from the 2005 American Community Survey, U.S. Census Bureau

Many diverse groups have worked together to aid women and minorities. Groups like the NAACP and the American Association of University Women still exist today to continue advocating for racial and gender <u>equity</u>. They work today to ensure that laws guaranteeing equality are enforced and that new laws are written so that everyone will have full educational, economic, personal, and political equity. You can join with a group or work alone to do your part.

Glossary

People in Societies B

affirmative action – a policy which gives opportunities to women and minorities because of past discrimination.

allies (ally) – friends, supporters; a group of countries joined together with a common purpose.

annex – to add; to add land to an existing country or state. For example, the state of Texas belonged to Mexico, but the United States annexed Texas in 1845.

assimilate – to act like; become like; fit in.

atrocity (atrocities) – a terrible, brutal, cruel action.

civil rights movement – movement (organized activities) to defeat legal racial segregation and discrimination.

coalition – a temporary alliance of different persons or groups with a common goal.

colonialism (colonial, colonized, colonists) – the policy of establishing a colony. For example, the European nations colonized Africa.

colonize – to start a colony.

communism (communist) – an economic system in which the businesses are owned and operated by the government. The government decides the type, quantity, and price of goods produced. They also decide what workers will make. Communism says it will provide for everyone's needs and get rid of social classes.

concentration camp – a guarded place where persons (prisoners of war, political prisoners, and refugees) are housed; used especially by the Nazis during World War II to confine, punish, and kill large numbers of Jews.

conflict – a disagreement, that could be violent, between people, countries, or ideas.

coup (coup d'état) – a sudden, often violent, overthrow of a government by a small group.

culture (cultural, culturally) – the way of life of a group of people, which includes their ideas, beliefs, customs, language, and traditions.

dictatorship (dictator) – a form of government in which the ruler (dictator) or ruler's power is not limited by citizens or a legislature. A dictator has absolute power that is enforced by an army and secret police.

discrimination (discriminate) – unfair treatment by a government or individual citizens, usually because of race, religion, nationality, sex, or certain disabilities; prejudice.

diversity – difference or variety.

emigrate (emigrant) – to leave one's country to live elsewhere. (a person who leaves his country to live elsewhere.)

equality (equity) – having the same rights and opportunity as anyone else regardless of race, religion, gender, or social class.

ethnic (ethnicity, ethnically) – having to do with a group of people who share a common culture, language, nationality, race, or religion. For example, new Chinese immigrants settled in a part of the city called China Town, so they could live with their own ethnic group.

ethnic cleansing – removing an ethnic group or groups from an area using force. It could include forced emigration and genocide.

exploit (exploitation) – to treat unfairly or meanly for one's own advantage.

extremist (extremism) – someone having extreme political or religious opinions.

facilities – something built which provides a service such as a hospital or restroom.

gender – one's sex; being a male or female.

genocide – the planned elimination of an ethnic group.

homeland – a separate territory or country that a group of people can control and call their own.

inherently – naturally built into; naturally forming an important part of something.

instability – the quality of being unstable, changeable, unsteady.

interact – act upon one another.

Islam – a religion based on a single god, Allah, and on the word of God as revealed to Muhammad during the 17th century and written in the Qur'an (Koran).

liberation (liberate) – setting someone or something free.

liberty – freedom from control by others.

literacy test – a reading and writing test. It was one of the voter registration procedures used to deny blacks in the South the right to vote.

lynching – death at the hands of a mob.

malnutrition – a medical condition usually caused by a poor diet. It is often the result of starvation.

massacre – to cruelly kill or slaughter people.

median – the middle number in a set of numbers arranged from least to greatest.

migrate (migration) – to move from one location to another. It is often used to describe people who move within their own country.

militant – aggressive; combative; willing to fight for a cause.

monarchy (monarch) – a form of government in which the ruler (monarch) is a king, queen, emperor, or empress. A monarch usually inherits the title and holds power for life.

Muslim – a person who practices Islam.

Nazism (Nazi) – the beliefs and practices of Adolf Hitler's National Socialist German Workers' Party including racial superiority, government control of society and the economy, and loyalty to one's nation or people above all else.

oppression – treating people in a cruel, unjust, or harsh way.

Orthodox – a Christian religion originally centered in eastern Europe and the Middle East. Today, examples include the Orthodox Church in America (formerly Russian Orthodox), the Orthodox Church of Poland, and the Ethiopian Orthodox church. Eastern Orthodox are mostly Greek.

poll tax – a tax which must be paid in order to vote. Since the poll tax cost more than most poor whites and African Americans could pay, it kept many from voting.

quota – a number or percentage that is set as a maximum or minimum amount. For example, immigration laws often set limits on the number of immigrants from different countries allowed into the United States.

ratify (ratified) – to confirm or approve, usually by a vote.

refugee – a person who runs away for safety, usually to another country.

region (regional) – a geographic area defined by some characteristics or features not found in surrounding areas. Northwest Ohio, the coal-mining region of Ohio, and the Arctic region are examples.

reparations – the debts a nation must pay for the harm done during a war.

reservation – land set aside for a special purpose, especially in the United States for Native Americans (American Indians) to live on.

segregation (segregate) – the law or practice of separating and isolating people by characteristics such as race, religion, or nationality.

status – position or rank in comparison to others.

stereotype – an unfair, unproven belief that certain people must be or act in a certain way.

suffrage (suffragist) – the right to vote. (a person, male or female, who supports giving women the right to vote.)

tradition (traditional, traditionalist) – inherited, established, or usual pattern of thought, action, or behavior.

urban – having to do with cities or towns.

People in Societies C

CULTURAL DIFFUSION

Analyze the ways that contacts between people of different cultures result in exchanges of cultural practices.

DIFFUSION: THE IMPACT OF ADVANCES IN COMMUNICATION AND TRANSPORTATION

People are affected by what they see and hear and do. You know that you are influenced by friends and family, by new ideas, sights, and tunes, even by the weather. Groups of people and their leaders also change. Sociologists study groups of people and their cultures—how they interact and how they change.

Sociologists ask questions like, "What causes cultures to change?" One answer to that question is cultural diffusion, which is the spread of ideas, technology, and other elements of culture over time and space. A good example of cultural diffusion is the introduction of sugar-growing in the Americas. It led to riches for a few Europeans and Americans and slavery for millions of Africans.

Foods are often good examples of cultural diffusion. Sixty years ago very few people in the United States had tasted pizza. We adopted pizza from Italians, who developed pizza thanks to the tomato they adopted 500 years ago from the Spanish, who found them grown by Indians in Mexico and South America. We modified the Italian's pizza recipe to agree with our tastes.

Today cultural diffusion happens more often and takes place more rapidly because of advances in communication and transportation. These advances have an impact on globalization, cooperation and conflict, the environment, collective security, popular culture, political systems, and religion.

Globalization

Globalization is the increasing interaction and interdependence among people and businesses in nations throughout the world. Advances in communication and transportation since the end of World War II have increased the pace of globalization. That trend has grown even faster since the 1990s. Every day people worldwide buy Japanese and Korean cars, cameras, and computer equipment, French wine, Columbian coffee, and carpets from India. Satellites used for broadcasting television signals let us see events happening live throughout the world. Computers, fax machines, and cell phones give us quick and easy access to people and businesses worldwide. Improvements in transportation have lowered costs and travel time for both passengers and products. Charles Lindberg's solo, non-stop flight from New York to Paris in 1927 took 33.5 hours. Today, commercial passenger flights from New York to Paris take about 4 hours.

Advances in communication and transportation encouraged businesses and individuals to offer products and services to national and international markets. Large and small businesses use cable television services and the Internet to advertise, make presentations, and make sales. There has been a growth in the number of multinational corporations, which are businesses with branches, plants, or other businesses in many other countries. For example, McDonald's restaurants are found throughout the world, including Beijing, Moscow, Paris, Singapore, and Melbourne, Australia. Sony is one of the largest electronics and entertainment businesses in the world. Its headquarters are in Japan, but branches, plants, other businesses it owns are found in China, France, Spain, the United Kingdom, the United States, and many other countries.

Globalization has also influenced people to look seriously at global problems. Fast and easy access to information about our world and more travel to other countries have helped people understand that some problems, such as global warming, disease, hunger, poverty, and avoidance of war, affect everyone and need to be addressed by the global community.

Conflict and Cooperation

Often cultural groups avoid conflict when they work together for a common goal. Fast communication and transportation can aid in cooperation. In 1933 President Roosevelt used weekly radio broadcasts to reassure U.S. citizens that they would see better days and to explain how his policies would help them. Today, nations cooperate on space projects such as Spacelab, a program of science experiments operated by 10 European nations and the United States. For over 10 years, 16 nations have worked together on the International Space Station. Russia and the U.S. started the first phase with the Russian Mir-U.S. shuttle missions in 1995. The world comes together to send aid to people who suffer from natural disasters, such as the tsunami in Indonesia (2004) and Hurricane Katrina in the U.S. (2005).

Communication can incite people to take action. In Rwanda in 1994, radio broadcasts stirred people to genocide and ethnic cleansing. During the Vietnam War, the evening news showed the war as it happened. The images moved U.S. citizens to call for a change in national policy and withdrawal from Vietnam. U.S. government officials accuse Al Jazeera, a television network in Qtar, of broadcasting news stories and images that encourage support for terrorists and strong anti-American feelings that prolong the War in Iraq.

Advances in communication and transportation can also lead to conflict. Some advances were used to create improved weapons for war such as the cruise missile, that can carry a nuclear weapon. Al-Qaeda terrorists used Boeing 767 passenger jet airliners as weapons in the September 11, 2001 attacks. Fast communication and transportation give people the power to act very quickly, perhaps even before they fully understand a problem.

Environmental Impacts

Nations also cooperate to solve problems affecting the worldwide environment. Transportation contributes about one-third of the total CO_2 emissions, a big cause of global warming.

Clearing forests, (deforestation), contributes another 20%. Businesses in some countries like Brazil have bought equipment and cut down large forests to sell worldwide. They know this is a fast way to earn money. Brazil's deforestation causes worldwide environmental change. The United States is also a large contributor to global warming due to emissions from its many cars, trucks, and power plants. Truck and auto manufacturers have to meet lower emissions standards set by the U.S. government. The United Nations (UN) has established a market in energy credits to encourage emissions reductions and control <u>pollution</u>.

Can countries work cooperatively to avoid problems that affect everyone? In 1992 the United Nations held the largest gathering of nations in history. One hundred seventeen heads of state and representatives of 178 nations met to reconcile problems of worldwide <u>economic development</u> with protection of the environment. Although the countries came to some agreements, conflicts divided the <u>developed countries</u> of the North from the <u>developing countries</u> of the South.

Collective Security

During the 20th century, advances in communication and transportation have brought the nations of the world closer together and made them more interdependent. It also made war between distant nations easier. This increased the need for <u>collective security</u>. In the 1930s world diplomats began to "telephone" each other, using radiophones. Airplanes made travel easier, and heads of state and diplomats began to meet more often. During the 1960s the U.S. and the USSR agreed to cooperate to avoid nuclear war. The U.S. president and the USSR premier each installed a telephone wired directly to the other. They knew they could quickly confirm or deny an attack and avoid mistaken reports. The main mission of the UN is to preserve collective peace and security. UN translators convey translations in six official languages through headphones to delegates from 192 member states.

Language is an important component of a culture. It includes how people think, not just what they think and how they express it. By understanding a culture's language, we may see a problem differently, or they may provide a solution because they see the problem another way. Language has also been a barrier to communication. Although there are computer translation services available on the Internet, they are useful mainly for casual use to learn about other cultures, rather than for diplomatic translation.

World nations watched the televised September 11, 2001 disaster and responded to help the United States. For the first time in its history, NATO, an international group that provides collective security for 26 nations, responded militarily to defend one of its member nations. More than 360 flights over the U.S. by 13 member nations helped the U.S. with security for eight months following the disaster. NATO nations continue to cooperate with naval operations in the Middle East to prevent movement of terrorists or weapons of mass destruction and to ensure shipping security.

Popular Culture

U.S. citizens enjoy televised regional festivals, hear regional accents, and learn to cook regional foods. Midwestern markets sell seafood flown in fresh from Massachusetts or flash frozen and shipped from Australia or Alaska. Local stores sell fruits and vegetables trucked across the nation or flown in from Latin America or Israel. Regional cultures are easily shared across the nation and around the world.

Advances in communication and transportation enabled popular culture (pop culture) to spread worldwide. The international distribution of films has made international stars, such as Jackie Chan, Julia Roberts, and Bruce Willis. Television series such as *I Love Lucy*, *The Muppet Show*, and *Lost* are shown in countries around the world. World tours by singers and bands such as Madonna, Julio Iglesias, Michael Jackson, The Rolling Stones and U2 also spread popular culture worldwide. Professional sports celebrities such as tennis players Venus and Serena Williams, basketball player LeBron James, golfer Tiger Woods, and soccer player David Beckham became role models. Popular culture also spread with easy access to music downloads and sports events via cable television and satellite transmission.

Availability of goods and services makes popular culture global, especially in the developed countries. Today hip hop is found on every continent except Antarctica. CocaCola can be bought in about 200 countries, McDonalds sells hamburgers in more than 100 countries, Wal-Mart operates in 15 countries, Gap sells clothes in 9 countries, and Walt Disney theme parks operate in 4 countries. Clothes, food, music, and DVDs can be bought on the Internet and are delivered worldwide.

Political Systems

Today people around the world have greater access to information about their country and other countries because of advances in communication. Books, the media, and the Internet provide information about the freedom or lack of freedom in all countries. In 1989 people around the world saw the Germans tear down the Berlin Wall and celebrate in the name of freedom. That same year people saw students challenge the Chinese government by demonstrating in Tiananmen Square. And in 1994 they saw the long lines of black South Africans patiently waiting for hours to vote for the first time. These events inspired many people, especially those who live in countries with little freedom.

Dictatorships and totalitarian governments do not want their citizens to know about freedom in other countries and work to suppress information. Governments in countries like North Korea limit access to the Internet, restrict foreign news broadcasts, censor the media, and silence critics. The government does everything within its power to keep North Korea the most isolated country in the world. But it is difficult to control all the news and information in a country. Radio, the Internet, and inexpensive CDs make it hard to suppress ideas that lead to political change.

People in poor nations know their economic disadvantage by comparing their life with the lives of those they see in the mass media. They have become very resentful about the large gap between the rich countries and the poor. That gap and the knowledge of a better life in the United States are major reasons for the large number of immigrants and illegal immigrants that come to the United States.

Religion

Some people in the world think there is a large divide between Christians and Muslims. Whether this is true or not, the fact that groups think it is causes concern about conflict and terrorism. It is easy to spread this fear through mass communication. As with other information, religious ideas and beliefs are easily researched on the Internet. Those who want to get along need to know what the others believe. Those who want to find knowledge can use the Internet to find complete religious texts by word or by subject, engage in online chats with others, or find the nearest worship group. Indeed, we have a wide choice of ideas, knowledge, images, and sounds that are easily available by Internet, radio, television, cell phone, mp3 player, and a long list of other electronic devices. With knowledge of the other culture, the two groups can work toward joint solutions for current world problems.

Advances in transportation and communication have helped the spread of some religions. The Christian music industry has grown dramatically and offers a variety of choices including gospel and contemporary music. There are over 1,600 radio and television stations representing different religious organizations in the United States alone. They present sermons, teachings, discussions, music, and news from a religious perspective. One of the largest broadcasters is The Christian Broadcasting Network (CBN), which offers religious programming and national and international news programs. On Sunday mornings many commercial stations present religious programming as well. These radio and television programs have a wide appeal and continue to grow in popularity. They have helped promote the growth of Christianity worldwide.

Using Our Understanding of Cultures

Fast communication and international distribution of

products force us to make choices and to evaluate sources. Are the electronic sources we use reliable and credible? Is the information accurate? Do these electronic sources give us unbiased information? Do they use propaganda? Do they tell us the whole story, or do they show or tell us things we know are not true? Who are the authors, and what are their sources of information? You may trust one brand of jeans will fit, but not be sure about another. In the same way, you must look at the source of information on the Internet or television. Who said it? Why did they say it? What is their cultural perspective? You must make these judgments. Nations also must use knowledge of cultures and toleration when they adopt policies that balance nationalism with globalism.

DIFFUSION: THE EFFECTS OF IMMIGRATION ON SOCIETY IN THE UNITED STATES

A Nation of Immigrants

Cultural diffusion also happens because of immigration. The United States has always been a nation of many immigrants and, therefore, many cultures. Each group has made cultural contributions which helped define the culture of the United States. These cultures have mixed due to education, mass media, and a desire to share in the American dream of freedom, opportunity, and prosperity. Many also preserve their cultural identity.

Many immigrants arrived in the United States with few resources, but lots of hope for a better life. Today, immigrants continue to come to the United States in search of freedom and opportunity.

The chart on the following page shows the number of immigrants who came to the United States from 1820 to 2006. Sometimes immigration was encouraged and other times it was discouraged. During the early twentieth century, there was a great demand for workers. Based on the next chart, in which year between 1895 and 1925 did the U.S. receive the greatest number of immigrants? During the difficult years of the Great Depression, many people needed jobs. There was little demand for immigrant labor. About how many legal immigrants came to the U.S. in 1932? Today, immigration numbers are rising. About how many legal immigrants came to the U.S. in 2006?

U.S. Legal Immigrants 1820 - 2006

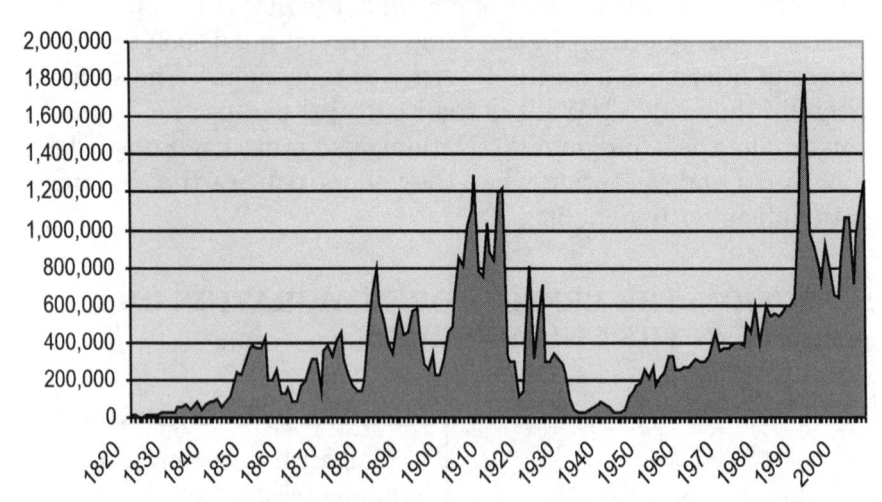

Source: U.S. Department of Homeland Security, *Yearbook of Immigration Statistics, 2006, Table 1*

The United States experienced three major waves of immigration. Each had different characteristics. The first wave came between 1830 and 1860. Most of the immigrants were from northern and western Europe especially from Great Britain, Germany, and Ireland. The second wave came between 1880 and 1920. Most of these immigrants came from southern and eastern Europe especially Italy, Poland, and Russia. Most were Catholics or Jews. The third wave came during recent decades. Especially large numbers came from Asia, Latin America, and the Middle East.

Today about 1,000,000 immigrants come to the United States each year. The majority of those immigrants come from Latin American and Asia. In 2006 Mexico, China, the Philippines, and India provided the largest number of immigrants. Most settle in one of seven states including California, New York, and Florida. In addition, there are more than 1 million illegal immigrants each year and between 12 million and 20 million illegal immigrants presently living in the United States. The effect of immigration is evident in housing patterns, politics, schools, work, and religion.

Housing Patterns

Most people who immigrated to the United States between 1880 and 1920 settled in cities and worked factory jobs. Their labor was needed to help sustain the economy of the growing nation. Many were from southern and eastern European countries. They were usually Catholic or Jewish and did not speak English. Most chose to live near others from their home country, and they continued to speak their native language and practice their religion and customs. The result was the creation of ethnic ghettoes in major cities such as Cleveland, Chicago, and New York. Many cities still have a neighborhood called "China Town" and perhaps another called "Little Italy." Cleveland also has a neighborhood called "Slavic Village" and other areas with high concentrations of Lithuanians, Czechs, Germans, Poles, Russians, and others.

As immigrants prospered and their children gained more education, many left their ethnic neighborhoods. They valued larger homes and services more than living among others of their ethnic group, or in some cases whole ethnic groups moved to a better neighborhood. As people moved from ethnic neighborhoods, they were replaced by African Americans migrating from the South and Hispanic immigrants. The result was often tension and sometimes violence.

Political Affiliations

Immigrants established political affiliations (connections) that often were different from many native-born, middle-class residents, especially employers. Some urban political leaders viewed the new immigrants as potential voters. Political bosses emerged, such as William Marcy Tweed in New York City. He gained power and influence by helping immigrant families find jobs, a place to live, and other favors, especially during hard times. In turn, Tweed expected them to vote for Democratic Party candidates. The Republican Party had political bosses too, but was usually not interested in winning the support of immigrant voters or supporting issues important to immigrants. The result was that in local elections immigrants and the working class usually supported Democratic candidates.

Language

Immigrants usually spoke their native language at home. Larger cities often had enough immigrants from one country to support a native-language newspaper, radio station, and church services. However, immigrants needed to learn English to communicate on the job, talk to their neighbors, use medical and government services, and to become citizens. Settlement houses appeared in many cities to help new immigrants. Jane Addams started Hull House in 1889 in Chicago. Addams and her volunteers, who were mostly young college-educated women, set up a day nursery and kindergarten to help take care of young, immigrant children while their mothers and fathers worked. Addams and others also offered adult education classes. Public schools also began to offer adult education classes during the evening. During the day many young immigrant children struggled to learn English while in school or were sent home until they could speak English. Today our education system offers English instruction to children whose parents have immigrated to the United States. These courses are known as ESL (English as a Second Language). The ESL programs are quite expensive to operate, and the federal government does not fully fund these programs.

Immigration had a major impact on the English language. Many foreign words have become an accepted part of the English language, such as the Spanish words *bronco*, *guerrilla*, *tornado*, and *tango*. Today, there are many Spanish newspapers, magazines, radio stations, and television channels. Today Hispanics account for the largest number of new immigrants and are the largest minority group in the United States. In response, hospitals and government offices print forms in both English and Spanish and pay translators to help immigrants. Many businesses provide services and instructions in English and Spanish.

Labor Practices

During the last half of the 19th century, emigrants frequently signed on with a factory employer before they left their home country. This, of course, left them at a disadvantage. They may not have had current information on wages, working conditions, or housing. Others arrived with no job and little or no education or skills. They took any job available, and that meant unskilled, backbreaking jobs with low pay, long hours, and poor working conditions. Immigrants with skills, such as carpenters, bakers, shoemakers, and tailors, found better-paying jobs, and their lives were much easier.

Immigrants made up a large percentage of laborers and the urban working-class population. In 1900 two-thirds of Cleveland's population was immigrants or the children of immigrants. Some Americans complained about the number of immigrants coming to America and called for restrictions. Some, who had been immigrants not long before, complained that the new immigrants lived in miserable, dirty, unhealthy conditions that lowered everyone's standard of living. They claimed these new immigrants were a drain on public services. Some unions complained that immigrants were cheap labor that took jobs away from Americans. They also complained that industry and business used immigrants as strikebreakers. The same complaints are heard today.

Most immigrants were not able to join unions because they were unskilled workers. The Knights of Labor was a union that accepted skilled and unskilled workers and blacks as well as whites. However, it collapsed. The American Federation of Labor (AFL), the most successful union, accepted only white, skilled workers into their union. Unskilled workers were included in a few unions such as the Congress of Industrial Organizations (CIO), the United Mine Workers (UMW), and the United Farm Workers (UFW).

Religion

Immigrants contributed to religious diversity in the United States. During various time periods, immigrants tended to come from specific countries or areas and brought their religious faiths with them. In the United States, they built houses of worship that remain in city centers today.

In 1800 most Americans were <u>Protestants</u>. During the first wave of immigration, between 1830 and 1860, increasing numbers of immigrants were Catholics or Jews. In the second wave of immigration, between 1880 and 1920, the number of Catholic, Jewish, and <u>Orthodox</u> immigrants grew dramatically. The recent, third wave of immigration included increasing numbers of Buddhist, Hindu, Muslim, and Sikh immigrants. Today most Americans are still Protestant, but the largest Christian religion is Catholic, and Islam is the fastest growing religion in the United States.

Immigration brought religious diversity to Cleveland, Ohio. Before 1865 in Cleveland, most churches were white and Protestant. In 1865 the Cleveland city directory listed 50 churches and 29 (58%) were white and Protestant. By 1929 only 45% of the city's 480 churches were white Protestant, and by 1986 the number had decreased to 25%. While the number of Protestant churches declined, the number of Catholic cathedrals, Jewish synagogues, Buddhist temples, and Muslim mosques increased. Within each religion, several groups clung to their native language and had separate services. Many depended on their church to help preserve their customs.

Generally, in Cleveland religious groups have practiced <u>tolerance</u> and cooperation. The workplace and schools adjusted their schedules to accommodate holidays previously unknown to most. In Cuyahoga County many Eastside public schools accommodate their large Jewish populations and close for the major Jewish holiday of Yom Kippur. Other public schools consider such religious holidays excused absences or personal days for employees and students who stay home to observe the holidays.

Future U.S. immigration policy will be shaped by our understanding of how past immigration has influenced our society. Questions about our ability to accommodate immigrants are as important now as in the past. New policy also will be influenced by answering the question, "Can our economy continue to support the number of people wanting to emigrate here?"

Glossary

People in Societies C

collective security – an agreement among nations 1) to not attack each other and 2) to defend each other against an attack.

credible (credibility) – believable, convincing.

cultural perspective – how a person views and understands a subject, based on his/her ideas, beliefs, customs, language, and traditions.

culture (cultural, culturally) – the way of life of a group of people, which includes their ideas, beliefs, customs, language, and traditions.

developed countries (developed world) – highly industrialized countries; countries in which most people have a high standard of living.

developing countries – countries with very little industry; countries in which most people have a low standard of living.

dictatorship (dictator) – a form of government in which the ruler (dictator) or ruler's power is not limited by citizens or a legislature. A dictator has absolute power that is enforced by an army and secret police.

diversity – difference or variety.

economic development – changing the way products are made by using technology to make more products and better products; using resources and people productively. Economic development is more than economic growth. The idea of economic development goes beyond increasing individual income to include things like health, education, safe environment, and freedom, in other words the quality of life.

emigrate (emigrant) – to leave one's country to live elsewhere. (a person who leaves his country to live elsewhere.)

ethnic (ethnicity, ethnically) – having to do with a group of people who share a common culture, language, nationality, race, or religion. For example, new Chinese immigrants settled in a part of the city called China Town, so they could live with their own ethnic group.

ethnic cleansing – removing an ethnic group or groups from an area using force. It could include forced emigration and genocide.

genocide – the planned elimination of an ethnic group.

ghetto – any neighborhood or section of a city where many members of a racial group live.

global (globalization, globalism) – worldwide, referring to the whole world.

immigrant (immigration) – a person who enters a country and makes it his home, often becoming a citizen of his new country.

incite – to stir up; urge to act.

interdependence (interdependent) – depending on or requiring assistance from one another.

media (mass media) – movies, newspapers, radio, television, and other forms of mass communication to the general public.

Muslim – a person who practices Islam.

nationalism (nationalist) – loyalty to one's own nation or country; especially putting one nation above all others, with major emphasis on promotion of its culture and interests.

nuclear – involving atomic weapons and atomic energy.

Orthodox – a Christian religion originally centered in eastern Europe and the Middle East. Today, examples include the Orthodox Church in America (formerly Russian Orthodox), the Orthodox Church of Poland, and the Ethiopian Orthodox church. Eastern Orthodox are mostly Greek.

perspective – point of view; how a person views and understands a subject.

political boss – a person who helped immigrants in the cities in exchange for their votes in elections.

pollution – dangerous substances released into the air, water, or soil.

popular culture (pop culture) – the culture of common, everyday people (the mainstream population) which can include cooking, clothing, media, entertainment, sports, and literature. Pop culture is often criticized as being sensationalism or pushing consumerism.

propaganda – selective facts, ideas, or information used to win support for a cause or a person. It usually has a strong emotional appeal.

Protestant – a Christian who is not Catholic or Eastern Orthodox, such as a Baptist, Lutheran, or Methodist.

reliable (reliability) – dependable, trustworthy.

settlement house – an institution that provides community services. Hull House in Chicago and Hiram House and Karamu House in Cleveland are examples of settlement houses started in the late 1800s and early 1900s.

standard of living – level of well-being of individuals or groups, based on characteristics such as education, income, healthcare, life expectancy, and available goods and services.

strikebreaker – a person who accepts employment to work in place of a striking worker.

terrorism (terrorist) – using fear and violence for political purposes.

tolerate (tolerance) – respecting the beliefs, customs, and physical differences of others.

toleration – an official policy that recognizes that others have the right to continue with their customs; a government policy of tolerance.

totalitarian – governed by a system which wants absolute control over all aspects of a person's private and public life. Individual freedoms must be sacrificed for the good of the state.

unbiased – without bias or prejudice; impartial; fair.

union – a number of persons joined together for a common purpose, such as better pay and better working conditions. They may use negotiation, picketing, and going on strike in order to get what they want from their employer.

urban – having to do with cities or towns.

Geography A

PLACES AND REGIONS

Analyze the cultural, physical, economic, and political characteristics that define regions and describe reasons that regions change over time.

Geographers study the interrelationship between the physical environment and human activity. They focus on regions. A geographic region is an area with common characteristics or features that set it apart from surrounding areas. Its people have a sense of identity. A region can be as small as a neighborhood within a city or as large as several continents.

Regional Characteristics

People within a specific region have at least one common cultural, physical, economic, or political characteristic. Here are some examples of regions.

Cultural Region	Cleveland's neighborhoods are cultural regions. Little Italy got its name because families emigrated from Italy, all spoke Italian, and they settled together in the same neighborhood.
Physical Region	All the people who live near Lake Erie live in the Great Lakes region. The Amazon Rainforest is the world's largest rainforest. It is located within eight South American countries.
Economic Region	The rust belt is a region of the U.S. with an economy based on heavy industry and manufacturing such as steel and automobile factories. The European Union (EU) creates an international region of 25 countries that use a common currency called the Euro.

| Political Region | Counties, states, and provinces are political regions. Mexico is a country divided into 31 states. Canada is a country divided into ten provinces and three territories. |

Comparing Regions

Geographers compare different regions. How does life in a coal-mining region in Germany compare with life in a coal-mining region in the United States? How does life in Ohio compare with life in Alabama? Geographers find answers to these big questions by breaking them down and answering simple questions. Using the answers, they compare regions.

Geographers begin by collecting and analyzing <u>data</u>. They use data to answer their questions. Geographers comparing life in Brazil, Haiti, and the United States ask questions such as: How healthy are these people? To answer that question they collect data about a region's <u>birth rate</u>, <u>infant mortality rate</u>, <u>death rate</u>, and other health factors. That data can be used to compare one region to another. Based on the chart below, how would you compare the health of the people of Brazil, Haiti, and the United States?

Health	Death Rate / 1,000	Birth Rate	Infant Mortality Rate	Life Expectancy	HIV/AIDS Rate (%)	Doctors per 100,000
Brazil	6.17	16.56	28.6	71.97	0.7	206
Haiti	12.17	36.44	71.65	53.23	5.6	25
U. S.	8.26	14.14	6.43	77.85	0.6	549

Geographers also compare education levels, poverty, and access to clean water. They research factors such as <u>literacy rate</u> and the population below the poverty line. Look at the chart below. How would you compare the literacy and poverty rates in Brazil, Haiti, and the United States?

Education & Poverty	Literacy Rate (%)	Population Below Poverty Line (%)	Access to Improved Water Source (%)
Brazil	86.4	22	87
Haiti	52.9	80	46
U. S.	99	12	100

Geographers would also compare the economies. They compare average incomes by looking at factors such as per capita gross domestic product (GDP (PPP)). They also look at labor force by occupation, electricity production, and unemployment rate. Look at the chart below. How would you compare the economies in Brazil, Haiti, and the United States?

Economy	GDP (PPP) per Person	Labor Force by Occupation (%) Agriculture Industry Services			Electricity Production (kWh per person)	Unemployment Rate (%)
Brazil	$8,400	20	14	66	2,060.3	9.8
Haiti	$1,700	66	9	25	65.7	67.0
U. S.	$41,800	0.7	22.9	76.4	13,041.0	5.1

Now, let's put all our tables together. Using the statistics in the large table below, compare life in Brazil, Haiti, and the United States. How would you compare the health, education, and economies of the three countries?

Indicators	Country		
	Brazil	Haiti	U. S.
Health			
Death Rate / 1,000	6.17	12.17	8.26
Birth Rate	16.56	36.44	14.14
Infant Mortality Rate	28.6	71.65	6.43
Life Expectancy	71.97	53.23	77.85
HIV/AIDS Rate	0.7	5.6	0.6
Doctors per 100,000	206	25	549
Education & Poverty			
Literacy Rate (%)	86.4	52.9	99
Population Below Poverty Line (%)	22	80	12
Access to Improved Water Source (%)	87	46	100
Economy			
GDP per Person (PPP)	$8,400	$1,700	$41,800
Labor Force by Occupation (%)			
Agriculture	20	66	0.7
Industry	14	9	22.9
Services	66	25	76.4
Electricity Production (kWh per person)	2,060.3	65.7	13,041.0
Unemployment Rate (%)	9.8	67	5.1

Regional Conflict

Differing points of view can lead to regional conflict.
- Native Americans living on the Great Plains during the 1800s were hunters who depended on the buffalo as their main source of food. They killed only what they needed. White American hunters saw buffalo as a source of profit and slaughtered millions for their hides. The killing of the buffalo and the increasing number of ranchers and settlers moving onto the plains led to a series of battles and massacres.
- Sunni Muslims and Shiite Muslims are followers of Islam, but have different beliefs concerning who should lead the Muslim community. Today in Iraq, the Sunnis and Shiites fight for control of the government and many fear a civil war.
- In the province of Quebec, Canada, French is the main language for most of the people. Some French-speaking Canadians want to secede from Canada where the majority of the people speak English.
- A major cause of the American Revolutionary War (1775-1783) was conflict surrounding laws the British government passed to tax the thirteen colonies. The British government insisted they had the right to tax the colonists, but many colonists argued that they could only be taxed by the representatives they elected to their colonial legislature.
- After World War II, the United Nations decided to divide the territory of Palestine into an Arab state and a Jewish state. Arabs rejected the plan. Jews accepted the plan and created the State of Israel. Arab states refused to recognize the right of Israel to exist. Since that time Israel has fought many wars with neighboring Arab states.

Regional Cooperation

People in regions often solve problems together.
- They can cooperate economically.
  - Countries in the European Union decided to use a common form of money and to work toward common

policies in <u>immigration</u>, security, <u>technology</u>, and justice.
- Canada, the United States, and Mexico agreed to free trade among their countries. The agreement is called NAFTA (North American Free Trade Agreement).
• Competition for resources can lead to agreements.
- Disagreements about rights to drinking water have led to court battles and then eventually to agreements among western states like California, Arizona, and Nevada.
- Similarly, countries in the Middle East have made agreements about how much water one country can take from a river, or they have set their country borders so each country has a share of available water.

Regional Change

History is a story about changes – how people migrate, invent, discover, create, cooperate, and disagree. Characteristics of a geographic area also change.
• <u>Industrialization</u> brought changes to regions. It caused many farmers to move from <u>rural</u> areas and take factory jobs in <u>urban</u> areas. About 5% of the U.S. population lived in urban areas in 1800. Today, about 80% live in urban and <u>suburban</u> areas.
• Immigration and migration bring changes to a region. New ethnic groups settle in communities and bring new foods and languages. At the West Side Market in Cleveland, the ethnic groups selling food products reflect the changes in the city's ethnic population.
• Economic conditions of a region can change. Car manufacturers began to use less steel to build cars. As a result, many steel mills closed in cities like Cleveland. Workers lost their jobs and had to learn new skills. Some people moved to find work elsewhere. The region needed to replace the steel work with new types of jobs, perhaps in service or technology.

- Technology changes regions. The automobile helped change urban areas. Cities have spread across large areas with more people living in single-family homes and driving to work instead of using public transportation. The landscape looks different with fewer trees and more houses and roads.
- Wars cause changes in regions. Wars can wipe out vegetation or natural resources. Often a treaty to end a war changes the boundaries of a country or leads to the creation of a new country.

Our ideas and opinions about a region can change. Early settlers wanted good farmland. Today most people do not own farms or even work in factories. They live in urban regions and value some land for its beauty and for recreation. For example, parts of the Cuyahoga Valley National Park were swampy and bad farmland, but now we enjoy the land as a nature preserve. The region may be the same, but our viewpoint of it has changed.

Learning about a region may change people's opinion about that region. Appalachia is a good example. It is a region of the Appalachian Mountains between New York and Alabama. The people who live there have long been described as hillbillies. Recent historians and scholars described Appalachian contributions to American culture and the economy. Even the media is presenting a more positive image in their movies and news reports. Country music and entertainers are very popular. Many people enjoy the *down home cookin'* of restaurants such as Bob Evans and Cracker Barrel.

Ideas and opinion about a region can change over time. In 1800 Ohio was a territory with a population of about 44,000 and Cleveland's population was 7. Ohio and Cleveland were considered a part of the western frontier. Today, Ohio is a state with a population over 11,000,000 and Cleveland's population is about 478,000. Ohio is the seventh largest state, and Cleveland is the headquarters for many large corporations and a leader in the area of healthcare and services.

Glossary

Geography A

birth rate – frequency of births; the number of live births in a year for every one thousand people. If 148 babies are born in a community of 10,200 people, the birth rate is 148 ÷ 10,200 x 1,000 = 14.5.

conflict – a disagreement, that could be violent, between people, countries, or ideas.

continent – one of the seven large land masses of the world. The United States is located on the North American continent. The other continents are South America, Europe, Asia, Africa, Australia, and Antarctica.

culture (cultural, culturally) – the way of life of a group of people, which includes their ideas, beliefs, customs, language, and traditions.

data – information, facts, and numbers.

death rate – the number of deaths in a year per 1,000 people; the frequency of deaths. If 84 people die in a community of 10,200 people, the death rate is 84 ÷ 10,200 x 1,000 = 8.24.

emigrate (emigrant) – to leave one's country to live elsewhere. (a person who leaves his country to live elsewhere.)

European Union (EU) – an inter-governmental organization of 25 European countries established in 1992. Each of the member countries is independent, but they share common laws to make trade and commerce between them easier. For example, EU members agreed to a common currency and a common tariff (tax on imports).

gross domestic product (GDP (PPP)) – GDP is the total value of goods and services produced in a nation during a specific period of time, usually one year, excluding income earned from investments abroad. The per capita gross domestic product is the gross domestic product divided by the number of people in the country. Purchasing power parity (PPP) shows how much of a country's currency is needed in that country to buy what $1 would buy in the United States. GDP (PPP) is a good way to compare average income or consumption between counties.

immigrant (immigration) – a person who enters a country and makes it his home, often becoming a citizen of his new country.

industrial (industry) – the making and distributing of products using machinery; manufacturing.

industrialization – the change from an economy dominated by agriculture (farming) to one dominated by manufacturing with machines in factories in urban areas.

infant mortality rate – frequency of babies dying before reaching age one; for every 1,000 live births, the number of babies that die each year before reaching the age of one.

interrelationship – the relationship or interaction between two things that affect or influence each other.

Islam – a religion based on a single god, Allah, and on the word of God as revealed to Muhammad during the 17th century and written in the Qur'an (Koran).

literacy – ability to read and write.

literacy rate – the frequency of adults who can read and write; the number of adults who can read and write per thousand of the population.

mortality rate – death rate.

Muslim – a person who practices Islam.

per capita – for each person.

region (regional) – a geographic area defined by some characteristics or features not found in surrounding areas. Northwest Ohio, the coal-mining region of Ohio, and the Arctic region are examples.

rural – relating to or characteristic of the country, country people, or country life. An example of rural people is farmers.

rust belt – an economic region in the United States roughly between Chicago and New York City and northern West Virginia and the Great Lakes. Much of the region's economy was based on heavy industry such as steel. Because many of their goods are produced for less in other countries, many businesses and factories were abandoned and closed. Machinery left behind rusted.

secede – to withdraw from an organization, political party, or federation. Eleven Southern states seceded from the United States at the time of the Civil War.

suburb; suburban (suburbanite) – a community or land near a city, with easy access to the city. (a person who lives in the suburbs.)

technology – machines, equipment, and procedures to use them to improve manufacturing and production; practical use of scientific knowledge especially in engineering.

urban – having to do with cities or towns.

Geography B

HUMAN ENVIRONMENTAL INTERACTION

Analyze geographic changes brought about by human activity using appropriate maps and other geographic data.

Geographers study how people affect the environment. They want to understand what causes regions to change, so we can make informed decisions. Regions can change because of wars, weather, economic conditions, new technology, and human migration.

Causes of Urbanization

Industrialization led to urbanization. During the 1800s increasing numbers of people in Europe and the United States worked in factories, including women and children. Workers needed to live close to the factory to work long hours each day. Between 1814 and 1850 in New England, factory owners built boardinghouses or dormitories for single-women employees. Having a safe place to live that was close to work encouraged families to allow young single women to leave their homes to work in factories.

As industrialization developed rapidly, so did urbanization. The use of steam power as an energy source encouraged manufacturers to build their factories in urban areas. There, transportation, local markets, and workers were available. The growing demand for factory workers encouraged people to leave farms and small towns. It also encouraged immigration. Between 1870 and 1920, over 26 million people came to the United States and many took factory jobs. In urban regions like Cleveland, many lived close to the steel mills and other factories so they could walk to work.

Cities grew larger and population density increased as merchants set up shops to supply food, laundry, clothing, and entertainment for workers. Large centers of industry and technology developed as factory suppliers clustered nearby. Universities provided educated workers such as engineers, economists, and scientists. In 1790 the United States was 5.1% urban. In 2000 it was 79% urban. Look at the chart. What conclusions can you draw about urbanization in the United States?

Percentage Urban & Rural Population of the United States: 1790 to 2000

Year	Urban	Rural
1790	5.1	94.9
1800	6.1	93.9
1810	7.3	92.7
1820	7.2	92.8
1830	8.8	91.2
1840	10.8	89.2
1850	15.4	84.6
1860	19.8	80.2
1870	25.7	74.3
1880	28.2	71.8
1890	35.1	64.9

Year	Urban	Rural
1900	39.6	60.4
1910	45.6	54.4
1920	51.2	48.8
1930	56.1	43.9
1940	56.5	43.5
1950	64.0	36.0
1960	69.9	30.1
1970	73.6	26.3
1980	73.7	26.3
1990	75.2	24.8
2000	79.0	21.0

Social Effects of Urbanization

During the second half of the nineteenth century, cities grew rapidly and without plans. A shortage of housing meant overcrowding and a lack of privacy. Cities had problems meeting growing demands for services such as fire and police protection and regular garbage collection. Industrial waste and sewage polluted rivers and drinking water. Disease spread easily. Cities were dirty, noisy, and over-crowded. Roads were

Main city streets often had buildings with store fronts on the first floor and apartments on the floors above. Rundown tenements (apartments) were packed with people. As many as eight people lived in a two-room apartment. City streets were crowded with carts, littered with garbage and horse manure, and with little or no lighting at night. Children played in the streets and alleys.

built wherever they were needed. Streets were muddy much of the year and so crowded that sometimes people died trying to cross them. Fights often broke out among groups of long-time city dwellers and the new city people. Migrants such as farmers, rural southern blacks, and immigrants fought among themselves. Crime and poverty were problems. Family members no longer lived close and could not help care for one another.

As transportation improved, people moved away from factories. By the 20th century, buses, streetcars, and cars meant people could work in the city and live in the suburbs. After World War II, more people moved to the suburbs. Cleveland is a typical example of this movement. Look at the following chart. What conclusions can you draw about suburbanization in Cleveland?

Cleveland City and Suburbs 1910 – 2000

	Cleveland	Cuyahoga County	City as % of County
1910	560,663	637,425	88%
1920	796,841	943,495	84%
1930	900,429	1,201,455	75%
1940	878,336	1,217,250	72%
1950	914,808	1,389,532	66%
1960	876,050	1,647,895	53%
1970	750,879	1,720,835	44%
1980	573,822	1,498,400	38%
1990	505,450	1,412,140	36%
2000	478,403	1,393,978	34%

Suburbanites liked living on the edges of the urban area where the air was cleaner and they had room for gardens and parks. Their life was more peaceful in the suburbs. Each suburban community had its own local government, fire and police protection, ambulance service, schools, swimming pools, and garbage collection. Gradually, some factories and smaller businesses moved from the center of the city to the suburbs. Some people moved even farther from the city center. The building of the interstate highway system after World War II made such moves easier. Today 80% of the U.S. population lives in cities and suburbs.

Urbanization continues today. Worldwide, more people are moving from rural areas to urban areas. Look at the next chart. What conclusions can you draw about urbanization in the world from 1975 to 2002?

Region	Population Density (people per square kilometer)		Percent of Population in Urban Areas	
	1975	2002	1975	2002
World	30	46	37.9	47.0
Asia	91	140	23.6	34.6
Europe	29	31	67.3	74.8
Middle East & North Africa	16	33	43.0	60.6
Sub-Saharan Africa	13	27	20.9	34.3
North America	12	16	73.9	77.2
Central America & Caribbean	39	66	55.5	66.3
South America	12	20	64.1	79.8
Oceania (South Pacific)	20	23	68.5	73.7
Developed Countries	20	23	68.5	73.7
Developing Countries	38	63	26.7	39.6

Some of the world's largest cities grow so fast, they double in size in 20 years.

Population of the World's Largest Cities 1996				
City, Country	Population (thousands, 1995)	Annual Growth Rate (%)	Percentage Increase for	
			1975-1995	1995-2015
Tokyo, Japan	26,959	1.45	36.36	7.15
Sao Paulo, Brazil	16,533	1.84	64.56	22.91
New York City, U.S.	16,332	0.34	2.85	7.78
Mumbai (Bombay), India	15,138	4.24	120.79	73.19
Seoul, South Korea	11,299	1.92	70.52	11.81
Beijing, China	11,802	0.87	32.23	37.82
Lagos, Nigeria	10,287	5.68	211.73	139.53

Environmental Effects of Urbanization

Urbanization greatly changed the physical characteristics of regions. Wilderness once covered by trees was cleared for houses. Farmland once covered with crops was covered with houses, factories, roads, and railroads. Trees that cool and clean the air and anchor the soil were gone. Deforestation meant an increase in air pollution and soil erosion.

Scientists track emissions each year from deforestation and fossil fuels. Here is a chart that compares average emissions from different sources during a 5-year period. Deforestation accounts for about 20% of the total emissions.

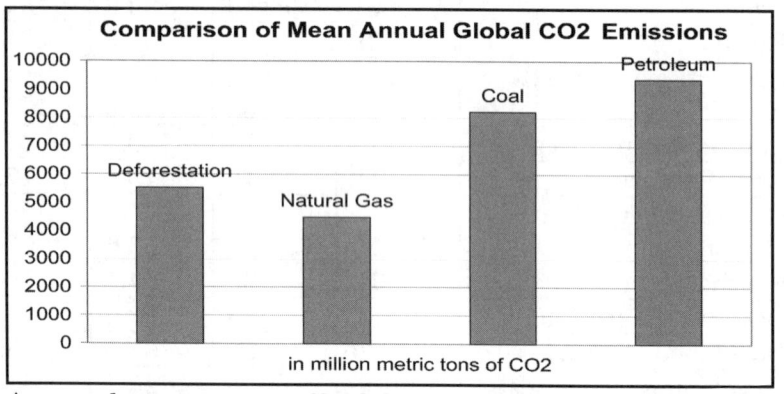

Comparison of Mean Annual Global CO2 Emissions

Source	Emissions (million metric tons of CO2)
Deforestation	~5500
Natural Gas	~4500
Coal	~8000
Petroleum	~9500

As cars became more affordable, more people in urban areas drove to work. Burning fossil fuels for cars and residential use produces carbon dioxide (CO_2), the main source of excess greenhouse gases that cause global warming. The pie chart shows that more than half of the CO_2 comes from residential use and transportation.

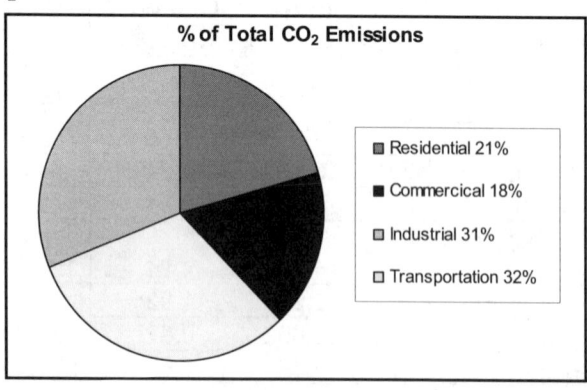

% of Total CO_2 Emissions

- Residential 21%
- Commercical 18%
- Industrial 31%
- Transportation 32%

As more people move to urban areas, pollution increases

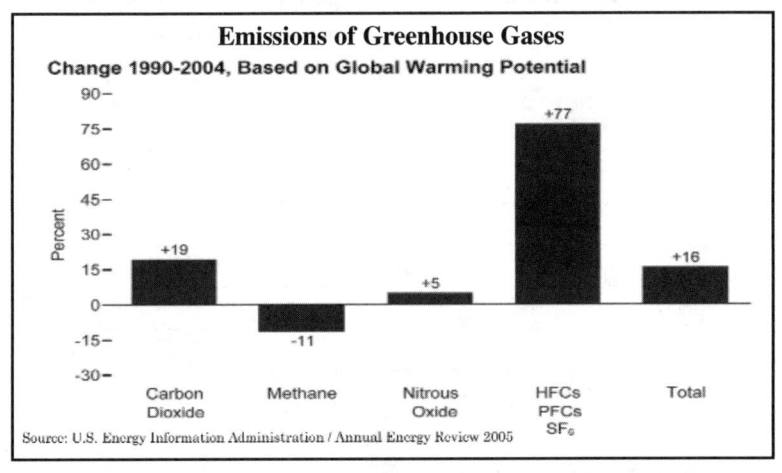

Emissions of Greenhouse Gases
Change 1990-2004, Based on Global Warming Potential

- Carbon Dioxide: +19
- Methane: -11
- Nitrous Oxide: +5
- HFCs PFCs SF₆: +77
- Total: +16

Source: U.S. Energy Information Administration / Annual Energy Review 2005

Urbanization affects a region's wildlife. Often animals are forced to look for food in other places. That explains why you may have skunks near your garbage can or under your porch in the city, and why deer eat plants and trees in suburban gardens. In some regions, even bears or alligators wander near houses and garbage dumps to search for food.

Scientists and geographers use maps and graphs to study the effects of urbanization. They use graphs to show how a region's population grows. Geographers measure population density or the number of people per square mile. The population density is high in urban areas. This population density map shows urban centers as dark areas. Scientists compare population maps with temperature maps to study global warming.

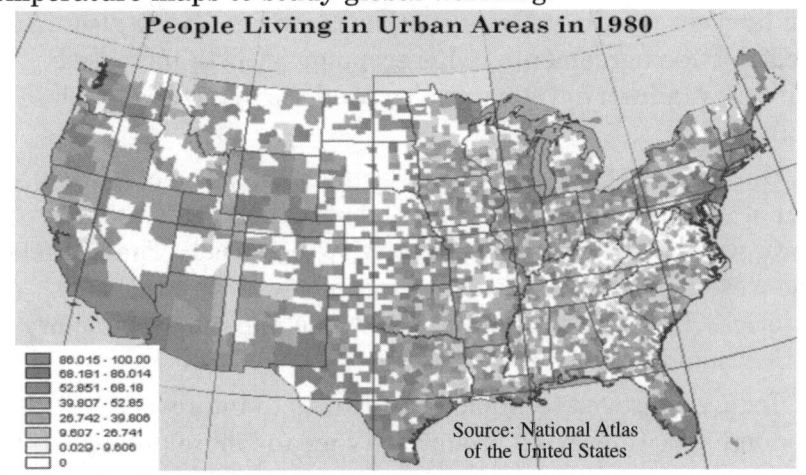

People Living in Urban Areas in 1980

Legend:
- 86.015 - 100.00
- 68.181 - 86.014
- 52.851 - 68.18
- 39.807 - 52.85
- 26.742 - 39.806
- 9.807 - 26.741
- 0.029 - 9.806
- 0

Source: National Atlas of the United States

Global Temperature Changes (1861–1996)

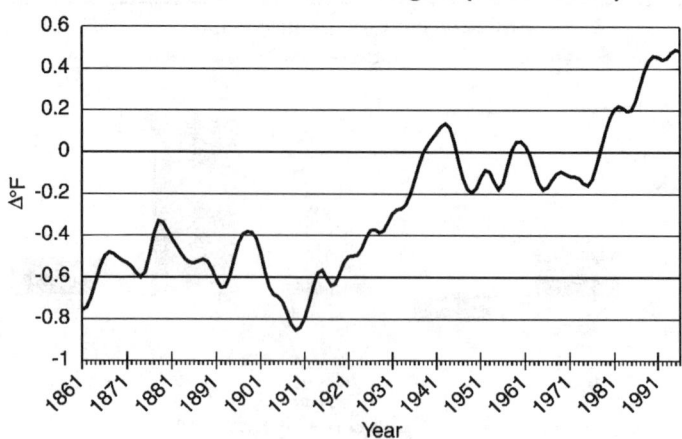

Source: IPCC (1995), updated

Effects of Economic Development

Urbanization and industrialization also change a region's economy. Economies changed from hunting and fishing to farming and then to industry. Industries made many more products than the local people could use. They needed to sell and transport their products across this country. They also needed to sell them to people in other countries. To sell products in other countries, industry had to hire someone who could speak a different language and travel to sell their products. They hired accountants who could work with other currencies and lawyers who knew laws of other countries. They also needed trade agreements. This economic growth increased profits for industry. Industry also used technology to increase profits.

During the 1800s new machines took the place of a great deal of manual labor. Each farm laborer then could produce more. In other words, his productivity increased. The workers who were no longer needed on the farms went to work in factories. Industries improved their machines so each factory worker could produce more.

Today, improved technology continues to improve productivity. Improving productivity means more products from fewer resources. More products means lower prices and a higher standard of living. Countries with a higher productivity and standard of living, such as the United States, are called developed countries. Countries with lower productivity and standard of living, such as Haiti, are called developing countries. Economic development has noticeable effects on the environment including air, water, and noise pollution. Industry and cities need to use technology to reduce pollution. Even more important than increased income, economic development usually leads to more freedom, equity, better healthcare, education, and a safer environment.

Effects of Technology, Transportation, and Communications

During the 1800s, transportation changed regions like Cincinnati and Cleveland. River traffic and later trains brought pigs to market in Cincinnati. The city became a center for hog butchering. Soon industries like Proctor and Gamble used the leftover animal fat to make soap. The Ohio and Erie Canal made water transportation between the Great Lakes and the Ohio River possible. It helped Cleveland grow into an important trade center. Great Lakes shipping and trains made Cleveland a steel center by bringing together ore from Michigan and coal from Pennsylvania. Companies like UPS now use jet airplanes to transport parts, materials, and products worldwide. Quick supply has reduced the need to store materials and products in warehouses.

As businesses grew, they needed more office space on the same amount of land. In the mid 1800s, the first safe elevator made it practical to build buildings with more than four floors. When people learned how to make iron into steel that was both strong and lightweight, they could build even taller buildings. Skyscrapers met the need for more office space close to industry.

As scientists and engineers found new ways to make products, they often used new materials. When the demand for a natural resource dropped, some regions lost their source of income. Michigan no longer mines much iron because new cars use less steel.

Technology changed the way people work. Research and technology for the space program led to the development of plastics and satellites, which are used by all of us. Technology that can be used many different ways changed lives even more. By using telephones, airplanes, computers, and the Internet, industries no longer need to be clustered together in a large urban area. A single business can locate some of its business and manufacturing processes in different countries and regions. They can operate as several small businesses. Employees can even work at home.

Glossary

Geography B

boardinghouse – a place to stay which provides a room and meals.

deforestation – the cutting of all or nearly all of the trees; the clearing of forests.

developed countries (developed world) – highly industrialized countries; countries in which most people have a high standard of living.

developing countries – countries with very little industry; countries in which most people have a low standard of living.

dormitories – rooms for sleeping; especially large rooms with several beds. Today colleges have dormitories with rooms for individuals or groups, often without a private bath.

economic development – changing the way products are made by using technology to make more products and better products; using resources and people productively. Economic development is more than economic growth. The idea of economic development goes beyond increasing individual income to include things like health, education, safe environment, and freedom, in other words the quality of life.

economic growth – increasing a country's economy by using more of its resources or by using them more efficiently. Economic growth is usually measured as a change in the value of the goods and services produced in one year (the gross national product (GNP) or the gross domestic product (GDP)).

equality (equity) – having the same rights and opportunity as anyone else regardless of race, religion, gender, or social class.

erosion – washing away, or wearing away, usually by the action of water or wind.

fossil fuel – a fuel, such as oil, coal, or natural gas, formed in the earth from plant and animal remains.

immigrant (immigration) – a person who enters a country and makes it his home, often becoming a citizen of his new country.

industrialization – the change from an economy dominated by agriculture (farming) to one dominated by manufacturing with machines in factories in urban areas.

migrate (migration) – to move from one location to another. It is often used to describe people who move within their own country.

New England – the northeastern part of the United States that includes Connecticut, Maine, Massachusetts, New Hampshire, Rhode Island, and Vermont.

pollution – dangerous substances released into the air, water, or soil.

population density – a measure of the number of people living in a given area, usually the number of people per square mile.

productivity – the amount produced by each person.

region (regional) – a geographic area defined by some characteristics or features not found in surrounding areas. Northwest Ohio, the coal-mining region of Ohio, and the Arctic region are examples.

standard of living – level of well-being of individuals or groups, based on characteristics such as education, income, healthcare, life expectancy, and available goods and services.

suburb; suburban (suburbanite) – a community or land near a city, with easy access to the city. (a person who lives in the suburbs.)

suburbanization – growth of suburbs.

technology – machines, equipment, and procedures to use them to improve manufacturing and production; practical use of scientific knowledge especially in engineering.

urban – having to do with cities or towns.

urbanization – the development or growth of cities or towns.

Geography C

MOVEMENT OF PEOPLE, PRODUCTS, AND IDEAS

Analyze the patterns and processes of movement of people, products, and ideas.

People move. They migrate from one region to another. They move from one continent to another. A major theme in the history of the world is the story of human migration.

Some people move voluntarily. People choose to move to find a better job or a better home. They are attracted to a new region. Other people move because they have to. Sometimes people move because they are forced out of a region. Often people move to get away from something. The reasons people move have always been affected by social, economic, political, and environmental factors.

Social Factors

People move for social reasons such as ethnicity, race, or religion. These people are persecuted or experience discrimination. Other people hurt, kill, or threaten them, and do not allow them to work and live as they choose. In the 1600s Pilgrims and Puritans left England because they were persecuted for their religious ideas. During much of the 20th century, many African Americans moved from the South to the North and West to escape racism. When Nazis began to persecute and kill Jews before and during World War II, many Jews fled Germany. Beginning in the 1970s, some Iranians left Iran because the government demanded they live according to Shiite Islamic rules and law. They were not allowed freedom to work, dress, or live as they wanted. Many Tutsis fled Rwanda to escape Hutu killings that became genocide.

Economic Factors

People move because of a lack of food or physical resources. During the 1840s the Irish came to the United States during the potato famine to escape starvation in Ireland. One of the strongest hurricanes in history, Hurricane Katrina, struck the

Gulf coast of the United States in August 2005. Over 1,800 people lost their lives and hundreds of thousands lost their homes, possessions, and jobs. Many people from New Orleans were moved to cities, such as Houston, Texas and Mobile, Alabama, that offered to provide food and shelter. Some people have decided not to return to New Orleans.

People move in search of jobs and economic opportunity. Much of the labor to build the trans-continental railroad in the United States during the 1860s came from China and Ireland. Italian stonemasons came to the United States between 1880 and 1914 for jobs building cathedrals, concert halls, and office buildings. In that same time period, many other Europeans came for <u>industrial</u> jobs. During the 20th century, millions of African Americans moved from southern farms to find northern industrial jobs. Many Mexicans moved to the United States during the twentieth century because they could find jobs, especially as farm workers. Doctors, engineers, and scientists often have moved to find specialized professional jobs.

Political Factors

People move because of their political beliefs. They move in search of freedom. Some left <u>communist</u> countries in search of freedom. After World War II, East Germans fled to West Germany to escape the new communist government. After the Cuban Revolution, many Cubans came to the United States to escape the rule of Fidel Castro. Politics can affect migration in other ways. Some European Jews decided they could escape persecution and be safe only if they lived in their own country. In the 1890s a few bought land and moved to Palestine, their homeland in ancient times. By 1939 many more Jews wanted to migrate there to escape <u>Nazism</u>. In 1948 the modern state of Israel was born.

Wars also shape migration. After World War II, millions of people had been forced to leave their homes and possessions. Camps for these displaced persons were set up to provide temporary food and shelter. Some displaced persons returned to their country of origin, while others moved to a new country to start over again. When the United States invaded Afghanistan in 2001 and Iraq in 2003 during its War on Terror, some Afghans and Iraqis left for neighboring countries.

Environmental Factors

Climate can influence migration. <u>Industrialization</u> in the United States began in the Northeast and remained concentrated there for a hundred years. But when oil prices skyrocketed in the 1970s, the cost to operate a factory skyrocketed as well. Industries relocated to warmer climates in the Sun Belt (the South and Southwest) where the cost of living was lower. Factory owners saved on heating and building costs and on salaries. Workers from the Northeast were encouraged to follow, both because they needed the jobs and because they, too, could save on heating.

Climate can influence migration more directly. In a year of very low rainfall or bad storms, farmers can lose all their crops. Often they are forced to migrate to find food and employment in another region or city. During the 1930s a severe drought led to a mass migration of farmers to California from states surrounding Oklahoma. Droughts also caused famines in Ethiopia and led to the migration of masses of people.

Today, migration still causes population to increase much more in some U.S. states than others.

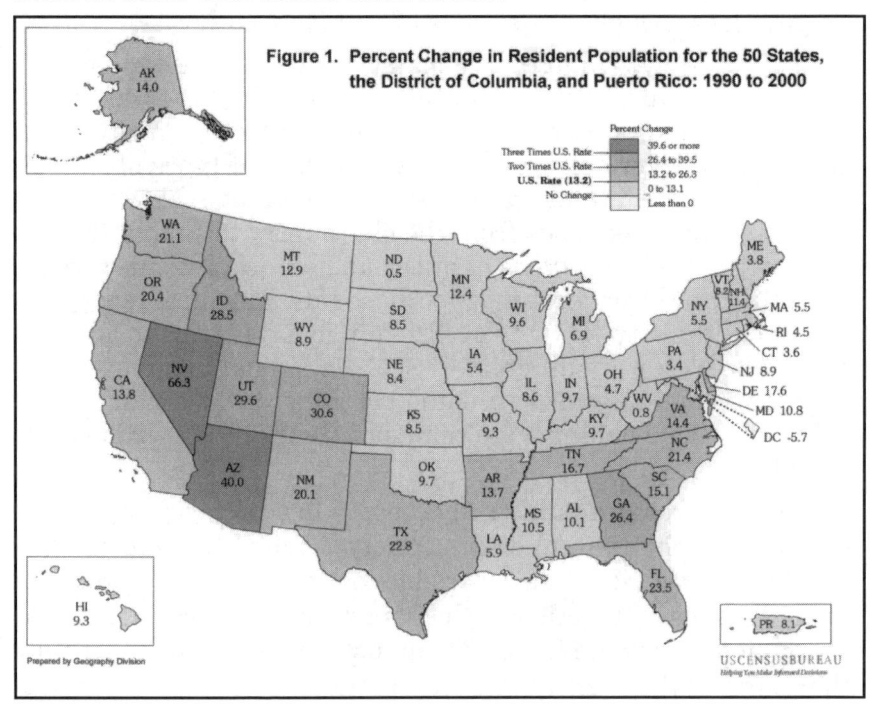

Figure 1. Percent Change in Resident Population for the 50 States, the District of Columbia, and Puerto Rico: 1990 to 2000

Percent Change:
- 39.6 or more (Three Times U.S. Rate)
- 26.4 to 39.5 (Two Times U.S. Rate)
- 13.2 to 26.3 (U.S. Rate 13.2)
- 0 to 13.1 (No Change)
- Less than 0

State	%	State	%	State	%
AK	14.0	WA	21.1	ME	3.8
MT	12.9	ND	0.5	VT	8.2
OR	20.4	MN	12.4	NH	11.4
ID	28.5	SD	8.5	NY	5.5
WY	8.9	WI	9.6	MA	5.5
CA	13.8	MI	6.9	RI	4.5
NV	66.3	NE	8.4	PA	3.4
UT	29.6	IA	5.4	CT	3.6
CO	30.6	IL	8.6	NJ	8.9
AZ	40.0	IN	9.7	DE	17.6
NM	20.1	OH	4.7	MD	10.8
KS	8.5	WV	0.8	VA	14.4
OK	9.7	KY	9.7	NC	21.4
TX	22.8	TN	16.7	DC	-5.7
MO	9.3	MS	10.5	SC	15.1
AR	13.7	AL	10.1	GA	26.4
LA	5.9	FL	23.5	HI	9.3
PR	8.1				

Prepared by Geography Division — U.S. CENSUS BUREAU

Changes in American Society

During the nineteenth century and the twentieth century, industrialization changed the nation from an agricultural economy to an industrial one. It caused the shift from a rural society to an urban one. Tall buildings housed many people in a small area. As incomes rose and transportation improved, many people and businesses left crowded, noisy cities and moved to suburbs. Some people moved even farther away and created communities beyond the suburbs in rural areas called exurbs (extra urban). They use high-speed highways to get to work. Meanwhile, central cities declined. They lost tax dollars, shopping, and entertainment centers to the suburbs.

Not only did the physical appearance of the land change, but social life and the family unit also changed. On farms, large extended families lived near one another and worked together. Factory work did not need large families working together. Families separated and lived as smaller, more isolated units consisting of an individual or just parents and children. Cities offered more stimulation than farms – more to see and do, and more people to do things with. People made their own choices and gave less thought to opinions of family or authority.

Immigration and migration changed urban areas by making them more culturally and ethnically diverse. Blacks from the South and immigrants moved to northern and western cities. They brought their culture with them. Different types of restaurants and churches appeared on city streets. New businesses imported foods from the old country to supply the newcomers. Different types of music and entertainment were available. However, most neighborhoods remained segregated by race or ethnicity. City dwellers often found it hard to accept people who were very different or spoke a foreign language. Immigrants and migrants resented prejudice and discrimination. Fights and name-calling were common. Tensions sometimes led to riots.

The shift from an industrial economy to a post-industrial economy also changed American society. Technology improved industrial work and made it possible for each worker to produce more. Technology together with changes in transportation and communications made it easy for industry to locate some jobs in other parts of the country or even in other countries. The result is that there are fewer factory jobs. Today, there are more service industries and <u>white-collar workers</u> than factories and <u>blue-collar workers</u>. The fastest growing part of the service sector now is in knowledge and information-based fields like business services, communications, education, healthcare, and research and development. People who work in these jobs need more education and training than many who worked in factories. The largest private employer in Cleveland today is the Cleveland Clinic, and the largest public employer is the Cleveland Municipal Schools.

Migration continues to change American society. Improvements in transportation made it easy for people to move and for industries to ship products worldwide quickly. Our world is becoming smaller and more interdependent. Job opportunities, warm climates, and air conditioning encourage people to move to Sun Belt states. California and Texas are the states with the largest populations. Florida, the home of many retirees, is the fourth largest state. Many universities specialized in a few fields and attracted the best researchers, teachers, and students to move there. Now with the widespread use of telephones, e-mail, and the Internet, ideas move among people freely, quickly, and worldwide, making change even more rapid.

Glossary

Geography C

blue-collar worker – someone from the working class, often a factory worker or a person who does heavy work or works with his/her hands.

communism (communist) – an economic system in which the businesses are owned and operated by the government. The government decides the type, quantity, and price of goods produced. They also decide what workers will make. Communism says it will provide for everyone's needs and get rid of social classes.

culture (cultural, culturally) – the way of life of a group of people, which includes their ideas, beliefs, customs, language, and traditions.

discrimination (discriminate) – unfair treatment by a government or individual citizens, usually because of race, religion, nationality, sex, or certain disabilities; prejudice.

diverse – different; having distinct characteristics.

ethnic (ethnicity, ethnically) – having to do with a group of people who share a common culture, language, nationality, race, or religion. For example, new Chinese immigrants settled in a part of the city called China Town, so they could live with their own ethnic group.

famine – extreme lack of food.

genocide – the planned elimination of an ethnic group.

immigrant (immigration) – a person who enters a country and makes it his home, often becoming a citizen of his new country.

industrial (industry) – the making and distributing of products using machinery; manufacturing.

industrialization – the change from an economy dominated by agriculture (farming) to one dominated by manufacturing with machines in factories in urban areas.

migrate (migration) – to move from one location to another. It is often used to describe people who move within their own country.

Nazism (Nazi) – the beliefs and practices of Adolf Hitler's National Socialist German Workers' Party including racial superiority, government control of society and the economy, and loyalty to one's nation or people above all else.

persecution (persecuted) – constant mistreatment, especially because of race, religion, sex, or political beliefs.

post-industrial (post-industrialization) – (the shift from) an economy where most people work in industry to an economy where most people work in the service sector (the part of the economy that provides services such as healthcare, education, information, entertainment, and tourism).

region (regional) – a geographic area defined by some characteristics or features not found in surrounding areas. Northwest Ohio, the coal-mining region of Ohio, and the Arctic region are examples.

segregation (segregate) – the law or practice of separating and isolating people by characteristics such as race, religion, or nationality.

Shiite – a member of the Shia branch of Islam.

suburb; suburban (suburbanite) – a community or land near a city, with easy access to the city. (a person who lives in the suburbs.)

technology – machines, equipment, and procedures to use them to improve manufacturing and production; practical use of scientific knowledge especially in engineering.

urban – having to do with cities or towns.

white-collar worker – usually someone from the middle class who has a clerical, business, or professional job.

Economics A

MARKETS

Compare how different economic systems answer the fundamental economic questions of what goods and services to produce, how to produce them, and who will consume them.

Economics is the study of how <u>goods</u> and <u>services</u> are produced and distributed. Economics is also about <u>scarcity</u>. There are never enough goods and services to satisfy everybody's wants. That is because the world has limited <u>resources</u>. Yet people's wants are unlimited. For example, the world's supply of oil is limited. But the world's demand for oil keeps growing. After awhile, there will be no oil left.

Scarcity is a basic problem of every nation. No nation is economically independent. All nations have wants they cannot satisfy, because they have limited resources. Nations depend on trade with one another to satisfy their wants. Nations sell the goods and services in which they specialize and buy from nations that specialize in the goods and services they want. This interaction of buyers and sellers exchanging goods or services is a market. Today many markets are worldwide.

We live in an <u>interdependent</u> world. Japan is a good example. It is one of the world's great economic powers. Yet, it produces no oil. Japan specializes in products like cars and electronics. It builds many such products for sale to other countries. Japan uses some of the money from these sales to buy oil from other nations like Saudi Arabia. Saudi Arabia uses money from selling oil to purchase the products it needs from other countries. Trade helps nations like Japan and Saudi Arabia satisfy their needs.

Faced with the problem of scarcity, every society must answer three basic questions:

- What should be produced?

- How should it be produced?
- Who should get what is produced?

Over time, three economic systems have evolved to answer these questions. They are called <u>traditional</u>, market, and command economic systems. Command and market systems rarely, if ever, exist in their pure forms. Many nations have characteristics of more than one economic system. Thus, economists also talk about mixed economic systems.

Rules for production and distribution develop as part of a society's overall social structure. Except for certain command economies, societies do not decide consciously to be of one type or another.

In a *traditional economy*, people keep on producing goods and services just as their ancestors have always done. All the basic economic decisions follow custom, habit, beliefs, religion, and the physical surroundings. If land is fertile, people are farmers. If animals are plentiful for food, they are hunters and gatherers. Sometimes they can be both.

Although there are important exceptions, a traditional economy often means <u>subsistence farming</u>, poverty, and <u>barter</u>. Today, traditional economies are found in <u>rural</u> non-industrial <u>region</u>s of Africa, Asia, and South America.

In traditional agricultural economies, most people are <u>peasant</u> farmers. A farmer may or may not own his own small plot of land. Either way, people usually must also work as <u>tenant</u> farmers for a few wealthy landlords who own large estates. This means the peasants farm the land and pay rent to the landlords, either in money or by giving them part of the crop. Besides growing food, most people make for themselves the other things they need. This includes housing, clothing, and tools. Some items such as metal tools, weapons, horseshoes, and blacksmith services require special skills. A few people specialize in making these products and trade them for food and other needs.

Sometimes people in traditional economies are well off and do not wish to change. But sometimes conditions are such that they have no other choice. This was true in much of western

Europe during the Early Middle Ages. People lived in small villages. Farming was crude, and there weren't enough people to grow all the food that was needed. Things changed sometime around the twelfth century. With improved farming methods and a growing population, people could grow much more than they needed to survive. Once there was enough food, some people decided to specialize in making other things. Some became bakers, weavers, builders, and finally even artists. People could make the products they made best and sell or trade with others for things they wanted or needed. Soon people began trading not only with others in their own village, but also with people in other villages. This was the beginning of a market economy.

A *market economy* is one in which individuals make their own economic decisions about what products to make or services to offer. People usually decide to make a particular product if they believe they can sell that product for more than it cost to make and for more than they could earn by making and selling some other product or service. The difference between the cost to make a product and the selling price is called profit. In a market economy, government interference, if any, is extremely limited. Producers decide what to make, how much of it to make, and what the price should be. Producers own the means of production as private property, and they get to keep the profits. They also take risks.

Producers can't sell what consumers don't want to buy. Thus, in a market economy, consumers really decide what is produced. Often several individuals or companies will want to make the same product. Consider automobiles. If more people want to buy one make than another, then the first company will be able to build more cars and earn more profit. If the difference is great enough, then the second company will eventually go out of business. However, the second company might create a more popular design and win back some customers. Or it might learn how to build cars at a lower cost and therefore sell them at a lower price. In that case, many people might decide to buy the second car even if they like the first car better. Then they could buy something else with the money saved. In a market economy, the basic economic questions are answered almost automatically by this "give and take" between producers and consumers and between different producers. Generally, consumers decide what is produced, and producers decide how. The question of for whom is decided through the setting of wages and salaries. Some people have skills that are more in demand than others. Some will invent new products that become very popular. These people will receive more money for their efforts and be able to buy more products.

Trade is essential in a market economy. It would not make sense for people who repair televisions to grow all their own food and make their own clothing too. People specialize in what they can do most profitably and trade for things they do not make, just as nations do. When people specialize, they improve. They make things faster and with fewer raw materials. This raises their productive capacity, which just means they can make more product with the same inputs. For example, specialization in manufacturing carried to extremes led to the assembly line.

Henry Ford made many improvements to the manufacturing assembly line and, in 1913, became the first to use it on a large scale. By 1914 he had reduced the time to build a Model T chassis from 12 1/2 hours to 93 minutes. A larger productive capacity means more product can be made at lower cost. More product leads to more trade over a wider geographic area. Goods become available that cannot be made locally. Lower cost and wider selection raise everybody's standard of living.

Ford 1913 assembly line for magnetos (electrical generators). Henry Ford drastically reduced the time to build a Model T. He did this by using interchangeable parts, a moving assembly line that brought work to the workers, specialization in which each worker performed only one operation over and over, and careful attention to reducing wasted effort.

There is a cost for trade, especially trade with partners far away. Building and maintaining roads uses economic resources (labor and materials) that could be used for other things. Moving goods to remote locations also requires resources. Transportation takes time, vehicles, fuel for vehicles or feed for animals, packaging, and protection for goods and crew during travel. There may be costs for advertising to attract customers. And there is always the possibility that goods will be damaged or will not be in demand.

Free choice and private property are also essential for a market economy. The system would not work if consumers were not free to choose what to buy and producers were not free to decide what to make and how to make it. There would be no reason to work hard if producers did not own the means of production and have the right to keep the profits. The chance to earn more by working harder or smarter leads people to invent new products and to find better ways of making old products.

Besides traditional and market economies, the third basic economic system is the command economy. For most of the twentieth century there were two competing economic systems in the developed world. The United States, Western Europe, and Japan had a market economy. The Soviet Union, Eastern Europe, and China had a command economy.

A *command economy* is one in which the government or ruler decides what should be produced, who should make it, and who should receive what is made. After the Russian Revolution in 1917, the Soviet Union changed a traditional economy into an industrial one through government action. The government took control of all factories and other production resources. They made a series of five-year plans describing what should be produced and in which factories. The government also set wages and salaries. This partly determined who could afford to buy what. Workers were told what to do and how to do it. There was little or no opportunity to "get ahead" by working hard or suggesting new ways to do things. Thus, there was no incentive for workers to improve productivity.

It is hard to predict how much of each product to produce in a large and complex society. It is also hard to respond quickly to unexpected problems. Sometimes there were shortages of consumer goods and hardship for the people. Other times there were overproduction and wasted resources. The more complex the society, the harder it is to plan effectively.

Most countries with a command economy became, or adopted features of, a market economy. In 1989 the countries of Eastern Europe broke away from the Soviet Union and began to build democratic institutions and market economies. In 1991, because of the failing economy and other serious problems, the Soviet Union collapsed into fifteen separate countries. The command economy came to an end. Since 1979 China, too, has been phasing-out of its command economy in favor of one that is market-based. Today Cuba and North Korea are two countries that still have command economies.

Most economists believe that certain goods and services can only be provided by government. These include national defense, a system of justice, police and fire protection, water and sewer systems, and roads. A *mixed economy* is one in which both business and government produce goods and services. In the United States, the federal and state governments regulate trade and provide social services such as disaster relief and Social Security. They also enforce laws that restrict business but are supposed to be for the public good. Examples include the Clean Air Act and rules about working conditions.

The Economic Impact of Special Interest Organizations

Before governments made laws about work rules, working conditions were harsh for many people. Wages were low. Adults and children were required to work 10-12 hours per day, six or seven days a week. There was little concern about workers' safety. Individual workers had little power to correct these conditions. If many people wanted jobs, business owners could just fire those who objected to the abuses and hire someone else. So workers joined together in unions to bargain as a group for fairer wages and better working conditions. The idea is that an employer can replace one or two unsatisfied workers, but it is much harder and more expensive to replace everybody. Unions bargain for groups of employees, and they also work to get favorable laws passed by government.

For years employers and government fought against unions. Employers used weapons such as armed guards, blacklists, court injunctions, lockouts, strikebreakers, and yellow-dog contracts to break strikes and punish union members. Some strikes were ended by troops sent by the state or federal government. Laws and court decisions usually supported employers and restricted unions.

In the United States, attitudes started to change during the Great Depression. The National Labor Relations Act of 1935, or Wagner Act, gave unions the right to organize and bargain collectively. It also established the National Labor Relations Board, which had the power to punish unfair labor practices. This law was challenged in the courts. In 1937 the U.S. Supreme Court in the *National Labor Relations Board v. Jones and Laughlin Steel Corporation* ruled that the law was constitutional.

Today, unions are accepted. They have won many benefits including the 8-hour workday and 40-hour workweek, restrictions on child labor, minimum wage laws, paid vacations and holidays, and rules about safety in the workplace.

Farm workers have also organized to get the same protections that labor unions have won for factory workers. In the 1960s and 1970s, Cesar Chavez organized California grape and lettuce pickers into a union that later became the United Farm Workers of America. But most farms in America are not like large factories where a few owners hire many workers. Mostly the owners themselves organized in order to get fair prices for their crops and to work for favorable laws.

In 1929 a group now known as the National Council of Farmer Cooperatives (NCFC) was formed. It works to pass laws farmers want. Farmers have also formed some very successful cooperatives (co-ops) to process and market their own products. They do this to get the best prices and eliminate costly "middlemen." Well-known co-ops include Sunkist citrus products, Land O'Lakes dairy products, Sun-Maid raisins, and Welch's grape products.

Business, too, has an organization, called the Chamber of Commerce, which works to influence laws and provide other assistance to member businesses. Chambers of Commerce are found in cities, towns, and countries. There is also an International Chamber of Commerce.

Glossary
Economics A

barter – a system of trade in which goods and services are traded directly for other goods and services without the use of money.

blacklist (to blacklist) – a list of people or groups that are under suspicion or being punished. They are usually denied jobs or privileges.

Clean Air Act – any of a series of U.S. laws designed to limit the amount of harmful substances in the air in order to protect public health and welfare. These laws set national standards for air quality and deadlines for meeting those standards by reducing harmful discharges from sources such as factories, power plants, and motor vehicles.

co-operative (co-op) – a business owned and managed by those who use its services.

developed countries (developed world) – highly industrialized countries; countries in which most people have a high standard of living.

goods – products offered for sale or trade.

Great Depression – global depression of the 1930s when businesses, banks, and the stock market failed, and many people lost their jobs. It was the longest and most severe depression ever experienced by the industrialized Western world.

industrial (industry) – the making and distributing of products using machinery; manufacturing.

injunction – a court order forbidding some activity.

interdependence (interdependent) – depending on or requiring assistance from one another.

lockout – the closing of all or part of a business until employees accept employer demands.

peasant – an agricultural laborer or small farmer, often uneducated.

profit – the amount of money left after all the costs of running a business have been subtracted from all the money earned.

region (regional) – a geographic area defined by some characteristics or features not found in surrounding areas. Northwest Ohio, the coal-mining region of Ohio, and the Arctic region are examples.

regulate (regulation) – to make and enforce rules or laws that control conduct or practices.

resources – In economics, resources are the items required to produce a product. They are raw materials (such as wood or metal), labor, and capital (machinery, buildings, etc.). Information is also sometimes included in this list.

rural – relating to or characteristic of the country, country people, or country life. An example of rural people is farmers.

scarcity – insufficient supply of goods or services to satisfy demand.

services – work performed for another, usually for pay or in trade for other goods or services.

Social Security – the U.S. Federal Old-Age, Survivors, and Disability Insurance program. Social Security provides monthly cash payments to retired and disabled workers and to survivors of insured workers. The Social Security programs also provide healthcare benefits for eligible individuals through Medicare and Medicaid.

standard of living – level of well-being of individuals or groups, based on characteristics such as education, income, healthcare, life expectancy, and available goods and services.

strikebreaker – a person who accepts employment to work in place of a striking worker.

subsistence farming – a form of farming that produces all or nearly all the goods required by the farm family, but little more to store or trade.

tenant – a person who rents land or housing.

tradition (traditional, traditionalist) – inherited, established, or usual pattern of thought, action, or behavior.

yellow-dog contract – an employment contract in which the employee agrees, as a condition of employment, not to join a union. Yellow-dog contracts have been illegal in the United States since 1935.

Economics B

GOVERNMENT AND THE ECONOMY

Explain how the United States government provides public services, redistributes income, regulates economic activity, and promotes economic growth and stability.

The United States government is involved in the economy of our nation in many ways. The U.S. government provides public services such as national parks, interstate highways, and federal food inspection. It <u>redistributes</u> wealth by taxing income, providing welfare to those in need, and setting a minimum wage. It also <u>regulates</u> economic activity and promotes economic growth and <u>stability</u> by setting standards for banking and regulating businesses and trade. Continue reading to learn how the government is directly involved in our economic life.

Protectionism

<u>Protectionism</u> is a policy in which a country tries to protect certain <u>domestic</u> products from foreign competition by means of <u>tariffs</u>, <u>quotas</u>, or other measures.

Tariffs are special taxes charged against particular products when they come into a country for sale. To make a <u>profit</u>, the <u>importer</u>s must add the tax to the price of their goods. This makes the imported goods more expensive compared with the same goods produced locally. Tariffs do not work well if consumers are willing to pay higher prices in order to get the foreign products.

Tariffs may protect a particular domestic industry, but they do so at the expense of other parts of the domestic economy. Suppose, for example, the United States places a large tariff on imported steel that otherwise could be sold for less than the cost of domestic steel. This will raise the cost to produce all products that use steel. These products include large buildings, cars, tools, and many others. Higher costs will mean higher prices. Some people will be unable to buy these other products (especially construction) at higher prices. Fewer sales will reduce profits and may even cause producers to employ fewer workers. These negative effects of a tariff can be very serious.

Quotas are like tariffs except that they limit the amount of product that can be imported. Quotas are more effective than tariffs because people cannot buy as much as they want even if they are willing to pay more. Quotas are sometimes used by one country to punish another for policies it does not like. By limiting imports, a major country that is a major market can reduce the trade of another country enough to cause economic hardship.

Blockades are total bans on trading some or all goods with another country. Blockades are usually used only when one country wishes to punish another. In 1962 U.S. president John F. Kennedy was informed that Soviet nuclear missiles capable of striking U.S. cities were installed on Cuba. He ordered a naval blockade against Cuba and demanded the Soviet Union remove all missiles. The Cuban Missile Crisis was resolved and the blockade ended. However, the U.S. kept its embargo on Cuba. Since 1960 the United States has banned almost all trade with Cuba. This has caused hardship and many shortages in Cuba, including food, medicine, and automobiles. U.S. citizens have been unable to travel to Cuba or buy popular Cuban products like sugar and cigars. Although the United States still does not trade with Cuba, Canada and many European nations do. A U.S. law passed in 2000 permits the sale of some food and medicine to Cuba.

Many countries, including the United States, have used protectionism for various reasons in the past and still do. While these practices may benefit particular industries for a while, most economists agree they do more harm than good.

The Federal Reserve System

Congress established the Federal Reserve System (often called "The Fed") in 1913 to "smooth out" the economy in times of overly high or low activity. Here's why.

Banks receive funds from depositors for safekeeping. To attract customers, banks pay the depositors a percentage of the deposit, called interest, from time to time. Thus, the value of the account grows, and the depositor "earns" money. It is unlikely that all or even many depositors will want their money all at the same time. (Unfortunately, this *does* happen, as we shall see.) So banks keep enough money on hand or in larger banks to cover their expected needs for cash. This money is called reserves. The rest they lend to people or businesses that want to buy expensive things like houses, cars, or machinery. Banks earn their profits by charging more interest for the money they lend than they pay depositors for the money they have "borrowed."

Before the National Bank Act of 1864, there was little regulation of banks in the United States and almost no federal control. Most banks operated under state charters. Some were even run by private individuals. Each bank issued its own currency. At one time there were more than 10,000 different forms of paper money, and they were easy to counterfeit. Some banks were well run and maintained adequate reserves, and others did not. Many banks failed. That is, they did not keep enough reserves to pay their depositors when many people tried to get their money at about the same time. Such times are called banking panics. The depositors lost their money, and the banks went out of business.

In 1864, Congress passed the National Bank Act. This and other laws provided for a system of regulated and supervised "national banks." National banks were required to keep substantial reserves and could only issue currency in proportion to those reserves. These laws also taxed state bank currencies, which soon disappeared.

The National Bank Act corrected many problems with the banking system, but it was not enough. Major banking panics still occurred in 1873, 1884, 1893, and 1907. In each case, even the national banks did not have enough reserves quickly available. There were more bank failures. The banking system needed a more flexible way to handle reserves.

In 1913 Congress set up the Federal Reserve System with broad powers to manage the banking system. The Fed does this by controlling the money supply, interest rates, and the reserve requirements of its member banks. The Fed has the sole authority to print U.S. currency and place it in circulation or take it out. It makes loans on short notice to member banks to increase their reserves so they can meet temporary needs for cash. Through its open market operations, the Fed can also increase or decrease the reserves that banks have available and thus the amount of money they can lend. This, in turn, controls total demand for goods and services and inflation. (Inflation is a general increase in prices when the money supply increases and the supply of goods and services does not.) With these powers, the Fed can actually stabilize the entire economy in times of financial crisis. The Federal Reserve System is the most important financial power in the United States. In recent years its policy has been to maintain full employment and low inflation.

The Great Depression, World War II, and the United States Economy

The Great Depression brought the economy to a standstill. It began with the stock market crash of 1929. Many banks and businesses failed and many people were out of work.

Before 1929 the United States government did little to control business or the economy. Even the Federal Reserve was uncertain how to use its powers and was reluctant to do so. For months after the great crash, many economists and President Herbert Hoover believed the economic slump was a natural and necessary correction. It would take care of itself.

President Franklin D. Roosevelt took office in 1933. He asked Congress for many new laws to provide relief, recovery, and reform in the economy. He called this program the "New Deal." People disagree about how much these programs helped to end the depression. However, they did relieve much of the economic hardship. They also gave people hope. Several agencies were set up specifically to

Privately funded breadlines and soup kitchens fed thousands who were out of work and had no income even to buy food. The need for them declined after 1932 as government income support and food assistance programs were set up. Notice the line goes right past a restaurant advertising hot lunch and extra beer which these men cannot afford to buy.

give people jobs on government projects. These agencies included the Public Works Administration (PWA), the Civilian Conservation Corps (CCC), and the Works Progress Administration (WPA).

Several other New Deal programs are still important today. The Federal Deposit Insurance Corporation (FDIC) insures deposit accounts at banks. The Securities and Exchange Commission (SEC) regulates the stock market. It requires companies selling stock to provide investors with complete and accurate financial information. Social Security provides old-age pensions and medical care for workers. The National Labor Relations Act guarantees workers the right to organize and join unions.

The economy did not recover completely until World War II. During the war, manufacturing increased and all available workers had jobs. This was necessary to produce materials and equipment for the war. To pay for the New Deal and World War II, the government spent more money than it raised in taxes. It borrowed the rest, mainly by selling government bonds. This is known as deficit spending.

After the war, the government retained a much larger role in the economy than ever before. Government taxing and spending as a percentage of the gross domestic product grew from about 3% in 1929 to 32% in 1945. As the graph shows, it has remained between 15% and 23% ever since.

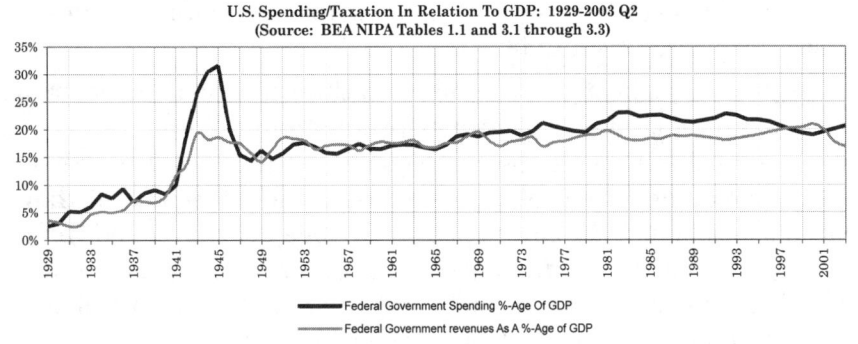

U.S. Spending/Taxation In Relation To GDP: 1929-2003 Q2
(Source: BEA NIPA Tables 1.1 and 3.1 through 3.3)

— Federal Government Spending %-Age Of GDP
— Federal Government revenues As A %-Age of GDP

Source: Bureau of Economic Accounts, United States Department of Commerce

Leaving the economy alone did not help correct the depression. Government spending during the depression and the war did improve the economy. Government continues to spend so the economy will grow and people will prosper. Since the war the government has tried to level out economic shifts by increased spending in slow times and decreased spending in good times.

There is another reason for the expanded role of the federal government after World War II. The United States found itself in a struggle with the Soviet Union known as the Cold War. The space programs of both countries reveal the political and (expensive) economic competition between the two countries. There was also a real fear that the Cold War might turn into a hot war with nuclear weapons. Because of this, the United States now maintains a powerful military force during peacetime for the first time in its history.

Taxes, antitrust legislation, and environmental regulations

All governments and all levels of government—federal, state, and local—use taxes to raise revenue. Taxes take money away from businesses and individuals. Some is used to pay for essential public services like police, firefighters, roads, and defense. Some is used to implement government policies. Spending to prevent economic recession helps everybody. So does spending to enforce environmental regulations. Other programs like unemployment benefits and price supports for farmers help certain groups at the expense of others. In these cases, taxes redistribute income.

Antitrust legislation prohibits two things. One is "conspiring in restraint of trade." Sometimes people from different businesses that provide the same goods or services get together and agree among themselves what prices should be so that they can make as much money as possible. Today this is called "price fixing," and antitrust laws make it illegal. Antitrust laws also prohibit monopolies, where one company tries to get control of all production of some product. A monopoly also allows one company to set prices so it can make as much money as possible. Laws prohibit this because the company may charge unfairly high prices. They also prohibit monopolies because monopolies concentrate too much wealth in the hands of too few people.

Those people can then do things to help themselves but which are harmful to the whole society.

Environmental regulations make the environment healthier and safer for everyone. Many businesses complain that these regulations increase the cost of doing business. They complain that it is expensive to install equipment to clean wastewater or remove pollution from air. Studies have shown that this may not actually be true in the long run. Some companies have also found that being environmentally aware is good for business.

Glossary

Economics B

antitrust legislation – laws opposing or intending to regulate business monopolies, including trusts, to prevent their use of unfair business practices to reduce competition and control prices throughout an industry. (A trust is a group of companies that cooperate with each other to reduce competition and control prices.)

ban – to stop, forbid, prohibit; a legal order prohibiting something.

blockade – the closing off of an area to keep people or supplies from going in or out.

charter – a document giving permission to create an institution such as a city or bank.

Cold War – the global struggle for power and influence between the United States and the Soviet Union following World War II. There was no direct fighting or military combat.

currency – money in circulation (being used), especially paper money.

deficit spending – government spending more money than it receives; spending that puts the government in debt and forces it to borrow money.

deposit – money left with a bank for safekeeping and to earn interest.

depression – a time when businesses do badly and many people lose their jobs. The stock market crash of October 1929 was the beginning of the Great Depression. The effects of the Great Depression were partly responsible for World War II. See economic slump, recession.

domestic – of or relating to one's own country.

economic slump – a short-term decline in business activity (employment, industrial production, wholesale and/or retail sales). See recession, depression.

embargo – a government ban on certain trade or on all trade with a foreign nation. For example, some Arab nations placed an oil embargo on the United States and other countries in 1973.

Great Depression – global depression of the 1930s when businesses, banks, and the stock market failed, and many people lost their jobs. It was the longest and most severe depression ever experienced by the industrialized Western world.

gross domestic product (GDP) – the total value of goods and services produced in a nation during a specific period of time, usually one year, excluding income earned from investments abroad.

implement – to carry out; to start.

imports (imported, importer) – products brought in from a foreign country.

inflation – a general increase in prices when the money supply increases and the supply of goods and services does not; a decrease in the purchasing power of money.

interest – a payment for the use of money. Banks pay interest to their depositors and charge a higher rate of interest to customers who borrow money.

money supply – the total amount of money available in an economy at a given time. As defined by the Federal Reserve, the money supply essentially consists of cash in circulation plus all types of checking and savings accounts in banks.

monopoly (monopolies) – exclusive control of a product or service by a single company.

panic – a sudden intense fear. A financial panic is a widespread fear about financial conditions that often causes a rush to sell property.

pension – a fixed amount of money paid regularly to a person.

profit – the amount of money left after all the costs of running a business have been subtracted from all the money earned.

prohibit – prevent or forbid.

protectionism – the policy of using quotas or tariffs (taxes) on foreign products to protect domestic companies.

quota – a number or percentage that is set as a maximum or minimum amount. For example, immigration laws often set limits on the number of immigrants from different countries allowed into the United States.

recession – an extended decline in general business activity including employment, industrial production, wholesale and/or retail prices.

redistribute – distribute some resource again, in a different way; reallocate.

regulate (regulation) – to make and enforce rules or laws that control conduct or practices.

reserve – something set aside or saved for future use. Bank reserves are funds that banks set aside to meet the demands of their depositors.

restraint – a limitation. In business, a restraint is an action that tends to limit free competition, such as the formation of a monopoly.

revenue – the income received by a government through taxes, duties, customs, and other sources.

stabile or stable (stability, stabilize) – not changing and not likely to change.

stock (stock market) – share of ownership in a corporation. (the business of buying and selling stocks.)

stock market crash – a drastic and rapid decrease in the value of corporate stocks over a wide cross-section of the market. Crashes tend to be driven by panic as much as by real, underlying economic conditions. The most famous and severe stock market crash began on Thursday, October 24, 1929. Its negative effects continued through much of the 1930s.

tariff – a tax on products that come from another country.

Government A

CONSTITUTIONAL AMENDMENTS AND SUPREME COURT DECISIONS

Analyze the evolution of the Constitution through post-Reconstruction amendments and Supreme Court decisions.

AMENDMENTS

The U.S. Constitution is a living document because it can change. The U.S. Constitution can be changed by <u>amendment</u> or by the interpretation of the Supreme Court. Right now, there are 27 amendments. Several are listed below. Notice that four amendments expanded the right to vote (suffrage).

- 13th Amendment (1865) – <u>abolish</u>ed slavery in the United States and in all areas governed by the United States.
- 14th Amendment (1868) – declares any person born or <u>naturalize</u>d in the United States is a citizen, and all citizens are guaranteed equal protection under the law.
- 15th Amendment (1870) – provides that a citizen cannot be denied the right to vote because of race, color, or having been a slave.
- 16th Amendment (1913) – gives Congress the power to tax incomes.
- 17th Amendment (1913) – provides for the direct election of Senators by the people of each state.
- 19th Amendment (1920) – gives women the right to vote.
- 22nd Amendment (1951) – states that no president may be elected for more than two terms.
- 24th Amendment (1964) – states that citizens cannot be required to pay a <u>poll tax</u> to vote in federal elections.
- 26th Amendment (1971) – lowers the voting age from 21 to 18.

The 19th and 26th Amendments

These two constitutional amendments made the United States more democratic by enlarging the voting population. Both were passed after a long, difficult struggle. The 19th Amendment guaranteed women the right to vote. Today, women vote in national elections at a slightly higher percentage than men. The 26th Amendment guaranteed the right to vote to those between the ages of 18 and 20. However, the 26th Amendment did not guarantee that young people would actually register and exercise their right to vote. Today, those 18 to 24 have the lowest registration and voting percentages.

19th Amendment

In 1848 Lucretia Mott and Elizabeth Cady Stanton organized the first women's rights convention in the United States. The convention called for basic rights for women, including the right to own property, earn wages, divorce, and vote. Until the Civil War (1861 – 1865), conventions were held almost every year. But, the Civil War required sacrifice. Supporting the war effort would come first. The issue of women's rights would have to wait.

After the Civil War, women's rights supporters hoped their hard work and support would be rewarded. They were disappointed. The 14th Amendment put the word "male" in the Constitution. It was used in reference to voting rights. The 15th Amendment provided that a citizen cannot be denied the right to vote because of race, color, or having been a slave. It did not include sex. African American male citizens could vote, but not women.

In 1869, two women's rights organizations were formed. The National Woman Suffrage Association called for a national amendment to give women the right to vote. They also called for other reforms. The American Woman Suffrage Association focused on the right to vote. They called on individual states to give women the right to vote. That same year Wyoming became the first state to give women the right to vote in its state constitution. Other newly formed western states did the same.

In 1890 the two women's suffrage associations joined together to form the National American Woman Suffrage Association. Male and female supporters called themselves suffragists. They organized conventions, distributed literature, held parades, and made speeches to support their cause.

Support for women's suffrage grew. In 1916 Jeannette Rankin, a Republican from Montana, was the first woman elected to Congress. Also in 1916 Alice Paul helped organize the National Women's Party, which used <u>militant</u> tactics similar to those being used by suffragists in Great Britain to demand voting rights for women. In 1917 Alice Paul and ninety-six other suffragists were arrested and jailed. They went on a hunger strike and were <u>force-fed</u>. That same year the United States entered World War I. As more men entered the armed forces, more women began working and contributing to the war effort. By 1918 most members of the U.S. Congress and President Wilson supported women's suffrage.

A woman suffrage amendment was finally passed by the House and Senate in 1919. In 1920, the 19th Amendment was <u>ratified</u> by three-fourths of the states, and women voted for the first time in a national election. The National American Woman Suffrage Association became the League of Women Voters, which still seeks to educate the public about candidates and election issues. The National Woman's Party started work on an Equal Rights Amendment (ERA). The ERA has not yet been ratified.

26th Amendment

An amendment to grant voting rights to anyone eighteen years of age or older was first introduced into Congress in 1941 by West Virginia Congressman Jennings Randolph. Randolph argued that people who were old enough to fight and die for their country should also have the right to vote. During the 1950s and 1960s, Presidents Dwight Eisenhower and Lyndon B. Johnson supported the amendment, but the U.S. Congress was reluctant to lower the voting age. Several states did lower voting ages, and many citizens thought all states should do the same.

During the Vietnam War, many soldiers under the age of 21 died. People pressured Congress to lower the voting age. In 1971, Congressman Randolph re-introduced this amendment, lowering the voting age to 18. It was quickly passed by both houses of Congress and, later that year, by three-fourths of the states.

SUPREME COURT DECISIONS

In addition to the formal amendment process, the U.S. Constitution can be changed informally by federal court decisions. The <u>judicial branch</u> of government has the power to interpret the law, and the U.S. Supreme Court can abolish a law by declaring it <u>unconstitutional</u>. The three Supreme Court cases below show that constitutional law concerning <u>racial discrimination</u> has changed over time.

Plessy v. Ferguson (1896)

Louisiana passed a law ordering "separate but equal" <u>accommodation</u>s for blacks and whites on trains. Homer Plessy, a light-skinned black man who was seven-eights white and one-eighth black, was arrested for refusing to move from a "white" railway car. Plessy's lawyer argued that the law <u>violate</u>d the <u>equal protection clause</u> of the 14th Amendment. The U.S. Supreme Court ruled that public <u>facilities</u> that were "separate but equal" were constitutional. This decision encouraged the continued growth and development of <u>segregation</u>. <u>Jim Crow</u> laws spread throughout the South.

Brown v. Board of Education (1954)

In Topeka, Kansas, seven-year old Linda Brown lived five blocks from a "white" school, yet was forced to attend a "black" school about one mile away. NAACP attorney Thurgood Marshall and his legal team challenged that segregation law and the "separate but equal" ruling of *Plessy v. Ferguson* in the U.S. Supreme Court. He argued that segregation makes minority students feel inferior and interferes with their ability to learn. "Separate but equal" can never be equal and violates the equal protection clause of the 14th Amendment. The U.S. Supreme Court agreed and ruled that "separate educational facilities are inherently unequal." The ruling in the *Brown* case inspired Congress in its later passage of the Civil Rights Act of 1964, which made racial discrimination in public accommodations illegal.

Southern states and communities resisted the *Brown v. Board of Education* decision. Three years after the *Brown* decision, federal troops were necessary to escort the school's first black students into Little Rock Central High School. Each of the nine students had her or his own personal bodyguard throughout the first school year.

The Regents of the University of California v. Bakke (1978)

Alan Bakke, a white man, was denied admission to medical school at the University of California. Students with lower test scores were admitted under a special admissions program for minorities. The question in this court case was "Is it constitutional to set aside a certain number of seats in a medical school for minorities?" Bakke sued, claiming the medical school discriminated against him based on his race. The U.S. Supreme Court ruled quotas to create racial balance are illegal. The Court also ruled that race can be used as one of several factors in admissions decisions. Affirmative action programs are constitutional, but quota systems are not.

Glossary

Government A

abolish – to put an end to something.

accommodation – a service which satisfies a need, such as a room, food, or a seat on a train or bus.

affirmative action – a policy which gives opportunities to women and minorities because of past discrimination.

amendment – a formal change to a law or constitution.

discrimination (discriminate) – unfair treatment by a government or individual citizens, usually because of race, religion, nationality, sex, or certain disabilities; prejudice.

equal protection clause – all citizens have equal protection of the laws that can not be denied by federal or state governments; found in the 14th Amendment to the United States Constitution.

facilities – something built which provides a service such as a hospital or restroom.

force-fed – forced to eat, sometimes by having food poured down a tube in the throat.

inherently – naturally built into; naturally forming an important part of something.

Jim Crow – the term used for laws and practices that segregated (separated) blacks and whites in the United States.

judicial branch – the branch of the federal, state, or local government that interprets the law and decides the guilt or innocence of the accused. The Supreme Court is the highest federal court, made up of nine Justices. In the State of Ohio, the Ohio Supreme Court is the lead court. Cities, suburbs, and counties have local courts.

militant – aggressive; combative; willing to fight for a cause.

minority (minorities) – smaller group(s) of people, as opposed to a large group, the majority. Women, Hispanics, and African Americans are often thought of as minorities.

naturalize – to complete the process of a foreigner becoming a citizen.

poll tax – a tax which must be paid in order to vote. Since the poll tax cost more than most poor whites and African Americans could pay, it kept many from voting.

quota – a number or percentage that is set as a maximum or minimum amount. For example, immigration laws often set limits on the number of immigrants from different countries allowed into the United States.

racial discrimination – unfair treatment in education, employment, voting, or social events of one racial group by a different racial group.

ratify (ratified) – to confirm or approve, usually by a vote.

segregation (segregate) – the law or practice of separating and isolating people by characteristics such as race, religion, or nationality.

unconstitutional – not allowed by the Constitution; against the law.

violate (violation) – to break or disregard the law. (the act of violating.)

Government B

SYSTEMS OF GOVERNMENT

Analyze the differences among various forms of government to determine how power is acquired and used.

There is a variety of systems of government today. Most governments in the world claim they are a form of democracy. Other systems of government include dictatorship, monarchy, and theocracy.

Democracy is a form of government in which citizens are the source of power. Government is created and maintained with the consent of the people. There are two basic forms of democracy: direct democracy and representative democracy. In a direct democracy, people meet together in one place to make the laws. There are no direct democracies in the world today. In a representative democracy, or republic, people elect representatives to make and enforce the laws. There are two forms of representative democracies in the world today: parliamentary democracy and presidential democracy.

- **Parliamentary democracy** is a democratic government in which the chief executive, usually a prime minister, is chosen from the legislature (parliament) after each election. Members of parliament serve a specific number of years before another election. However, if a prime minister receives a vote of "no confidence" from the parliament at any time, a general election is held, and a new government is formed. (Canada and Israel)

- **Presidential democracy** is a democratic government in which the legislative branch and executive branch are separate and equal. Citizens vote separately for legislators and a president. Each serves a specific number of years before a national election is held. A president is the official head of state and chief executive. (United States and Mexico)

Monarchy is a form of government in which the ruler (monarch) is a king, queen, emperor, or empress. A monarch usually inherits the title and holds power for life. There are two basic forms of

monarchy: absolute monarchy and constitutional monarchy.
- **Absolute monarchy** is a form of monarchy in which the power of the ruler is not limited by law or a legislature. An absolute monarch claims to rule by <u>divine right</u>. The monarch claims the power to make, enforce, and interpret the law at will. (Saudi Arabia and Oman)
- **Constitutional monarchy** is a form of monarchy in which the power of the ruler is limited by law and a legislature. Often the monarch is the symbolic head of state. The prime minister is the official head of state and chief executive who runs the government. (Japan and United Kingdom)

Dictatorship is a form of government in which the power of the ruler or rulers is not limited by citizens or a legislature. A dictator has absolute power that is enforced by an army and secret police. Some dictators take power by a <u>coup d'état</u>, or <u>coup</u>, but they can also be elected, appointed by a ruling party, or inherit the position. (Cuba and North Korea)

Theocracy is a form of government in which political leaders rule according to religious laws. There is no separation of church and state. Political leaders are often religious leaders who claim to rule on behalf of their God. (Iran)

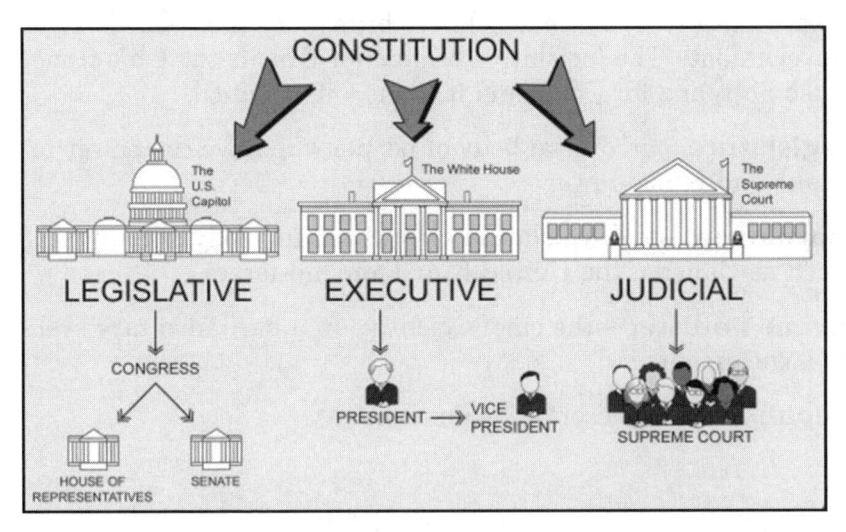

The U.S. government is a presidential democracy. Citizens vote separately for legislators in two branches of Congress, the Senate and the House of Representatives, and for the president and vice president together as a pair. Our Constitution provides for a third, separate and equal branch: the judicial branch (the courts). Generally speaking, the legislative branch makes laws, the executive branch enforces laws, and the judicial branch interprets laws.

Glossary

Government B

coup (coup d'état) – a sudden, often violent, overthrow of a government by a small group.

direct democracy – a form of government in which citizens vote directly on all laws and public issues.

divine right – belief that a monarch (king, queen, or emperor) received the right to govern from God and not from the people.

emperor – the ruler of an empire.

executive branch – the branch of government that is responsible for enforcing the laws. The president heads the executive branch of the federal government. The governor heads the executive branch of Ohio's state government. The mayor heads the executive branch of Cleveland's city government.

legislative branch – the branch of government that makes laws. The Congress (the Senate and the House of Representatives) is the legislative branch for the federal government. The legislative branch for Ohio is the Ohio General Assembly, and for Cleveland it is the City Council.

legislature – an official body of people who have the power to make and repeal laws.

parliament – the legislature or law-making body of countries such as Canada, the United Kingdom, and Israel.

prime minister – the chief executive in a parliamentary system of government.

republic – a representative democracy.

Citizenship Rights and Responsibilities A

CITIZEN ACTION AND PARTICIPATION

Analyze ways people achieve governmental change, including political action, social protest, and revolution.

THE INFLUENCE OF CITIZEN ACTION ON PUBLIC POLICY

Throughout history people used many ways to change government policies and laws. They influenced the government through political action, such as organizing <u>petition</u> drives, supporting political parties, and voting. People turned to social protest, including <u>boycotts</u>, marches, <u>sit-ins</u>, and <u>civil disobedience</u>. Sometimes they turned to revolution. The method that people chose depended on the system of government in place and the seriousness of the problems. As you read about the six important historical events below, notice how the actions of ordinary people influenced the government and public policy.

Non-violent marches and demonstrations, especially in Washington DC, are one way for citizens to influence public policy. When large crowds attended, these events have received a lot of media attention, making the whole country aware of the issues. This photo shows leaders of the civil rights march on Washington in 1963.

The French Revolution

During the eighteenth century, France was ruled by <u>absolute monarch</u>s. About 97% of the population was common people. Most were <u>peasant</u> farmers who paid almost half of their income in dues to <u>nobles</u>, <u>tithe</u>s to the church, and taxes to the government. They had few rights and no voice in the government.

During the 1780s anxiety and tension grew worse in France. Several years of poor crops created a food shortage. The price of bread doubled in 1789 and many feared starvation. In addition, the government was broke. King Louis XVI (16th) could not raise enough money to pay the government's debts and cover expenses. People needed help and wanted changes in the government. When changes did not come, common people began to revolt.

The French Revolution began with the storming of the Bastille. Rumors in Paris warned of an attack by royal troops. Fearful citizens gathered weapons. On July 14, 1789, several hundred people marched to the Bastille, a fortress used as a prison, in search of gunpowder. Soldiers fired into the crowd, killing 98 and wounding 73. The crowd located five canons, and the governor of the Bastille surrendered. The governor and several guards were killed.

Storming of the Bastille

The revolution spread. In the countryside peasants attacked food shipments and refused to pay taxes, tithes, and dues. Rumors spread that nobles were planning to steal their crops. The result was the Great Fear. Angry and fearful peasants raided nobles' homes and burned records of dues owed. In Paris over 6,000 hungry women walked to the Palace of Versailles to demand bread from the king and the national assembly. About 20,000 sympathetic soldiers followed. The crowd invaded the palace and killed several royal bodyguards. They demanded the king return to live in Paris. The next day the king and his family left the palace. Louis XVI was no longer an absolute monarch.

In 1792 the French Revolution entered a <u>radical</u> stage. The small shopkeepers, craftsmen, and city workers played an important role in the Revolution, but had gained little. They wanted a stronger central government that would pass laws to reduce the gap between the rich and the poor. In 1793 they used force to let the Jacobins, members of a political club, seize control of the government. The Jacobins fixed the price of important goods like bread and raised wages. They also imprisoned and executed all those considered enemies and <u>traitors</u> of the new French Republic. Many common people accepted the government's use of terror. Large crowds attended the public executions in Paris. By 1794, this Reign of Terror took the lives of about 40,000 men and women, including King Louis XVI and his wife, Marie Antoinette.

International movement to abolish the slave trade

For thousands of years, slavery was an accepted idea in most parts of the world. Nations often made slaves of the people they captured in war. Whenever there was a shortage of paid workers to do heavy and often dangerous work, slaves were used. <u>Colonization</u> of the Americas during the 16th century included the use of slave labor in mines and on <u>plantations</u>. By the 17th and 18th centuries, the Atlantic slave trade developed into an extremely profitable international business. During the same time, <u>Enlightenment</u> thinkers began writing about natural rights such as liberty. This led to questions about <u>abolish</u>ing slavery. In addition, religious groups such as the Quakers called for an end to slavery because all men were equal in the eyes of God.

In 1772, a judge ruled that slavery in Great Britain was illegal. This ruling did not apply to British colonies and did not affect the slave trade. In the late 1700s, antislavery societies formed in Great Britain and the American colonies to organize for political action. Most called for an end of the slave trade and the gradual <u>emancipation</u> of slaves. They held public meetings and published pamphlets and posters to educate the public about the evils of slavery and the slave trade. First-hand accounts such as *The Interesting Narrative of the Life of Olaudah Equiano, or Gustavus Vassa the African* influenced many. The slave trade was declared illegal in Great Britain in 1807 and in the United States in 1808.

By 1804 slavery was illegal in all northern states in the United States. However, slavery in southern states grew. During the early 1800s, <u>abolition</u> movements appeared. They called for the immediate emancipation of all slaves. To influence public opinion, abolitionists held meetings, gave speeches, supported antislavery newspapers, and wrote books. Books about slavery became popular reading, especially nonfiction such as Theodore Weld's *American Slavery as It Is: Testimony of a Thousand Witnesses* and *The Autobiography of Frederick Douglass*. Some books, such as Harriet Beecher Stowe's *Uncle Tom's Cabin*, were translated into different languages and read in countries around the world.

Some abolitionists took direct action to end slavery. In the United States, the Underground Railroad was organized to help slaves run away. The American Colonization Society formed to purchase freedom for slaves and send them and interested free blacks to colonize Liberia in Africa. Political parties, such as the Liberty Party, organized to elect antislavery candidates. Some planned slave revolts, such as former slave Denmark Vesey, slave Nat Turner, and white abolitionist John Brown. These revolts were unsuccessful and the leaders were captured, tried, and hanged.

The abolition movement grew and was successful. In 1833 slavery was outlawed in all British colonies. In 1840 the World's Antislavery Convention was held in London. By the beginning of the twentieth century, slavery had been abolished in much of the world, including France (1848), the United States (1865), and Brazil (1888). In 1948 the United Nations General Assembly passed the Universal Declaration of Human Rights, which says that no one in the world should be held in slavery or deal in the slave trade. However, children are sold into slavery in Asia and Africa today. Modern abolitionists are still working to end slavery in the world.

The Russian Revolution

Russia faced serious problems at the beginning of the 20th century. Most of the people were poor peasants, and industrial workers worked long hours for low pay. The best land and much of the wealth were controlled by the nobles. Russia was an absolute monarchy. Czar Nicholas II made and enforced the laws. People had few rights and no voice in their government.

A series of poor harvests in the early 1900s caused food shortages and rising prices. In January 1905 a large, peaceful group of workers and their families marched to St. Petersburg to ask Czar Nicholas for better working conditions and <u>democratic</u> elections. The police and the military opened fire on the marchers and, over 100 people were killed and 300 wounded. During this time, now called the Russian Revolution of 1905, riots and <u>strikes</u> broke out across the country. University students walked out of their classes in protest. Doctors, lawyers, and other members of the <u>middle class</u> demanded a legislative assembly to work on the problems. Czar Nicholas was forced to make changes. He agreed to the election of a legislative assembly, the Duma, and to civil rights for people, such as freedom of speech and trial by jury. However, whenever the Duma did not agree with him, the Czar closed it down. Little had changed.

World War I hurt Russia. The economy was unable to provide food, fuel, and other supplies for the armed forces and the people. Many soldiers died, prices rose to all time highs, and food was scarce. In March 1917, strikes broke out in the Russian city of Petrograd (St. Petersburg). <u>Demonstrations</u> and meetings led to clashes with the police and rioting. Some demonstrators stole weapons from police headquarters. The Czar sent troops to crush the <u>rebellion</u>, but soon many soldiers deserted. Taking their weapons with them, they joined the revolt. Without the support of the army, the Czar was forced to <u>abdicate</u>.

A new, <u>provisional</u> government was set up to run the country. Led mostly by the middle class, the provisional government wanted to continue fighting in World War I. Most Russians, especially the ordinary workers and soldiers, wanted Russia out of the war. They set up councils called "soviets" to run local governments. Some common people liked Vladimir Lenin and his group, the Bolsheviks. Many people liked the Bolshevik <u>slogans</u>, especially "Bread, peace, and land." In November 1917 the Bolshevik party led a group of workers, sailors, and soldiers to overthrow the weak and divided provisional government. There was little resistance. Russia became the world's first <u>communist</u> nation.

The independence movement in India

Between 1498 and 1757, the British, French, and other Europeans competed for trade and power in India. The British government held direct control over India for 90 years from 1857 to 1947. During that time, Great Britain gained so many riches from its colony it was called the "Jewel in the British Crown." Under British rule Indians were second-class citizens and faced British <u>racist</u> attitudes. Some Indians, especially the educated middle class, wanted independence. Two groups organized around the idea of <u>home rule</u>, the Indian National Congress in 1895 and the <u>Muslim</u> League in 1906.

When World War I began in 1914, the British expected Indian support. India provided over one million soldiers and laborers and suffered high casualty rates. They also sent large amounts of cotton for uniforms and wheat for bread to the <u>Allies</u>. Great Britain promised home rule to India after World War I, but was slow to keep that promise. Many British did not want to lose their rich "Jewel." Indians, especially returning soldiers, expected the British to keep their promise.

Great Britain feared a growing Indian <u>nationalist</u> movement, especially radicals who used violence. In 1919 the British Parliament passed laws permitting arrests without warrants and holding people in jail without a trial if they were suspected of <u>terrorism</u>. People protested against these unfair laws by signing petitions and attending public meetings. In a park in Amritsar, British Indian Army troops following the command of a British general fired into an unarmed group of men, women, and children, killing over 300 and wounding over 1,000. After the Amritsar Massacre, millions of angry people across India demanded complete independence.

In 1920 Mahatma Gandhi became a leader in the Indian National Congress and convinced them to follow a program of <u>nonviolent</u> resistance. Gandhi called on all Indians to participate in a nationwide protest, the Non-Cooperation Movement. He asked Indians to boycott British goods and businesses, refuse to pay taxes, take their children out of British schools, not use any British government services, and to give up jobs in the British government. He urged Indians to make and sell their own goods. He called on Indians to reject violence by accepting arrests and not striking back if attacked by police. Millions of Indians participated, hundreds of thousands were arrested, and thousands were wounded or killed. Because of increasing violence on both sides, Gandhi called for an end to the protest in 1922. Gandhi was sentenced to six years in prison, but was released after two years.

Other nationwide programs of nonviolent resistance followed, including the Great Salt March in 1930 and the Quit India Movement from 1942 to 1943. Thousands more were arrested and hundreds were killed. Indians still demanded complete independence. In 1946, the British government finally agreed to give India its independence as long as the two main political groups, the Indian National Congress and the Muslim League, could settle their differences. The Muslim League did not want to live in a majority Hindu state and called for a separate Islamic country. Nationwide Muslim demonstrations led to rioting and deaths. The result was the partitioning, or dividing, of India. On August 15, 1947 India and Pakistan became independent countries.

Fall of communism in Europe

In Soviet-bloc countries, people rebelled against communist rule in East Germany (1953), Hungary (1956), and Czechoslovakia (1968). With the military support of the Soviet Union, those rebellions were crushed, and many people were killed or jailed. By the 1980s the Soviet Union suffered from severe economic problems, including shortages of consumer products. It feared economic collapse. So when communist rule was threatened in Poland, the Soviet Union did not send military support. The Soviet Union had other more pressing problems.

In 1980, 50 trade unions in Poland formed a group called Solidarity, the first labor organization in a communist country. The number of union members grew to about one-half of the workforce. Solidarity's leader, Lech Walesa, called for more reforms, including free elections. The Polish government banned Solidarity and arrested over one thousand union members, including Lech Walesa. The citizens of Poland continued to support Solidarity and to insist on reform. Finally in 1988, strikes forced the government to recognize Solidarity and hold elections. In 1989 Solidarity's candidates won control of the parliament. The citizens of Poland voted to end communist government. This was the first in a series of revolutions that swept through Eastern Europe in 1989.

Shortly after the fall of the communist government in Poland, the Soviet Union announced it would not interfere in the affairs of countries in the Soviet bloc. Hungary began preparing to hold free elections and opened its borders. Over 30,000 East Germans quickly left their country through Hungary's open borders. Most went to West Germany. Mass demonstrations in several East German cities called for reforms. On the night of November 9, 1989, East Berliners heard a press conference announcing that they would be allowed to cross the border into West Berlin with proper permission. Thousands of East Berliners went to the Berlin Wall and demanded that guards let them cross. Afraid to fire on such large crowds, stunned guards opened their checkpoints allowing East Berliners to cross into West Berlin. They were soon met by excited West Berliners. Then, they danced for joy in the city streets. A few days later, the government began taking down the wall. Since 1961 it had been the symbol of the iron curtain between the communist and free countries of Europe. Now, it was gone.

One by one, citizens in Hungary, East Germany, Czechoslovakia, Bulgaria, and Romania united to overthrow their communist governments. These revolutions involved citizen calls for reform, massive demonstrations, and strikes. Most of these revolutions experienced little violence. One journalist called the revolution in Czechoslovakia the "Velvet Revolution." Only Romania experienced a large, violent uprising. It started with security forces firing on protesters and ended with the execution of the leader of the Romanian Communist Party and his wife. In 1990 free elections were held in all of these former communist countries, resulting in all non-communist governments. Then, on October 3, 1990, East and West Germany became one country.

The people of the Soviet Union watched as former satellite nations became independent and self-governing. The Soviet Union consisted of 15 republics and over 100 nationalities. Some began calling for independence. In 1991 a small group within the Communist Party wanted to prevent further changes and assert their power. They planned a coup. Soviet leader Gorbachev was held prisoner in his vacation home, and hundreds of tanks rolled into Moscow. However, most citizens did not support the coup, and there were large public demonstrations. Russian president Boris Yeltzen and most members of parliament joined the protesters in the street. Most troops sent to Moscow sided with the demonstrators, and the coup collapsed. Gorbachev was freed, but had little power or influence left. The presidents of Russia, Ukraine, and Belarus declared the Soviet Union dissolved. There were now fifteen newly independent non-communist nations.

The end of apartheid in South Africa

South Africa was colonized by the Dutch in the seventeenth century. Racial segregation immediately became an important part of South African life and allowed a small white minority to prosper and rule. During the nineteenth century, South Africa became a British colony, but black Africans continued to face segregation and discrimination. After World War II, the National Party of South Africa won control of the Parliament and passed laws creating a system of strict racial segregation. The policy was called "apartheid," which means apart or separate. Apartheid laws banned mixed marriages and grouped people by race: black, white, Asian, and colored (mixed). Laws also divided the country into different areas for different races to live. Blacks, who were about 80% of the population, had to carry identification papers with them at all times and were not allowed in white areas without special permission. Other laws segregated public services, including hospitals, restaurants, schools, and transportation.

The South African government claimed its policy of apartheid was necessary for different races to live together peacefully and described public services as separate but equal.

Most South Africans wanted to end apartheid because it made racial <u>discrimination</u> legal and treated non-whites as separate and unequal. About 10% of the population was classified as white, and only they could vote in national elections.

Unable to vote to change the laws, non-whites opposed apartheid by protest. Groups such as the African National Congress (ANC) and the Pan-Africanist Congress (PAC) organized boycotts, demonstrations, marches, strikes, and acts of civil disobedience. PAC called on black Africans throughout South Africa to go to their local police stations without their passes on March 21, 1960. In one town, Sharpeville, police opened fire on an unarmed crowd killing 69 and injuring over 160. Massive demonstrations followed. The government declared a national emergency, arrested over 18,000 people, and banned the ANC and PAC. Although they continued to support nonviolent protests, the ANC and PAC turned to armed resistance, including bombings and murder. In 1964 Nelson Mandela and seven leaders of the ANC were sentenced to life imprisonment for committing acts of terrorism. Other ANC leaders left the country.

During the late 1960s and 1970s, resistance grew stronger. The ANC continued <u>terrorist</u> activities, and new groups formed, including some by students. In the black township of Soweto, students went on strike to protest the government's new educational policies in 1976. Students organized a mass rally. Police fired tear gas, and some students threw stones. The police opened fire on the unarmed crowd. Several hundred were killed and over one thousand injured. Riots spread to other cities and so did police violence. Countries around the world were shocked and so were some white South Africans.

During the 1980s boycotts, demonstrations, and violence continued. The <u>media</u> followed these stories. Anti-apartheid movements grew in Europe and the United States. They called on their governments to pressure South Africa to end apartheid by using <u>economic sanctions</u>. They called on businesses not to trade or invest in South Africa. In 1990 President F. W. de Klerk began to end apartheid. He lifted the ban on the ANC and PAC and released many political prisoners, including Nelson

Mandela. Two years later 68% of white South African voters supported an end to apartheid. In 1994 free elections were held. The ANC won over 62% of the vote, and Nelson Mandela became the president of South Africa.

CITIZEN PARTICIPATION UNDER DIFFERENT SYSTEMS OF GOVERNMENT

Different systems of government offer different ways for people to participate. The more <u>authoritarian</u> a government is, the fewer opportunities people have to participate. Authoritarian governments include absolute monarchy, dictatorship, and theocracy. The more democratic a government is, the more opportunities people have to participate. Democratic governments include constitutional monarchy, parliamentary democracy, and presidential democracy.

An absolute monarchy considers its people subjects, not citizens. Some <u>monarch</u>s, such as the pharaohs of Ancient Egypt, are considered gods. Absolute monarchs, such as Louis XVI of France and Czar Nicholas II of Russia, claim to rule by <u>divine right</u>. God, not the people, chose them to rule. People might express their opinions or offer advice, but must be careful because they have no rights. Political action and protest are dangerous. It usually takes a revolution to bring major changes. The French Revolution (1789) and the Russian Revolution (1917) are good examples of successful revolts against absolute monarchs.

A <u>dictatorship</u> rules through force. Violence is used to take power and the military and secret police to stay in power. There are no free elections, and the only rights people have are those the dictator permits them to have at any given time. Those who oppose the government are brutally punished. Some are tortured and murdered. Political action and protest are dangerous. People usually have to revolt to change a dictatorship. A good example is the Romanian Revolution of 1989. Sometimes dictatorships end because of a war or invasions by foreign countries. Good examples include German Adolf Hitler, Italian Benito Mussolini, and Iraqi Saddam Hussein. Some dictators such as Cuba's Fidel Castro and North Korea's Kim Il-sung followed by his son Kim Jong-il have been in power for many years.

A theocracy rules through religious laws and in the name of God. Generally, there are no public elections. It is difficult for people to use political action or protest in a theocracy because they would be opposing the state and religion. Laws are strictly enforced and punishment is often harsh. Iran has many characteristics of a theocracy.

A constitutional monarchy is a limited monarchy. Usually it combines a hereditary monarch and an elected legislature. A constitution defines the powers of the monarch and the legislature. Most constitutional monarchies offer opportunities for citizen participation, including political action and protest. Most constitutional monarchies are also parliamentary democracies, such as the United Kingdom.

Parliamentary democracy and presidential democracy are systems of government found in most countries today. They have a constitution that defines and limits the powers of the government. Each country's constitution is different and some are more democratic than others, but all share common characteristics. All people are citizens and have rights guaranteed by law, such as freedom of speech and trial by jury. Political action and protest are possible. Citizens can freely contact their representatives to let them know what they want. Citizens can also participate by joining a political party, running for political office, and voting in elections. They can use a variety of nonviolent protest methods such as a boycott, demonstration, petition, picket, and strike. They may try acts of civil disobedience. Citizen participation can lead to peaceful governmental change, and that usually means revolution is not necessary.

USING PROPAGANDA TO INFLUENCE PUBLIC OPINION AND BEHAVIOR

Governments often use propaganda to gain support, especially during wars. Below are a few examples of U.S. propaganda from World War I and World War II.

- The United States government used propaganda during World War I urging Americans to support the war and to hate the enemy. The United States published more propaganda posters during World War I than any other country. These posters urged people to join the military, buy war bonds, and not waste food. One poster showed an ugly face in a German helmet. He was holding a rifle with a bloody bayonet and looking over the smoldering remains of a city. The poster said, "Beat Back the Hun with Liberty Bonds." Another poster said, "Little Americans, Do your bit. Eat Oatmeal, Corn meal mush, Hominy, other corn cereals, and Rice with milk. Save the wheat for our soldiers. Leave nothing on your plate."

- During World War II, the United States again put up posters to make Americans hate the enemy and support the war effort. Germans were called "Nazis" and "Krauts." The Japanese were called "Japs." Posters called on Americans to "Save freedom of speech, buy war bonds." Another said: "They're fighting harder than ever, are you buying more war bonds than ever?" The U.S. government had movies produced such as the *Why We Fight* series to convince the public to support the war effort. Films such as *The Negro Soldier* appealed to the patriotism of specific groups.

During the Cold War, propaganda was a major weapon used by both sides. Below are some examples.

- The United States broadcast propaganda to the Soviet Union on Radio Free Europe and Voice of America about the advantages of democracy and the disadvantages of communism. The Soviet Union used its station, Radio Moscow, to spread the opposite message.
- Accomplishments involving the arms race, the space race, and the Olympics were used by the United States and the Soviet Union to support claims of superiority.
- Cuban exile groups and the Central Intelligence Agency (CIA) used television and radio stations to aim anti-Castro propaganda at Cuba. Pro-Castro propaganda and Radio Moscow were broadcast by Radio Havana.

Propaganda is used in the War on Terror.

- In 2001 the United States airdropped leaflets over

Afghanistan, saying that the Americans were friends of Afghanistan and the Taliban were the enemies. The leaflets offered rewards for the capture of Osama Bin Laden, a terrorist linked to the 9/11 attacks in the United States.

- In Afghanistan, the Taliban spread anti-American propaganda. They called the Americans the enemy of Afghanistan and of Islam. Americans, they said, had invaded and occupied a peaceful Muslim nation, causing unnecessary death and destruction.

Propaganda is also used by other groups. Political parties, special interest groups, and political action committees (PACs) use propaganda to influence voters. Democrats claim that Republicans are the party of corruption whose policies favor the rich, while they are the party that supports American workers and the middle class. Republicans claim the Democrats are a party that is weak on terror and in favor of increasing taxes, and they are the party that supports a strong America and family values. This propaganda is delivered in speeches by politicians, in the media, and through mailings and taped telephone messages, especially during election years.

Totalitarian governments rely on propaganda to help control citizen beliefs, opinions, and behavior. Dictator Joseph Stalin used art, drama, literature, newspapers, radio, and movies to glorify the accomplishments of the Soviet Union. No criticism or negative comments were permitted. Critics were traitors and punishment for treason meant prison or execution. Propaganda is used in much the same way by some countries today, including China and North Korea.

Some people claim that advertising and public information campaigns are forms of propaganda. Many companies use advertising to influence people to buy certain products or services and to create a positive image of the product or company. Examples of public information campaigns include announcements that promote getting an education, avoiding drugs, and not littering.

THE INFLUENCE OF POLITICAL PARTIES, INTEREST GROUPS, LOBBYISTS, THE MEDIA, AND PUBLIC OPINION

In a democracy the opinions and support of voters is very important to elected officials. Government officials in the United States listen to the views of many individuals and groups concerning important issues. As you read through the next seven sections, notice how political parties, interest groups, lobbyists, the media, and public opinion influence government policy.

Extension of Suffrage: African Americans, Women, and Youth 18 to 21

In 1787 the writers of the United States Constitution decided to let states determine voting requirements. In most states only adult white male property owners could vote. African Americans, Native Americans, women, and young people aged 18 to 20 had to fight for the right to vote. Since 1787 five amendments to the Constitution, several court decisions, and some civil rights laws extended suffrage to other citizens.

The United States began as a nation of 13 states. As additional states entered the union, their constitutions did not include property requirements for voting. This signaled a change in public opinion about active citizen participation and voting rights. Older states began dropping property holding as a voting requirement, and by 1856 all states permitted adult white males to vote. However, African Americans and women had no political voice and had to fight for the right to vote.

The 13th Amendment (1865) freed the slaves and the 14th Amendment (1868) gave them citizenship. However, most states and Congress were not interested in guaranteeing African Americans the right to vote. After the presidential election of 1868, the Republican Party saw how important the African American vote was to their narrow victory. Fearing that Southern states would keep African Americans from voting, Republicans worked for the passage of the 15th Amendment (1870). The 15th Amendment says a man's race, color, or previous life as a slave cannot keep him from voting.

By the 1890s many southern states adopted a variety of ways to stop African American men from voting, such as the poll tax and literacy test. During the 20th century, interest groups organized to fight for equal rights. Civil rights groups such as the National Association for the Advancement of Colored People (NAACP), Congress on Racial Equality (CORE), Southern Christian Leadership Conference (SCLC), and the Student Nonviolent Coordinating Committee (SNCC) stressed the importance of voting rights. These groups sponsored voter education and voter registration programs.

During the 1950s and 1960s, civil rights groups turned to nonviolent direct action that would attract media attention. For example, the 1964 Freedom Summer campaign organized thousands of volunteers to register African Americans to vote in Mississippi. Three young civil rights workers were murdered. In 1965 a 54-mile march from Selma to Montgomery, Alabama, ended with a brutal attack by armed state troopers and local law enforcement officers. Shocked by the violence, angry citizens from around the country called the White House, wrote letters to Congress, and participated in protests in 80 American cities.

Media coverage led to changes in public opinion and changes in law. Two amendments to the U.S. Constitution were ratified. In 1963 the 23rd Amendment granted the District of Columbia, which has a large African American population, the right to vote in presidential elections. In 1964 the 24th Amendment prohibited the use of a poll tax as a voting requirement in federal and state elections. In 1965 the Voting Rights Act called for federal registration of voters where necessary and banned the use of the literacy test. Within four years, the number of black voters in the United States jumped from 23% to 61%.

Before the Civil War, few men or women supported women's suffrage. In 1848 the first Women's Rights Convention took place in Seneca Falls, New York. Elizabeth Cady Stanton's call for the right to vote shocked many. After the Civil War, women reformers hoped the women's hard work and support during the war would be rewarded. The 14th Amendment, however, used the word "male" concerning voting and the 15th Amendment extended voting rights to African American citizens, but ignored women.

In 1869, suffragists responded by organizing two interest groups: the National Woman Suffrage Association and the

The 1913 annual women's suffrage parade in New York City drew 10,000 marchers. One in twenty of them were men.

American Woman Suffrage Association. In 1890, the two women's suffrage associations joined together to form the National American Woman Suffrage Association (NAWSA). Other interest groups such as the Women's Christian Temperance Union and the National Association of Colored Women also supported women's suffrage. Together they organized conventions, distributed literature, held parades, and made speeches to support their cause. Their goal was to win support for a woman suffrage amendment by changing public opinion and lobbying Congress.

Public opinion was changing especially in the western territories where men and women worked together to survive on the frontier. When Wyoming became a state in 1869, the state constitution granted women the right to vote. Other newly formed western states did the same. In 1916 Montana elected the first woman to Congress, Jeannette Rankin.

Lobbying by suffragists had little effect on Congress. So Alice Paul helped organize the National Woman's Party to use militant tactics such as picketing the White House and hunger strikes. These activities increased the attention of the press and the public. After the United States entered World War I, President Woodrow Wilson decided to support the suffrage amendment as part of the war effort. With support growing, Congress finally proposed the woman suffrage amendment in 1919, and three-fourths of the states ratified it in 1920.

"Old Enough to Fight; Old Enough to Vote" is the World War II slogan that sums up the argument for the 26th Amendment. U.S. Representative and Senator Jennings Randolph from West Virginia tried for over 30 years to pass an amendment to lower the voting age to 18. Then during the Vietnam War, anti-war protests began. protesters asked why could a citizen be drafted into the military at the age of 18, but not be able to vote for those who caused him to be drafted. With so many young men fighting and dying in Vietnam, public opinion finally supported Randolph's amendment. He and a group of senators reintroduced the amendment in 1971, and within 4 months it was ratified.

Labor Legislation

Workers form labor unions to persuade employers to improve their working hours, wages, and job conditions. During the late eighteenth century, the first labor unions in the United States appeared. These unions were small, local organizations. After the Civil War, national unions appeared, such as the Knights of Labor and the American Federation of Labor (AFL). Unions often turned to strikes to win reforms from employers. Sometimes those strikes and demonstrations turned violent, such as the Haymarket Square riot (1886) and the Pullman strike (1894).

Labor unions did not have the support of the government or the public. Many people saw unions as large groups of workers organized to bully their employer who owned the business. Owners should run their businesses the way they wanted. If workers were unhappy with their jobs, they should quit. Violence was usually blamed on workers and their union because they chose to strike or protest.

At the beginning of the 20th century, attitudes about workers and unions began to change. Progressive Era reformers, such as Lillian Wald and Florence Kelley, protested against child labor. With other social reformers, they created the National Child Labor Committee in 1904. The committee showed pictures of children working under awful conditions and asked for child labor laws. Due to their work, Congress created the Federal Children's Bureau in 1912 to report on abuses against children.

During the Industrial Revolution, children as young as five or six worked 10-14 hour days for low pay in dangerous and unhealthy conditions. In this photograph, young children operate heavy rotating machinery. There were many accidents. Some reformers tried to pass laws abolishing child labor.

Labor unions worked hard to win the support of the

238 ■ CITIZENSHIP A: ACTION AND PARTICIPATION　　THE NEW LITTLE BOOK

government and the public. They lobbied Congress for laws to protect workers and asked their members to vote for those candidates who supported issues important to working people. During the Great Depression, the federal government under the leadership of the Democratic Party began to support workers and labor unions. Congress passed the National Labor Relations Act (1935) granting most workers the right to organize unions, participate in collective bargaining and strike. It also created the National Labor Relations Board where workers could report unfair labor practices. Also in 1935, the Social Security Act provided for old age pensions and unemployment insurance. Congress passed the Fair Labor Standards Act in 1938. It established a minimum wage, maximum hours, and a ban on child labor in industries involved in interstate commerce.

In 1955 the American Federation of Labor (AFL) and the Congress of Industrial Organizations (CIO) joined together. The AFL-CIO represented millions of workers and, therefore, millions of voters. Today, the AFL-CIO and other unions continue to ask their members to support candidates who best represent their interests.

Civil Rights Legislation

The Civil War ended slavery, but it did not end discrimination. Southern states passed laws, often called black codes, to control the recently freed slaves. For example, freedmen were not allowed to vote, serve on juries, testify in court against a white man, carry a weapon in a public place, or to work at certain jobs. In response, Congress passed several civil rights acts and the 14th and 15th Amendments.

Discrimination against African Americans continued. Terrorist groups such as the Ku Klux Klan used violence and intimidation to keep African Americans from using their rights, especially voting. Starting in the 1880s, southern states passed laws segregating railroad cars, buses, bathrooms, hotels, hospitals, restaurants, and schools. Civil rights groups formed to fight these Jim Crow laws. However, in 1896 the U.S. Supreme Court ruled in *Plessy v. Ferguson* that separate but equal facilities were constitutional.

African Americans organized to fight for equal rights in the courts and by lobbying Congress. Civil rights groups such as the National Association for the Advancement of Colored People (NAACP), the National Urban League, and the Congress of Racial Equality (CORE) formed. However, there was little success and little public support until after World War II. Then, public opinion began to change. In 1947 Jackie Robinson integrated baseball, and in 1948 President Harry Truman ended segregation in the armed forces. In 1954 the U.S. Supreme Court ruled in *Brown v. Board of Education* that "separate educational facilities are <u>inherently</u> unequal," and segregated schools were ordered to <u>desegregate</u>.

During the 1950s and 1960s, civil rights groups turned to nonviolent direct action that would attract media attention. Boycotts, sit-ins, freedom rides, marches, and voting registration drives brought media attention. All Americans read about and saw the ugliness of discrimination and <u>racism</u>. The 1963 March on Washington, especially Dr. Martin Luther King Jr.'s "I Have a Dream" speech, was televised worldwide. Feeling the pressure of public opinion and lobbying by civil rights groups, Congress passed the Civil Rights Act of 1964 that made discrimination based on race, color, religion, sex, or national origin in public facilities and employment illegal. Those who believed they faced discrimination could sue for damages.

The success of the civil rights movement inspired others to form interest groups to lobby for equal rights and their own civil rights legislation. These interest groups include the disabled, gays, Hispanics, Native Americans, and women.

Military Policy

Military policy involves the action plans a government develops for protecting its country from enemies. The U.S. Constitution makes the president the commander in chief of the armed forces, but gives Congress the power to declare war and control of the federal budget. So, the president and Congress must work together to make successful military policy. In addition, they both must also respond to public opinion.

Before the beginning of World War I and II, the majority of the public supported a policy of <u>isolationism</u>. The government's first response to both wars was neutrality. However, important events caused changes in public opinion and government's policy. In 1917, Germany's decision to return to unrestricted warfare and the publishing of the Zimmermann note changed the opinion of Congress, the president, and the majority of the public. President Woodrow Wilson asked for and received a declaration of war in 1917. The Japanese surprise attack on Pearl Harbor on December 7, 1941, shocked and angered American citizens. The next day President Franklin D. Roosevelt asked for and received a declaration of war. Public opinion supported both declarations of war, and men and women enlisted to fight for their country.

The Vietnam War was very different. U.S. involvement began when Presidents Eisenhower and Kennedy sent money, weapons, and military advisors to help South Vietnam train its own soldiers to fight communist North Vietnam. They feared one country after another in Asia would become communist if South Vietnam lost its civil war. In addition, they did not want the public to judge them as "soft on communism." In 1964 President Lyndon B. Johnson convinced Congress to pass the Gulf of Tonkin Resolution which gave him the power to use troops in Vietnam. In 1965 President Johnson used combat troops and expanded their size and role in Vietnam. Congress never did declare war.

Although some people began to organize against U.S. participation in the war, most of the American public supported it. As the Vietnam War dragged on, more Americans died and more were being drafted. Public opinion changed and more people participated in demonstrations, especially on college campuses. Media covered anti-war activities, reported the stories of innocent Vietnamese civilians killed, and gave daily body counts of Americans killed in action. By 1968 the majority of the public wanted to pull American military forces out of Vietnam. That same year President Johnson announced he would negotiate a peace. However, peace negotiations stalled and the war continued.

The anti-war movement grew. On October 15, 1969, about one million Americans, including 50 members of Congress, participated in peace vigils, anti-war demonstrations, and protests throughout the country. One month later, President Nixon announced plans to slowly withdraw the troops. When four students were killed by the Ohio National Guard during an anti-war demonstration at Kent State University in 1970, Congress again took note of the anti-war feelings in America. In 1973 the United States finally withdrew from Vietnam. In that same year, Congress ended the draft and made the armed services an all-volunteer military force.

Environmental Legislation

As people moved west during the 1800s, they wrote to their friends back east about the beauty of America. Believing that the federal government should protect the country's natural resources, Congress created the U. S. Department of the Interior in 1849. In 1872, Congress set aside land for Yellowstone National Park, the world's first official national park. John Muir, a conservationist who lived in Yosemite, wrote magazine articles about saving the area. Because of Muir's writings, Congress made Yosemite a national park in 1890. Muir then started the Sierra Club in 1892 to make sure the park and all other wilderness areas would be protected. President Theodore Roosevelt read John Muir's book, *Our National Parks*, and visited him in Yosemite to talk with him about conservation. During his presidency (1901-1909), Roosevelt encouraged Congress to create the National Forest Service, doubled the number of national parks from four to eight, set aside 125 million acres of land for federal forest reserves, and started 51 wildlife refuges and 16 national monuments.

After World War II, concerns about the environment turned from conserving natural resources to stopping pollution. When smog covered Donora, Pennsylvania for seven days in 1948, 20 people died and 7,000 became sick. People insisted the government should do something about air pollution. Congress passed the Air Pollution Control Act of 1955, a first step toward cleaning up the air. Many people read Rachel Carson's book, *Silent Spring*, (1962) about the dangers of pesticides. Environmentalist John McConnell went to his local city government in San Francisco with his idea for "a special day to remember Earth's tender seedlings of life and people, a day for planting trees and grass and flowers, for cleaning streams and wooded glens." The first Earth Day was celebrated in 1970 and spread quickly throughout the United States. Even the United Nations started a World Earth Day, and people still celebrate Earth Day every spring.

The Sierra Club and other interest groups lobbied Congress for action. Many government agencies were already working on environmental problems. In 1970 Congress set up the U.S. Environmental Protection Agency (EPA) to put all of these groups into one large agency, which answers directly to the president. The EPA works to reduce the damage caused by air and water pollution, pesticides, oil spills, and toxic chemicals. Its job is to protect human health and keep the natural environment safe.

Meanwhile Congress was also busy working on environmental problems. Congress passed the Clean Air Act of 1970 that required the EPA to name each dangerous pollutant in the air and find out how much of each pollutant a person would have to breathe to be harmed. Chemicals dumped into the Cuyahoga River in Cleveland fueled a fire on the river in 1966. This fire led to the Clean Water Act of 1972. Congress also passed the Endangered Species Act in 1973 and the Clean Water Act of 1987. Over the years, Congress passed laws to get lead out of gasoline and house paint, to stop the use of dangerous pesticides such as DDT, to get asbestos removed from schools and other public buildings, and to stop companies and cities from putting wastes into rivers and lakes. Today, our environment is healthier.

Media coverage of environmental disasters such as the land fill leaks polluting ground water in the Love Canal neighborhood, the escape of radiation from Three Mile Island nuclear power plant, and the 10.8 million gallon spill of oil from *Exxon Valdez* led to growing public support of environmental issues. Since the 1990s Americans have shown their concern for new environmental issues such as acid rain, drilling for oil in the Alaska wilderness, and global warming.

Business Regulation

The French phrase "laissez-faire" (pronounced lay zay fair) describes the U.S. government's economic policy for much of its history. Laissez-faire means leave alone. It means the government should not interfere in private economic decisions such as how many products to produce or what prices to charge. Government should focus on national security and protecting private property, but it should not try to regulate economic decisions of businesses or individuals. Laissez-faire policies support free trade and oppose protectionism such as tariffs.

After the Civil War, some people began to question the government's laissez-faire policies. Farmers were one of the first groups that asked the government to pass laws regulating some businesses. During the 1870s and 1880s, railroads were often unfair to western farmers who needed to take their products to markets in the big cities. So farmer organizations such as the Grange lobbied the government for laws to regulate the railroads. In response, Congress passed the Interstate Commerce Act (1887) that required railroad rates to be fair. It created the Interstate Commerce Commission (ICC), which had the power to investigate and prosecute any unfair practices.

In 1890 some farmers decided to organize their own political party, the Populist Party. During the 1890s they managed to elect several candidates as state legislators, governors, and U.S. representatives and senators. They also ran a candidate for president and in 1892 won over one million votes. Although the Populist Party died, some of its ideas about government regulation were adopted by Democrats and Republicans. One was the graduated income tax that became the 16th Amendment.

More business regulations came during the Progressive Era (1898-1918). A group of writers excited the public with books and newspaper and magazine articles. They were called muckrakers because they described terrible working conditions in factories and living conditions in slums, unfair business practices, and corrupt politics. For example, Upton Sinclair's book, *The Jungle* (1906), described dirty working conditions in the Chicago meat packing industry. Public disgust with the lack of cleanliness was so strong even some meat packers lobbied for regulations. Congress passed the Pure Food and Drug Act and the Meat Inspection Act in 1906. Other Progressive Era legislation responded to public anger about business abuses. The Clayton Antitrust Act (1914) made it easier to break up monopolies, and the Federal Trade Act (1914) created the Federal Trade Commission to investigate unfair business practices.

The impact of the Great Depression in the 1930s led to business regulations. Many people lost their farms, homes, jobs, and savings. Banks closed and businesses went bankrupt. The economy collapsed. Americans looked to the federal government for help. President Herbert Hoover expected private charities and voluntary cooperation from the business community would help until the economy adjusted on its own. President Hoover's policies offered too little, too late. In 1932 Americans elected Franklin D. Roosevelt to take his place.

President Roosevelt had promised Americans a new deal. The president and Congress created federal programs that established new business regulations in order to help working people. Employers were forced to accept unions, pay a minimum wage and overtime, and pay into Social Security. The Federal Deposit Insurance Corporation (FDIC) provided deposit insurance for checking and savings accounts, but placed requirements on banks that wanted to offer this benefit. The Securities and Exchange Commission (SEC) regulated the stock markets. Most Americans approved of such government involvement in the economy and elected Roosevelt president four times.

After World War II, regulation shifted to concerns of minorities, consumers, and workers. Civil rights organizations lobbied for a variety of laws. One of the most important was the Civil Rights Act of 1964. It banned discrimination based on race, color, religion, sex, or national origin for employment. Other legislation such as the Equal Pay Act (1963), the Americans with Disabilities Act (1990), and the Family and Medical Leave Act (1993) created additional regulations for businesses. Consumer groups such as the Consumers Union have lobbied for consumer protection laws such as the Truth in Lending Act (1968) and the Fair Credit Reporting Act (1971). The U.S. Surgeon General reported in 1968 that 65% of American workers were exposed to harmful chemicals on the job. Only 25% of the workers were protected from harm. After lobbying by the steelworkers, the unions, and <u>activist</u> Ralph Nader, Congress passed the Occupational Safety and Health Act (OSH Act of 1970) which set up an agency (OSHA) to get rid of dangers in the workplace and improve health programs for workers.

Educational Policy

Education is not mentioned in the U.S. Constitution. It was a responsibility left to individual states. State and local school boards decide most educational policies in the United States. Voting for good school board members is one way that citizens influence what schools teach and how schools are run. In the 1840s, for example, many people felt students should pay for a high school education. Charles Bradburn of Cleveland, Ohio disagreed. As a school board member, he lobbied for Ohio's first free, public high school. That school, Central High School, opened in 1846. The 1851 State Constitution of Ohio agreed with Bradburn's views, saying public schools supported by taxes should be set up throughout the entire state. In 1877 Ohio passed a compulsory education law, which said that parents must send their children age 8 to 14 to school for at least 12 weeks each year. Today, the compulsory school age is from 6 to 18 and the school year for students is 178 days.

Parents, of course, have a special interest in their children's schools. Two mothers, Alice M. Birney and Phoebe A. Hearst, started the Parent Teachers Association (PTA) in 1897 to help children and their schools. PTAs supported many health and education projects for children, including kindergartens, hot school lunches, a public health service, and child labor laws.

School <u>desegregation</u> brought the U.S. federal government into education issues normally controlled by state and local governments. The Supreme Court decision *Plessy v. Ferguson* (1896) said that separate but equal facilities were constitutional. Based on that court decision, many school boards set up separate schools for black and white children. However, they were not equal. In 1954 parents from school systems in four states and the District of Columbia, with the support of National

Association for the Advancement of Colored People (NAACP) lawyers, challenged that court decision. They said the schools were not equal and their children were not getting a fair education. In *Brown v. Board of Education of Topeka, Kansas* (1954), the Supreme Court ruled that the parents were right and the schools must desegregate.

During the 1960s many Americans supported government programs to eliminate poverty. They were influenced by reformers such as Michael Harrington, who wrote *The Other America*. Many believed education was one of the best ways to eliminate poverty. Local and state governments usually provide tax money to run schools, and low-income communities raise less money. President Lyndon Johnson, who was once a teacher, wanted to provide additional money to schools in low-income communities. As part of the Democratic Party's Great Society programs, Johnson signed into law the Elementary and Secondary Education Act of 1965 (ESEA). This act gave $1 billion to schools throughout the country for teaching materials and education programs such as Head Start.

During the 1980s and 1990s, many Americans were upset with the quality of education in the public schools. Some education reformers and politicians called for more school-wide testing to measure how much students are learning. In 2002 President George W. Bush signed a new federal law, No Child Left Behind Act (NCLB). It was supported by Democrats and Republicans in Congress. According to NCLB, schools must show adequate yearly progress in areas determined by each state, have "highly qualified" teachers as defined in NCLB, test all students in reading and math in grades 3 through 8 and once in high school, and each state must issue a report card describing the success of every school and district. Schools receiving ESEA funds that fail two years in a row will be listed as "in need of improvement" and the parents can choose to send their child to another school in the district. After a third failing year, schools must give the students extra tutoring and after-school study programs. Some people say that NCLB does not provide enough money to pay for all the extra programs and tutors that are needed.

The Impact of Civil Disobedience

If people disagree with a public policy, they can hand out flyers, give speeches, join a peaceful march, write letters to the newspapers, picket, boycott, lobby Congress, or wear symbols of their disagreement. These kinds of <u>dissent</u> are usually not against the law. Civil disobedience, on the other hand, is. Civil disobedience is a deliberate and public refusal to obey a law in order to protest its unfairness. With civil disobedience, people actually break the law to draw attention to it and they may be arrested, tried, jailed, and fined. People often turn to civil disobedience when all other means of protest have failed. It is usually nonviolent, but can lead to violent responses from authorities.

Carefully read these next three stories about civil disobedience. Focus on what happened and if civil disobedience was effective.

The Women's Suffrage Movement of the Late 1800s

In Rochester, New York, Susan B. Anthony was arrested because she voted in the presidential election. She pled not guilty based on the 14th Amendment to the U.S. Constitution. It states that no state can take away a citizen's rights. Voting, said Anthony, was one of those rights. Women were citizens, so they should be able to vote just like men. The judge did not agree. Anthony was found guilty of voting illegally and fined $100. She refused to pay the fine, but the judge did not force her to pay. He knew she would take her case to a higher court if she were arrested for not paying her fine. Although she lost in court, Anthony's civil disobedience provided publicity for the suffrage movement.

While attending college in England, Alice Paul joined the English suffrage movement. When Paul returned to the United States, she told others about militant suffragists who used acts of civil disobedience, such as shouting at sessions of Parliament and throwing stones through the prime minister's windows. Some of these women were arrested and went on hunger strikes in jail.

Paul and members of her National Woman's Party worked for a federal "Women's Right to Vote" amendment to the U.S.

Constitution. After lobbying efforts failed, the National Woman's Party turned to some of the militant activities used by English suffragists, including civil disobedience. Starting in January 1917, they picketed silently in front of the White House. In April the United States entered World War I, and some of the signs and banners were written to embarrass President Wilson. One said: "Democracy should begin at home." Another said, "Mr. President, how long must women wait for liberty?" The police arrested some of the women for interfering with traffic and jailed them for a few days. The women kept picketing and the arrests increased. The jail sentences got longer. President Woodrow Wilson and his staff ignored them.

After the police arrested Alice Paul for the third time, she was sentenced to 7 months in jail. When she went on a hunger strike, doctors force-fed her by pumping liquids through tubes in her nostrils. Officials attempted to have her committed to an insane asylum. She did not give up. Others joined her with their own hunger strikes. After being released from jail, she and her party members continued protesting. All these activities were reported in the newspapers, and readers were shocked by how the women were treated by government officials. This increased the pressure on the president to support women's suffrage. Finally, in August 1920, President Wilson signed the 19th Amendment to the Constitution, giving women the right to vote.

The Civil Rights Movement of the 1960s

The modern civil rights movement of the 1960s provided many examples of civil disobedience. In 1955 Rosa Parks, an African American, broke a Montgomery, Alabama law by refusing to give her bus seat to a white person. She was arrested and fined. Her action started a nonviolent bus boycott that lasted 382 days and finally ended segregated buses in Montgomery.

In 1960 four African American college students sat at a segregated lunch counter at Woolworth's in Greensboro, North Carolina. They were not served, but allowed to stay. Although they were insulted and intimidated, they did not leave until the end of the day. The next day more college students took seats at Woolworth's. Sit-ins spread to other states and involved other public places, including beaches, libraries, and theaters. Soon some white students and high school students participated. Some protesters experienced beatings and arrests. Many of those arrested refused bail, choosing to help fill the jails with protesters and call attention to their cause. Other protesters organized boycotts and pickets in support of the sit-ins. Stores and other public places throughout the South began to desegregate.

In 1963 the Southern Christian Leadership Conference (SCLC) protested to end segregation in Birmingham, Alabama. Boycotts of downtown stores, sit-ins at segregated lunch counters, and a march toward city hall led to over 70 arrests. The city went to court for an <u>injunction</u> banning any further demonstrations. The SCLC believed the injunction was unconstitutional and decided on a course of civil disobedience. They continued organizing marches. Many marchers, including Dr. Martin Luther King, Jr., were arrested. In need of marchers, students were asked to participate, leading to the arrest of over 600 young marchers. The next day another 1,000 students joined the march. This time they were attacked by police, police dogs, and fire hoses. Shocked Americans watched the violence on the national news and read about it in daily newspapers. A week later the SCLC and city officials reached an agreement that included desegregating downtown public services and an end to the demonstrations.

Student Protests and the Vietnam War

Vietnam anti-war protests began in 1965 with peaceful <u>teach-in</u>s on college campuses. Students, teachers, and others met at night to talk about the war. In early 1965 President Lyndon Johnson increased bombing raids and sent American ground troops to Vietnam. In April of that year, an estimated 25,000 college students, many of them members of Students for a Democratic Society (SDS), marched in Washington DC to protest the bombings. The police arrested four people that day.

As the fighting in Vietnam grew worse, more American soldiers were killed in battle and more people opposed the war. At the same time, more men between the ages of 18 and 26 were drafted. In 1967 the government drafted about 30,000 men a month. Anger and resentment grew. Many young men tried to avoid being drafted by going to college or graduate school. Thousands went to Canada. Some young people turned to acts of civil disobedience such as publicly burning draft cards, sit-ins at draft induction centers, and destroying official government draft records. In 1967 the March on the Pentagon was held in Washington DC. Over 600 of the 100,000 protesters were arrested for sitting down on the steps and around the grounds of the Pentagon. Two rounds of protests at Columbia University in New York erupted in 1968. Campus buildings were occupied by students who were violently removed. Over 800 were arrested. After the 1970 shootings at Kent State in Ohio that killed 4 and injured 9 and the shootings at Jackson State in Mississippi that killed 2 and injured 12, more than 900 colleges and universities were closed because of strikes or threats of strikes.

A more militant anti-war group, the Mayday Tribe, planned to shut down the government on May 3, 1971, by blocking the streets and bridges into Washington, DC. This protest did not succeed. Police in riot gear and troops were ready. They guarded every bridge and intersection. Police arrested 7,000 protesters that day, too many to put in jail. Those arrested were held instead at the Washington Red Skins practice field. This Vietnam War protest ended with the largest number of arrests ever made at one time in the United States. Protests continued until all U.S. troops were withdrawn from Vietnam in 1973.

Glossary

Citizenship Rights and Responsibilities A

abdicate – formally giving up an important office of power or authority.

abolish – to put an end to something.

abolition (abolitionist) – ending slavery.

absolute monarchy (absolute monarch) – a form of monarchy whose power is not limited by law or a legislature. (the ruler of an absolute monarchy.)

acid rain – rain or snow polluted by acids.

activist – someone who uses direct action to bring about change.

Allies (Allied Powers) – name of the group of countries that opposed the Central Powers during World War I and the Axis Powers during World War II.

authoritarian – demanding obedience and restricting freedom. Absolute monarchy and dictatorship are examples of two authoritarian types of governments.

ban – to stop, forbid, prohibit; a legal order prohibiting something.

boycott – an organized refusal to buy something or to participate in an event as a protest.

civil disobedience – a method of nonviolent protest. It is a deliberate and public refusal to obey a law and often leads to people being arrested.

Cold War – the global struggle for power and influence between the United States and the Soviet Union following World War II. There was no direct fighting or military combat.

collective bargaining – negotiations or talks between a company and a union concerning wages, hours, and working conditions.

colonization – a powerful government's sending of some of its citizens to claim and control a weaker country's land, resources, and people.

communism (communist) – an economic system in which the businesses are owned and operated by the government. The government decides the type, quantity, and price of goods produced. They also decide what workers will make. Communism says it will provide for everyone's needs and get rid of social classes.

conservation (conservationist) – protecting the land, its forests, and natural resources.

constitution – the basic principles, laws, and structure of a government. It is usually a written document.

constitutional monarchy – a type of monarchy in which the powers of the king or queen are limited by a constitution and a legislature elected by the citizens.

coup (coup d'état) – a sudden, often violent, overthrow of a government by a small group.

czar – the title of any of the emperors who ruled Russia before 1917; comes from the Latin word caesar.

democratic – allowing more people to participate in the decision-making processes of institutions such as government, colleges, or universities. For example, during the 1960s some students wanted to participate in the decisions to set student policies such as curfews and political activities.

demonstration – a public display of group feelings about a cause.

desegregate (desegregation) – to end segregation

dictatorship (dictator) – a form of government in which the ruler (dictator) or ruler's power is not limited by citizens or a legislature. A dictator has absolute power that is enforced by an army and secret police.

discrimination (discriminate) – unfair treatment by a government or individual citizens, usually because of race, religion, nationality, sex, or certain disabilities; prejudice.

dissent – difference of opinion; disagreement.

divine right – belief that a monarch (king, queen, or emperor) received the right to govern from God and not from the people.

draft (to draft) – a system which requires citizens to join their country's armed forces. (to call citizens to serve in the armed forces.)

economic sanctions – actions which limit the buying and/or selling of products in order to convince a country to change its policies.

emancipation – freedom; the act of making free.

Enlightenment – an intellectual movement of the 18th century in which the ordinary person rejected the authority of rulers and the church, and valued his own logic and ideas.

free trade – international exchange of goods and services without government taxes (tariffs).

global warming – steady increase in the earth's average temperature that threatens changes in climate.

hereditary monarchy (hereditary monarch) – a government run by a king or other ruler who inherited the office from another family member. (the ruler who heads a hereditary monarchy.)

Hinduism (Hindu) – 4,000-year-old religion followed by most of the people of India.

home rule – self-government.

inherently – naturally built into; naturally forming an important part of something.

injunction – a court order forbidding some activity.

iron curtain – a term used by Winston Churchill to describe the division between the communist and non-communist countries in Europe; a barrier.

Islam – a religion based on a single god, Allah, and on the word of God as revealed to Muhammad during the 17th century and written in the Qur'an (Koran).

isolationism (isolationist) – national policy of avoiding political or military agreements with other countries. (someone who supports such a policy.)

labor union – a group of workers organized to help improve wages, benefits, working hours, and working conditions.

legislature – an official body of people who have the power to make and repeal laws.

literacy test – a reading and writing test. It was one of the voter registration procedures used to deny blacks in the South the right to vote.

media (mass media) – movies, newspapers, radio, television, and other forms of mass communication to the general public.

middle class – all the people who are not rich or poor. Most have a comfortable standard of living.

militant – aggressive; combative; willing to fight for a cause.

military advisors – soldiers sent to a foreign country to help train that country's soldiers. Usually the advisors do not fight, but just give advice about how to fight.

minimum wage – according to the law, the amount of money which must be paid to a worker for each hour he/she works. An employer can pay more than the minimum wage but not less. Not all workers are covered by minimum wage laws.

monarchy (monarch) – a form of government in which the ruler (monarch) is a king, queen, emperor, or empress. A monarch usually inherits the title and holds power for life.

monopoly (monopolies) – exclusive control of a product or service by a single company.

muckrakers – a group of American writers (1900 to 1912), who reported the horrible working and living conditions for low wage workers and unfair political policies.

Muslim – a person who practices Islam.

national monument – a place of historical or environmental interest set aside by the federal government for citizens to visit, study, and enjoy. Devil's Tower in Wyoming and the Statue of Liberty in New York City are examples of U.S. national monuments.

nationalism (nationalist) – loyalty to one's own nation or country; especially putting one nation above all others, with major emphasis on promotion of its culture and interests.

natural resources – naturally occurring materials, such as mineral deposits, oil, water, forests, wildlife, air, climate, deserts, and mountains.

noble – person who has a high rank or title which is inherited. Lords, knights, and dukes are examples.

nonviolence (nonviolent) – the belief and practice of working actively for political and social change without using violence. Mahatma Gandhi and Dr. Martin Luther King, Jr. were both strong supporters of the philosophy of nonviolence.

parliamentary democracy – a form of government in which an elected parliament makes laws for a country.

patriotic (patriotism) – loving, defending, and supporting one's country and its interests.

peasant – an agricultural laborer or small farmer, often uneducated.

pension – a fixed amount of money paid regularly to a person.

pesticide – a chemical used to kill pests such as insects that attack food crops, cockroaches, or rats and mice. Many pesticides can also be harmful to humans.

petition – written request for change signed by several people; to request.

picket – to march as a protest group outside a work place or government building while carrying signs to explain your cause. Workers who belong to trade unions often picket during a strike.

plantation – a large farm that raises crops for sale such as cotton, tobacco, and sugar.

political action committee (PAC) – a committee formed by a group to raise money and donate to the campaigns of candidates who support the group's interests.

poll tax – a tax which must be paid in order to vote. Since the poll tax cost more than most poor whites and African Americans could pay, it kept many from voting.

pollution – dangerous substances released into the air, water, or soil.

presidential democracy – a form of government in which an elected president runs the country and a legislature makes the laws.

propaganda – selective facts, ideas, or information used to win support for a cause or a person. It usually has a strong emotional appeal.

protectionism – the policy of using quotas or tariffs (taxes) on foreign products to protect domestic companies.

provisional – temporary.

racism (racist) – the belief that one race is naturally superior to others; discrimination and prejudice against a group of people because of their race.

radical – a person, group, or idea that favors making extreme changes, usually political in nature.

ratify (ratified) – to confirm or approve, usually by a vote.

rebellion – openly resisting the government, often with weapons. Rebellions usually fail.

reform (reformer) – to improve or change something that is wrong or unsatisfactory.

satellite – (1) a smaller object that circles a larger object in the sky; (2) a country that is economically and politically controlled by a more powerful nation.

segregation (segregate) – the law or practice of separating and isolating people by characteristics such as race, religion, or nationality.

sit-in – a type of demonstration in which a group of people protest against something by sitting down in a place and refusing to leave; a peaceful protest.

slogan – a phrase used to win people's support.

smog – air pollution caused by fumes from cars, factories, electric power plants, incinerators, and dust from building sites.

Soviet bloc (Eastern bloc) – the Soviet Union and its allies during the Cold War, such as Bulgaria, Czechoslovakia, East Germany, Hungary, Poland, Romania, and Albania.

special interest group – a group of people, with similar interests and goals, who seek to influence political decisions.

strike – refusing to work, in order to achieve a goal such as higher pay or better working conditions.

suffrage (suffragist) – the right to vote. (a person, male or female, who supports giving women the right to vote.)

Taliban – an Islamic fundamentalist group that controlled Afghanistan from 1996 to 2001. After the September 11, 2001 attacks, they refused to deliver Osama bin Laden and other Al-Qaeda leaders to the United States. A U.S.-led coalition invaded Afghanistan and drove the Taliban from power. Osama bin Laden was not captured.

teach-in – a method of peaceful protest which began during the Vietnam War when university students and teachers met on college campuses to ask questions about the war and to explain why they were against it.

terrorism (terrorist) – using fear and violence for political purposes.

theocracy – a system of government in which a religious leader or a religious group rules in the name of God or a god.

tithe – one-tenth of a part of something paid voluntarily or as a tax, usually to a religious organization.

totalitarian – governed by a system which wants absolute control over all aspects of a person's private and public life. Individual freedoms must be sacrificed for the good of the state.

toxic – poisonous; very harmful to life.

treason (traitor) – betraying of one's own country. A traitor is a person who betrays his/her own country.

unemployment insurance – temporary payments by the government to unemployed workers.

voter registration – requirement that citizens sign up with the Board of Elections several weeks before the first election in which he or she wants to vote.

wildlife refuge – a protected place, set aside, where animals and plants can safely live without being hunted or hurt by people.

Citizenship Rights and Responsibilities B

INDIVIDUAL RIGHTS AND RESPONSIBILITIES

Explain how individual rights are relative, not absolute, and describe the balance between individual rights, the rights of others, and the common good.

Determining the Limits of Individual Rights

The U.S. Constitution was written and sent to individual states to be <u>ratified</u> in 1787. Many Americans believed it created a government too powerful and that individual rights would be restricted. To ease those fears, the supporters of the new constitution, the Federalists, promised to add amendments protecting individual rights. The Federalists kept their promise, and two years later ten amendments were added to the U.S. Constitution.

The first ten amendments are called the Bill of Rights. They guarantee our basic rights such as:

- freedom of speech
- freedom of the press
- freedom of religion
- freedom to assemble
- the right to keep and bear arms
- freedom from unreasonable search and seizure
- freedom from <u>self-incrimination</u>
- right to speedy public trial
- right to an <u>impartial</u> jury
- freedom from cruel and unusual punishment

Even though the Constitution gives American citizens these rights, they are <u>relative</u>, not <u>absolute</u>. A person's individual rights must be balanced with rights of other people and the common good of the community. For example, a person may have freedom of speech, but that does not give anyone the right to yell "Fire!" in a crowded school auditorium as a joke. Final decisions about the limits of citizens' rights are usually decided by the Supreme Court. The Court has used reasons such as clear and present danger, compelling government interest, libel and slander, national security, public safety, and equal opportunity to limit individual rights.

The clear and present danger standard was first used in *Schenck v. United States* (1919). The general secretary of the American Socialist Party, Charles T. Schenck, handed out anti-draft leaflets during World War I. He was arrested and found guilty of attempting to obstruct the war effort. Schenck's attorneys argued that he could urge young men to resist the draft because of his right to free speech. The Supreme Court disagreed; declaring what a person might say or write during peacetime could be dangerous to the nation during a time of war. Free speech, therefore, can be limited if it presents a clear and present danger. In *Debs v. United States* (1919), the U.S. Supreme Court upheld the conviction of socialist Eugene Debs for an anti-war speech also based on the clear and present danger standard.

Another reason to limit individual rights is compelling government interest. This usually refers to the government's attempt to protect the common good of the community. For example, freedom of religion is a First Amendment right. However, freedom of religion does not justify using drugs as part of a religious practice or ceremony. The government has a compelling interest in controlling the use of illegal drugs. The government also has a compelling interest in protecting children by censoring obscenity and pornography. In 2003 the U.S. Supreme Court agreed that a law demanding public libraries install internet filters on their computers was constitutional.

Although the Bill of Rights gives us the right to freedom of speech and press, courts have said that a person cannot ruin someone else's reputation by saying or writing lies about them. If spoken words damage a person's reputation, it is not free speech. It is slander. If those damaging words are written, it is called "libel." The victim can sue the liar in civil court.

Individual rights have been limited because of the needs of national security. During wartime, for example, the government censors private mail between the troops and their families to remove any sensitive military information that might aid the enemy. Increased national security was the goal of the USA Patriot Act (2001), which grew out of fear that there might be more terrorist attacks on the United States like those on 9/11. The Patriot Act expands the powers of the government in order to investigate and prevent terrorism. It made it easier for authorities to search a person's home without a warrant, wiretap phones, monitor e-mails, and request library, bank, and medical records. Critics claim the Patriot Act goes too far and is a threat to our right of privacy.

Individual rights have also been limited because of the issue of public safety. The government has the right to protect the public from violence. A speaker can express his opinion at a rally, but cannot encourage people to riot. People have the right to assemble and protest at an abortion clinic, but cannot stop others from entering the building. A protest group has the right to organize a march to city hall, but the government can limit the time and other conditions of the march to protect the rights of others.

The 14th Amendment to the United States Constitution guarantees all citizens equal protection of the law. All citizens have the freedom of speech and press to express themselves including opinions that support discrimination based on race, gender, religion, or sexual preference. However, that does not grant citizens the right to practice those ideas. An apartment owner or employer can express racist views, but not discriminate against tenants or employees based on race. Because of past discrimination, some colleges and companies use affirmative action programs to provide equal opportunity and create diversity. Critics claim affirmative action programs give minorities an advantage and discriminate against white Americans. The Supreme Court ruled in the *Regents of the University of California v. Bakke* (1978) that affirmative action programs using a quota system to create racial balance are unconstitutional. However, in *Grutter v. Bollinger* (2003) the Supreme Court ruled that race can be used as one of several factors in admissions decisions.

Restricting the Rights of Individuals

There are many instances in which the government restricted the rights of individuals in order to protect the common good. However, sometimes people were abused and mistreated. During World War I, about 65,000 men registered as <u>conscientious objectors</u>. Some were drafted and given non-combat duty. Because of <u>pacifist</u> or religious beliefs, about 2,000 conscientious objectors refused to cooperate with the military in any way. Some were given prison sentences in military facilities where they were mistreated. Two died of physical abuse.

The restriction of individual rights also occurred during the <u>Red Scare</u> (1917-1920). Because of the Russian Revolution (1917) and violent activities after World War I, many Americans feared that <u>radicals</u> were planning a revolution. U.S. attorney general A. Mitchell Palmer organized raids of <u>communist</u>, socialist, and <u>labor union</u> offices searching for radicals. The Palmer raids led to the arrest of over 10,000 people. Many were <u>immigrants</u>. The Palmer raids included mass arrests, illegal searches and seizures, arrests and wiretaps without warrants, false imprisonment, and physical abuse. About 600 people were <u>deported</u>.

A second Red Scare happened after World War II. As the Cold War developed, the Soviet Union and communism became the new enemies abroad and at home. Possible suspects included artists, civil rights leaders, college and university faculty, government workers, the movie industry, union leaders, and writers. Some employers and state legislatures required employees to take loyalty oaths. In 1947 President Truman began a loyalty review program for federal employees. The Federal Bureau of Investigation (FBI) completed background checks sometimes using burglaries, illegal wiretaps, and mail openings. Thousands of federal employees lost their jobs. Many were not permitted to know their accusers' identities or cross-examine them. That same year the House Un-American Activities Committee began investigating the motion picture industry. The "Hollywood 10," writers who refused to testify based on their rights of freedom of speech and assembly, were found guilty of <u>contempt</u> of court and given prison terms. Studios immediately made a list of people considered suspect. Over 300 blacklisted actors, directors, and writers could not find work.

By the late 1940s, many Americans feared there was a communist conspiracy to take over the government. In 1950 Senator Joseph McCarthy confirmed those fears by claiming he had a list of 205 communists working in the U.S. State Department. He never released the names or provided evidence to support his charges. Instead, he accused even more people of being communists. McCarthy labeled those who criticized him or defended those he accused as communists of being "soft on communism." McCarthy did not hesitate to use libel, slander, or manufactured evidence. Many people lost jobs and had careers destroyed. Some were imprisoned. McCarthy's influence and power grew, and most people, even Presidents Truman and Eisenhower, were afraid to criticize him. Today, publicly accusing someone of disloyalty without regard for evidence is called "McCarthyism."

African Americans also had their rights restricted by the government during the civil rights movement. Since the nineteenth century, Jim Crow laws created a segregated society that made African Americans second-class citizens. However, in 1954 the U.S. Supreme Court ruled in *Brown v. Board of Education* that segregation in public schools is unconstitutional. For several years many schools refused to integrate. The governor of Arkansas used the National Guard to stop nine African American students from attending all-white Central High School in Little Rock in 1957. To enforce the federal court orders, President Eisenhower sent troops to escort the students to school and between classes.

When African Americans protested, they were often arrested. Many local authorities permitted or participated in physical beatings of those who participated in sit-ins, freedom rides, demonstrations, and marches. In 1964 three young activists registering voters in Mississippi were kidnapped and killed by members of the Ku Klux Klan, including members of the county sheriff's department. In 1965 a peaceful march for the right to vote in Selma, Alabama was halted by a brutal attack of state troopers and local authorities using clubs and tear gas.

Glossary

Citizenship Rights and Responsibilities B

absolute – not limited; total; complete.

activist – someone who uses direct action to bring about change.

affirmative action – a policy which gives opportunities to women and minorities because of past discrimination.

blacklist (to blacklist) – a list of people or groups that are under suspicion or being punished. They are usually denied jobs or privileges.

communism (communist) – an economic system in which the businesses are owned and operated by the government. The government decides the type, quantity, and price of goods produced. They also decide what workers will make. Communism says it will provide for everyone's needs and get rid of social classes.

compelling – important, urgent.

conscientious objector – a person who refuses to participate in any military action because of religious or moral principles.

conspiracy – a secret plot or plan.

constitutional – in agreement with or allowed by the constitution.

contempt – disrespect or disobedience.

demonstration – a public display of group feelings about a cause.

deport – to force a foreigner to leave a country by legal means.

discrimination (discriminate) – unfair treatment by a government or individual citizens, usually because of race, religion, nationality, sex, or certain disabilities; prejudice.

draft (to draft) – a system which requires citizens to join their country's armed forces. (to call citizens to serve in the armed forces.)

freedom ride (freedom riders) – black and white activists riding interstate buses through segregated southern states in the 1960s to protest illegal racial segregation in bus stations.

immigrant (immigration) – a person who enters a country and makes it his home, often becoming a citizen of his new country.

impartial – fair; without prejudice.

integrate – to end segregation, to mix or blend together.

Jim Crow – the term used for laws and practices that segregated (separated) blacks and whites in the United States.

labor union – a group of workers organized to help improve wages, benefits, working hours, and working conditions.

obscenity – crude and vulgar words or phrases.

pacifism (pacifist) – the belief that violence and war are wrong. It is a reason for not participating in any military action.

quota – a number or percentage that is set as a maximum or minimum amount. For example, immigration laws often set limits on the number of immigrants from different countries allowed into the United States.

racism (racist) – the belief that one race is naturally superior to others; discrimination and prejudice against a group of people because of their race.

radical – a person, group, or idea that favors making extreme changes, usually political in nature.

ratify (ratified) – to confirm or approve, usually by a vote.

Red Scare – a widespread fear of communists in the United States and their secret plans for a communist revolution.

relative – depending on the circumstances; limited. The opposite of "relative" is "absolute."

segregation (segregate) – the law or practice of separating and isolating people by characteristics such as race, religion, or nationality.

self-incrimination – testifying against yourself.

sit-in – a type of demonstration in which a group of people protest against something by sitting down in a place and refusing to leave; a peaceful protest.

socialism (socialist) – any of various economic and political ideas that favor the government's ownership and administration of the means of production.

terrorism (terrorist) – using fear and violence for political purposes.

unconstitutional – not allowed by the Constitution; against the law.

warrant – a legal document giving authority. Warrants are issued by a judge.

Social Studies Skills and Methods A

EVALUATING SOURCES OF INFORMATION

Evaluate the reliability and credibility of sources.

Reading an article, book, or newspaper, listening to the radio, watching television, or talking to friends are ways to learn new information. But, are the sources of that new information reliable and credible? Were all the facts reported, and were they reported accurately? You know better than to believe everything you hear, see, or read, but too often we accept new information from a friend, a textbook, or television as the truth.

All information we receive comes from either primary or secondary sources. A primary source is a first-hand account of an event from an eyewitness or participant. Primary sources include autobiographies, diaries, e-mails, letters, journals, logs, speeches, photographs, film, video, and official records such as birth certificates and wills. A secondary source is an account created by someone who researches events and people. Secondary sources include biographies, history books, most newspaper and magazine articles, and textbooks. The best secondary sources use primary sources. For example, a good biography uses oral interviews and private papers, as well as public information to reconstruct the life of a person.

Primary and secondary sources always reflect a point of view. It is important for you to be able to detect point of view in order to evaluate the reliability and credibility of a source. Words usually reflect the historical, political, or cultural point of view of the person who chooses them. An author's purpose, thesis, and themes can often be found in the preface or introduction of a source. The title of a source can indicate a point of view. History books with the titles *The United States: Land of Freedom* and *The United States: Land of Freedom?* will probably not have the same point of view. Sometimes point of view can be found in the words chosen to describe a person or event. During the 1960s China's ruler, Mao Zedong, was often called "Great Teacher, Great Leader, Great Supreme Commander, Great Helmsman" in China. However, most Americans described him as a "ruthless communist dictator." The U.S. Civil War (1861-1865) was called the War of the Rebellion in northern states and the War of Southern Independence in southern states.

But who really cares who Mao Zedong was? After all, he lived in China and died in 1976. And the U.S. Civil war happened over 100 years before you were born. So what? Who cares? Will it help you get a job or buy a car? Will it pay for a prom dress or the latest shoes? What good is history and social studies anyway? Why do we have to study the past when we live in the present?

One reason we study history is to understand the present. All events and all people have their roots in the past. Why is there a War in Iraq, an AIDS crisis, and rising gasoline prices? Why do issues of race and color continue to be so important in the United States? The answers are found in our history. Author William Faulkner wrote: "The past is not dead. In fact, it's not even past."

Another reason we study history is to more fully understand ourselves. We were born into the world at a time and place that is not of our choosing. How would you and your life be different if you had been born an African American in the Jim Crow South during the Great Depression in 1933, a Russian Jewish daughter of an immigrant in New York City in 1890, or a Mexican American in Texas in 1986 to parents who were illegal immigrants? History helps define who we are and the world in which we live. It is often said that "A person with no history is like a tree without roots." The more we understand our roots the better we understand ourselves.

Studying history helps people make decisions and judgments. History shows our strengths and weaknesses. We see what wonderful things are possible and how those who came before us struggled and sacrificed. History also shows us what selfishness and evil are possible. Hopefully, we learn from past successes and failures. History helps us evaluate our choices for the future and the direction our leaders want to take us. Author George Santayana wrote: "Those who cannot remember the past are condemned to repeat it."

The goal of history is to tell the truth, to tell what actually happened. Historians must use sources that are reliable and credible in their search for the truth. Readers of history must always look at the historian's or writer's sources. To decide how reliable a source is, start by checking the date of publication. Has this information been published recently? Are the author's generalizations supported by facts? Are the facts accurate? Can the same facts be found in other sources? Does the author accurately identify his or her sources of information?

To decide if a source is credible ask yourself the following questions. What are the author's background, qualifications, and reputation? What motivated the author to create this source? Does the author express bias or use propaganda? Does the author use stereotypes? Does the author use logical fallacies? Are there any unstated assumptions? Is the author's argument consistent?

THIS IS THE ENEMY
Many Americans did not want to be involved in another war in Europe. U.S. propaganda tried to convince Americans that the new world war was a fight between good and evil. Nazism was anti-American. It opposed American values including the right to worship.

Many men openly opposed the women's movement. Most people, men and women, believed that a woman's proper place was in the home. They argued women didn't need more rights. They had fathers and husbands to protect them. Women did not belong in the public world, but in the private world at home. According to the cartoon, what does the women's rights movement really want?

In the search for the truth, you must be a critical reader. Everyone has opinions and the right to express those opinions. However, not every opinion is valid. Only after evaluating the reliability and credibility of sources should you decide if an author's opinions, point of view, and thesis are valid.

Glossary

SOCIAL STUDIES SKILLS AND METHODS A

accurately – without error; using only facts or a standard.

autobiography – a history of a person's life that is written by that person.

bias – favoring one point of view, whether it is fair or logical, over all others.

credible (credibility) – believable, convincing.

fact – knowledge or information about something that actually happened.

generalization – a statement that all things or persons in a group act a certain way.

logical fallacies – incorrect reasoning; conclusions drawn from incorrect reasoning or false assumptions.

opinion – a belief, often strongly held, that a person has about some subject.

point of view – one person's interpretation of something; one person's stand on a matter.

primary source – information from people who were there at the time something happened.

propaganda – selective facts, ideas, or information used to win support for a cause or a person. It usually has a strong emotional appeal.

qualifications – skills, education, training, or first-hand knowledge that make the person someone whose words can be trusted and believed.

reliable (reliability) – dependable, trustworthy.

reputation – what other people think about a person's honesty or capabilities.

research – to investigate a topic carefully and thoroughly.

secondary source – information from people who were not there at the time something happened, but studied and wrote about it.

stereotype – an unfair, unproven belief that certain people must be or act in a certain way.

thesis – an idea that a speaker or writer wants to prove. The thesis is often the main idea.

unstated assumption – a fact or idea accepted as true (assumption) and used but not stated by a source to support or prove some thesis. A speaker or writer might leave unpopular assumptions unstated to avoid turning opinion against his or her ideas.

valid – logical, reasonable.

Social Studies Skills and Methods B

HOW TO SUPPORT OR REFUTE A THESIS

Use data and evidence to support or refute a thesis.

Throughout your school years, you have been asked to write reports, make presentations, and complete research papers. No matter what the length of these assignments, they all should include certain basic ingredients: a topic, a thesis, and supporting evidence.

Here are the steps for a research project.

1. **Select a general topic.** Your teacher may provide you with a topic, or you may be able to choose your own.
2. **Narrow your topic.** After some reading, you need to narrow your topic to some point of particular interest. For example, a teacher may give the class the United States during the 1960s as a general topic. After some reading you decide to narrow your topic to the 1968 shootout in Glenville, a neighborhood in Cleveland, Ohio.
3. **Collect information and data.** Begin with secondary sources. Researching the shootout in Glenville could begin with reading an article in *The Encyclopedia of Cleveland History* and *Shoot-out in Cleveland* by Louis H. Masotti and Jerome R. Corsi.
4. **Develop a thesis.** Based on your reading and research, form a thesis about the causes of the shootout in Glenville. For example, "There were three major causes for the Glenville shoot-out in 1968."
5. **Continue to collect information and data.** Your evidence should increasingly rely on primary sources. For example, news accounts in the *Cleveland Plain Dealer*, the *Cleveland Press*, and the *Cleveland Call and Post* on July 23 through July 28, 1968 provide reporter's accounts and the names of eyewitnesses. Later articles on editorial pages of those newspapers provide analysis

and opinions. Using names found in your sources, arrange oral interviews with politicians, reporters, participants, and eyewitnesses. Remember, you always need to evaluate the reliability and credibility of your sources. Even eyewitnesses and participants in events do not necessarily agree about what happened.

6. **Write a logical and persuasive argument that uses data and evidence to support your thesis.** Make sure all your generalizations are supported by facts. You may discover that the data and evidence do not support your thesis. In that case, change your thesis.

Glossary

SOCIAL STUDIES SKILLS AND METHODS B

primary source – information from people who were there at the time something happened.

secondary source – information from people who were not there at the time something happened, but studied and wrote about it.

thesis – an idea that a speaker or writer wants to prove. The thesis is often the main idea.

Illustrations Source Information

1. **History**
   - **A –** The Enlightenment
     Library of Congress, Prints and Photographs Division
   - **B –** Industrialization
     Library of Congress, Prints and Photographs Division, National Child Labor Committee Collection; Wikimedia Commons
   - **C –** Imperialism
     Hoover Institution; University of Alabama Contemporary Map Collection
   - **D –** Twentieth Century Conflict: World War I to World War II
     Imperial War Museum (United Kingdom); Library of Congress, Prints and Photographs Division, Work Projects Administration Posters; United States Holocaust Memorial Museum, courtesy of Muzej Revolucije Narodnosti Jugoslavije
   - **E –** Twentieth Century Conflict: The Cold War and Contemporary Conflicts
     National Archives and Records Administration; National Archives and Records Administration through United States Holocaust Memorial Museum; Wikimedia Commons (shading added)
   - **F –** Domestic Affairs in the United States during the Twentieth Century
     Library of Congress Prints and Photographs Division; National Archives and Records Administration; Rosewood Forum, LLC and Displays for Schools, LLC Gainesville, FL; Wikimedia Commons

2. **People in Societies**
   - **A –** Cultural Perspectives
     University of Alabama Contemporary Map Collection; Wikimedia, copyright John Mullin, Directorate of Public Relations, East Punjab

    B – Cultural Interaction: Oppression, Discrimination, Conflict
        Library of Congress, Prints and Photographs; U.S. Census Bureau
    C – Cultural Diffusion
        National Archives and Records Administration; U.S. Department of Homeland Security

3. Geography
    A – Places and Regions
        CIA *World Factbook*; The World Bank, Washington DC data query at http://devdata.worldbank.org
    B – Human Environmental Interaction
        EarthTrends Data Tables: *Population Health and Human Well-being Demographic Indicators*, United Nations Population Division; *Encyclopedia of Cleveland History;* Library of Congress; United Nations, Department for Economic and Social Information and Policy Analysis;
        U.S. Census Bureau; U.S. Census Bureau, Department of the Interior www.nationalatlas.gov; U.S. Energy Information Administration; U.S. Environmental Protection Agency
    C – Movement of People, Products, and Ideas
        U.S. Census Bureau, Geography Division

4. Economics
    A – Markets
        National Automotive History Collection, Detroit Public Library
    B – Government and the Economy
        Library of Congress; U.S. Department of Commerce

5. Government
    A – Constitutional Amendments and Supreme Court Decisions
        Wikipedia

   B – Systems of Government
       Ben's Guide to U.S. Government, U.S. Government Printing Office

6. Citizenship Rights and Responsibilities
   A – Citizen Action and Participation
       Library of Congress Prints and Photographs Division; National Archives and Records Administration; Wikimedia, French National Library

7. Social Studies Skills and Methods
   A – Evaluating Sources of Information
       Library of Congress Prints and Photographs Division; New Hampshire State Library

Because Wikimedia allows editing of its material, we have attempted to verify that artwork used from this site does not differ in content from that of the same or similar items from other trusted sources. When possible we have chosen original-source artwork and unedited versions. Photos may be adjusted for printing; maps may be shaded for illustration.